100 GREATEST AMERICAN MEDALS AND TOKENS

Complete With Market Values

Katherine Jaeger and Q. David Bowers

Foreword by David T. Alexander and Russell Rulau

Whitman Publishing, LLC
Atlanta, GA

100 Greatest American Medals and Tokens

© 2007 Whitman Publishing, LLC
3101 Clairmont Road • Suite C • Atlanta GA 30329

All rights reserved, including duplication of any kind or storage in electronic or visual retrieval systems. Permission is granted for writers to use a limited number of brief excerpts and quotations in printed reviews, magazine articles, and numismatic catalogs, provided credit is given to the title of the work and the author. Written permission is required for other uses, including in books, any use of illustrations, and any use of any information or illustrations in electronic or other media.

Correspondence concerning this book may be directed to the publisher, at the address above.

ISBN: 0-7948-2260-6
Printed in China

Disclaimer: No warranty or representation of any kind is made concerning the accuracy or completeness of the information presented, or its usefulness in numismatic purchases or sales. The opinions of others may vary. The authors may buy, sell, and sometimes hold certain of the items discussed in this book.

Caveat: The price estimates given are subject to variation and differences of opinion. Especially rare medals and tokens trade infrequently, and an estimate or past auction price may have little relevance to future transactions. Before making decisions to buy or sell, consult the latest information. Grading of medals and tokens is subject to wide interpretation, and opinions can differ. Past performance of any item in the market is not necessarily an indication of future performance, as the future is unknown. Such factors as changing demand, popularity, grading interpretations, strength of the overall market, and economic conditions will continue to be influences. The market for a given medal or token can fall or it can rise.

Advertisements within this book: Whitman Publishing, LLC, does not endorse, warrant, or guarantee any of the products or services of its advertisers. All warranties and guarantees are the sole responsibility of the advertiser.

For a complete catalog of numismatic reference books, supplies, and storage products,
visit Whitman Publishing online at www.whitman**books**.com

CONTENTS

Foreword
   Medals *by David T. Alexander* iv
   Tokens *by Russell Rulau* v
Grades and Estimated Market Values vi
Introduction vii

100 Greatest American Medals and Tokens, No. 1 to No. 100

1. 1776 Libertas Americana Medal 2
2. Washington Before Boston Medal 4
3. Jefferson Indian Peace Medal 6
4. 1837 Feuchtwanger Coinage 8
5. 1792 Washington Peace Medal for Red Jacket 10
6. 1796–1798 Washington "Seasons Medals" 12
7. 1737 and 1739 Higley Coppers 14
8. 1826 Erie Canal Medal 16
9. 1757 "Kittanning Destroyed" Medal 18
10. 1838 "Am I Not a Woman & a Sister" Token 20
11. 1800 Washington Funeral Medal by Perkins 22
12. 1820 North West Company Beaver Token 23
13. George II Indian Peace Medal 24
14. 1862 Encased Postage Stamps 25
15. Patriotic Civil War Tokens 26
16. Civil War Store Cards 27
17. 1790 Washington Manly Medal 28
18. 1900–1901 Lesher "Dollars" 29
19. 1930–1995 Society of Medalists Issues 30
20. 1796 P.P.P. Myddelton Token 31
21. 1764 "Happy While United" Indian Peace Medal 32
22. 1896 Bryan "Cartwheel" Dollar 33
23. 1793–1795 Ricketts's Circus Token 34
24. 1805 Washington Medal by Eccleston 35
25. New Yorke in America Token 36
26. 1801 Thomas Jefferson Inaugural Medal 37
27. 1905 Theodore Roosevelt Inaugural Medal 38
28. 1860–1977 Assay Commission Medals 39
29. 1777 Franklin Americain Medal 40
30. Carolina and New England Elephant Coppers 41
31. 1787 Columbia and Washington Medal 42
32. 1766 William Pitt Token 43
33. 1714 Gloucester Court House Token 44
34. Satirical Hard Times Tokens 45
35. 1779 John Paul Jones Medal 46
36. 1794 and 1795 Talbot, Allum & Lee Tokens 47
37. 1790 Albany Church Penny 48
38. 1925 Norse-American Octagonal Medal 49
39. Circa 1785 Bar Copper 50
40. 1812–1815 P.B. Counterstamp on Cut Coin Segment 51
41. 1832 Andrew Jackson Presidential Campaign Medalet 52
42. 1783 Felicitas Britannia et America Medal 53
43. War of 1812 Congressional Medals 54
44. 1836 First Steam Coinage Medal 55
45. 1797 Washington Medal by Getz 56
46. Atwood's Railroad Hotel Token 57
47. 1860 "We All Have Our Hobbies" Medalet 58
48. 1824 Washington/Lafayette Counterstamps 59
49. Medal for the 1857 Loss of the SS *Central America* 60
50. 1778–1779 Rhode Island Ship Token 61
51. 1796 Castorland Medals 62
52. Official U.S. 1876 Centennial Medal 63
53. 1893 Columbian Exposition Award Medal 64
54. Sutlers' Tokens of the Civil War 65
55. 1821 Peale's Philadelphia Museum Medal 66
56. Horatio Gates at Saratoga Medal 67
57. Abraham Lincoln Indian Peace Medal 68
58. Charles I. Bushnell Medalet 69
59. 1778 Washington "Voltaire" Medal 70
60. 1844 "Vote the Land Free" Counterstamp 71
61. Congressional Medal of Honor 72
62. 1848 Congressional Medal to Winfield Scott 73
63. 1860 "The Smoker" Medalet 74
64. 1860 Wealth of the South Tokens 75
65. 1824 Franklin Institute Award Medal 76
66. Declaration of Independence Medal by C.C. Wright 77
67. John Quincy Adams Indian Peace Medal 78
68. Houck's Panacea Counterstamp 79
69. 1807 "1776" American Beaver Medal 80
70. 1739–1741 Admiral Vernon Medals 81
71. 1783 Washington C.C.A.U.S. Medal 82
72. 1792 Washington "Born Virginia" Medal 83
73. The Diplomatic Medal 84
74. Stonewall Jackson Medal of 1864 85
75. 1860 Washington Cabinet Medal 86
76. 1817 Amelia Island "Green Cross" Medal 87
77. 1850s J.L. Polhemus Counterstamps 88
78. 1808 Washington Benevolent Society Medal 89
79. 1915 Pan-Pacific Exposition Medal 90
80. 1746 Annapolis Tuesday Club Medal 91
81. 1944 O.P.A. Red and Blue Point Tokens 92
82. Sales-Tax Tokens 93
83. "Good for a Scent" Civil War Token 94
84. 1861 Pioneer Base Ball Club Medal 95
85. 1835 New York and Harlaem Rail Road Token 96
86. Beck's Public Baths Token 97
87. 1850s Scovill Manufacturing Co. Token 98
88. 1904 to Date, Carnegie Hero Medal 99
89. The Theatre at New York Token 100
90. 1809 Madison Indian Peace Medal 101
91. 1800 Thomas Truxtun Naval Medal 102
92. 1792 Washington "Roman Head" Cent/Token 103
93. Charles Carroll of Carrollton Medal 104
94. Elongated Nickel of the Columbian Exposition 105
95. Washington / Column Indian Peace Medal 106
96. 1818 New Spain Jola 107
97. 1919 to Date, the J. Sanford Saltus Medal 108
98. Store Cards of Augustus B. Sage 109
99. Sir Francis Drake's Globe Circumnavigation Medal 110
100. 1861 Fort Sumter Medal 111

Appendix: What Might Have Been—No. 101 to No. 200 112
Notes 115
About the Authors 117
Credits and Acknowledgments 117
Selected Bibliography 118

FOREWORD

MEDALS

By David T. Alexander

Medal collecting is enjoying a renaissance in the United States today, echoing the vast popularity medals enjoyed in the pioneer era of American numismatics in the mid-19th century. Medals occupied an honored niche in all of the great collections from the first stirrings of numismatic interest in the 1850s until the 1890s triggered the sudden and all-consuming focus on U.S. coins by date and mintmark.

After that time, medals underwent decades of neglect, despite the virtually limitless topical interest they offer. Medals span the worlds of art, history, biography, science, and industry and are unmatched in the colorful variety of sizes, shapes, and metals in which they are struck or cast. The medal was popular with European collectors since its 15th century reinvention by Antonio Pisano (called Pisanello) in Italy. Medals were a recognized medium for the expression of fine art and commemoration in Italy, the German States, the Netherlands, France, and Britain.

Medals relating to American colonial history were cataloged by C. Wyllys Betts, although his researches were published in 1894 after his death, and the items he included are still referred to as "Betts medals"—to the occasional amusement of our European colleagues. The Continental Congress fathered the new nation's first official medals, the famous Comitia Americana series, hailing Revolutionary War heroes beginning with a medal commemorating George Washington's role in the British evacuation of Boston.

These earliest medals were struck at the Paris Mint, since the struggling United States would have no operating mint until 1793. Enterprising merchants Jacques Manly and Joseph Sansom created the earliest privately issued medals on what became a favorite national theme, the life and career of George Washington. A key factor that caused American medal collecting to lag behind has been the lack of adequate guides and catalogs, but Washingtonia is a notable exception. This area flourishes today thanks to William S. Baker's classic *Medallic Portraits of Washington*, first published in 1885, updated in modern times by Russell Rulau and Dr. George Fuld.

The infant Philadelphia Mint soon played a major role in developing the American medal through its series of Indian peace, presidential, military and naval, exposition and award, and other medals of all kinds. U.S. Mint medals have become another well-charted area, made accessible to today's collectors by R.W. Julian's masterful *Medals of the United States Mint: The First Century, 1792–1892*, published in 1977.

Outside the Mint, private medalists of the 19th century added to the corpus of America's medallic treasures: the exceptionally talented engraver Charles Cushing Wright, Robert Lovett Jr., his prolific brother George Hampden Lovett, Boston's Joseph Merriam, and John Adams Bolen of Springfield, Massachusetts, among them. The Civil War triggered a major flurry of activity in the form of award and commemorative medals for battles, heroes, and veterans' organizations on both sides of the blue-gray divide.

As the 20th century dawned, the U.S. Mint faded from leadership in medallic art. The honors passed to private companies, notably Whitehead & Hoag of Newark, New Jersey, and the youthful Medallic Art Company of New York City. Although it struck a vast array of medals, the Newark firm deliberately avoided any emphasis on the artistic component of its medals, preferring to emphasize the utilitarian business and industrial aspects of the products.

Medallic Art, on the other hand, based its total business strategy on the closest possible interaction with the art community. The firm was born just as the art medal came into its own with the creation in 1908 of the Circle of Friends of the Medallion by Robert L. Hewitt and Charles DeKay. Until 1915, the Circle issued two art medals a year inserted in hardbound books, with Medallic Art producing the first and last issues.

This two-medal-per-year format was revived by George Dupont Pratt when he launched the Society of Medalists (SOM) in 1928 and issued its first art medals in 1930. This greatest series of true art medals continued into the 1990s. Produced with the stated goal of fostering excellence in American medallic sculpture, SOM medals offer the bas-relief art of many legendary artists whose work in any other form would be prohibitively expensive today.

Some nonprofit organizations produced a medal series, notably the New York City–based American Numismatic Society. Their first medal in 1866 by Emil Sigel was dedicated to the memory of Abraham Lincoln. Producing this ultra-high-relief medal nearly bankrupted the young society, but it rallied and went on to issue many outstanding medals into the 21st century, continuing today.

Medallic Art Company issues covered a wide spectrum of events and subjects, including state and local anniversaries, most of the finer issues of the American Revolution bicentennial, and medals for colleges and universities, business and industry, aviation and space, railroads and shipping, learned societies, and organizations of all descriptions.

Its work for numismatic groups included the convention and award medals of the American Numismatic Association (ANA) over several decades. Typical of its work for smaller organizations is the nearly century-old series of presidential medals of the New York Numismatic Club, now struck by Medalcraft Mint of Green Bay, Wisconsin.

Medallic Art was a major producer of presidential inaugural medals. The U.S. Mint struck those of Herbert Hoover to Harry S. Truman, but Medallic Art struck most of the classic designs into the 1990s, beginning with Dwight D. Eisenhower in 1953. This specialized area was galvanized by the catalogs of Richard Dusterberg, Neil MacNeil, and H. Joseph Levine, which created a collecting boom in inaugural medals in the mid-1970s.

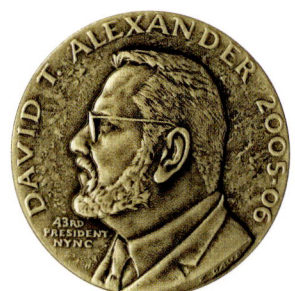

Medal issued in 2006 (shown actual size, 38 mm) to observe David T. Alexander's presidency of the New York Numismatic Club. Light brass with antiqued finish. Art by sculptor Eugene Daub.

The world of the medal was impacted by the meteoric rise of the Franklin Mint after 1967. This merchandising giant aggressively marketed its coin-relief, proof-surface products as "medals" to a wide spectrum of non-numismatic buyers. Franklin Mint pieces were only tangentially related to high-relief art and historical medals, and their lamentable secondary-market performance gave medals a bad name to a public unaware of such distinctions.

Numismatic auctions have played a pivotal role in reigniting collector enthusiasm for American medals. Sales of the great Garrett family collection by Bowers and Ruddy Galleries in 1979 through 1981 electrified many series, including privately issued 19th-century medals and issues of the U.S. Mint. The great inaugural-medal and U.S. Mint col-

FOREWORD

lection of David W. Dreyfuss was sold by Bowers and Merena in combination with Presidential Art and Antique Co. (headed by medal pioneer H. Joseph Levine), and introduced Michael J. Hodder to medal cataloging. Johnson & Jensen of Danbury, Connecticut (which featured David T. Alexander as cataloger 1981–1983), was important in its time.

The oldest U.S. numismatic auctioneer, Stack's of New York City, initiated high-quality medal auctions beginning in 1990, including its annual Americana sales. Stack's recently launched a series of sales offering the vast collection of the late dealer-collector John J. Ford Jr. (1925–2005). In his busy lifetime, Ford built collections in numerous areas—including Betts medals and general U.S. Mint and Indian peace medals—that were the greatest ever assembled by a private collector.

Organizations serving medal collectors appeared only in the second half of the 20th century. The Token and Medal Society (TAMS) was organized in 1960, and its *Journal* featured many high-quality medal articles, especially in its early years. The Orders and Medals Society of America (OMSA) was formed in 1950 to serve collectors in these specialized areas.

Interested medallic sculptors and collectors, including the present writer, organized the American Medallic Sculpture Association (AMSA) in 1982. That organization soon directed most of its effort into the areas of actual medal sculpting and production. There was still no organization specifically focused on the needs of medal collectors, although an attempt was made in 1972 when the short-lived Collectors of Art Medals blazed across the horizon.

The long-standing need was met in August 1998, when Medal Collectors of America (MCA) was born at the ANA convention at Portland, Oregon. Under the leadership of presidents David T. Alexander and John W. Adams, MCA has achieved solid growth and launched publications that are full of promise for the medal field.

It can be safely said that the future for medal collecting is bright in the 21st century, enriched by organizations and publications, of which the present volume is a significant example.

TOKENS

BY RUSSELL RULAU

The full flourishing of medallic beauty in the American token field occurred in the 19th century, as a host of great diesinkers and engravers embellished our substitutes for small change. It was a time when the private token was needed either to supplement the U.S. Mint's output or to replace it altogether when hoarding of coins took place. To the 21st-century American the word *token* has a greatly reduced significance, limited to streetcar or bus fare pieces, or tokens used to activate bridge, tunnel, or turnstile admittance.

Tokens began to be used in America when the 13 colonies thrust aside their allegiance to England. Soon afterward these pieces were needed to supplement the early Philadelphia Mint's coinage from 1793 through about 1843, or the end of the Hard Times period. During the Civil War (1861–1865) there was massive hoarding of all coinage—gold, silver, and copper based. In the years 1862 to 1864 almost all small change in circulation was privately issued by tradesmen and speculators, including the tokens and encased postage stamps featured in this book. The 19th century also saw the use of tokens for another purpose: advertising. We hobbyists call these *store cards*, *advertising checks*, or similar names to distinguish them from the money tokens. Tokens as a supplement to the legal-tender coinage saw service from the late 18th century, expanding during the Hard Times and Civil War eras, and continuing through the end of World War II in 1945 down to the present time.

The book before you, the product of the pen of one of America's greatest numismatists, Q. David Bowers, and of the energetic researcher Katie Jaeger, herself a descendant of the great Lovett family of engravers, is the first ever to present tokens in full color in a format understandable to everyone able to read English. The Bowers-Jaeger team was assisted by a chosen group of exonumists. The courage of Whitman Publishing in creating this lavish coffee-table book on U.S. tokens and medals has been backed up by the votes of a large number of experts in selecting the "100 Greatest" of the hundreds of thousands of varieties known. This book is not just another book on tokens and medals. Its hallmark is that of Bowers himself: deep, innovative research techniques that bring the reader facts never before gathered in one venue.

I used the word *exonumist* above. It's a word comfortable to me, as I coined it from classical roots in 1960 and had it accepted by Webster's dictionary in 1965. It simply means a collector of tokens, medals, and similar noncoin items. The field is thus called *exonumia*, and that term is in general use within numismatics.

Beauty is in the eye of the beholder, and many selections within these pages may not conform to the reader's idea of magnificent medallic art, but the word *greatest* must be accepted in its numismatic context: rarity, desirability, and popularity, as well as eye appeal. As the author of the *Standard Catalog of United States Tokens 1700–1900*, now in its fourth edition of 1,200 pages, I have collected, studied, and popularized our token emissions since I first became fascinated with them in 1939. Thus, when Dave Bowers asked me to write the tokens foreword to this opus, the request could not be denied. Never once could I have envisioned a full-color background study book such as this, especially with the imprimatur of the 75-year-old numismatic publishing firm of Whitman upon it.

Well-known experts nominated their idea of the "100 Greatest," and the publisher's staff then collated more than 300 nominees to be submitted for vote by an even larger group of experienced exonumists. The result is a collage of the best thinking of folks who have spent much of their lives in this field—dealers, collectors, curators, scholars, and writers.

Personal medal struck by the Pobjoy Mint for Russell Rulau (shown actual size, 39 mm). Issuing their own medals has been popular with numismatists ever since the late 1850s.

A separate medals foreword has been written by my friend and colleague Dave Alexander, which readers should peruse with care. The two fields are in actuality closely related: one can hardly collect tokens without some knowledge of medallic art, and medal collectors learn appreciation for token design. As the text explains, there are many issues that can be called either tokens or medals, although most are clearly in one class or the other.

Coin collectors, who far outnumber token collectors, eventually become numismatists in the full sense, and at this point many add tokens to their holdings of coins and paper money. There are many more collectors of tokens than of medals, due in part to the ever-growing popularity of Hard Times tokens (1832–1844) and Civil War tokens (1861–1865). It was not always so, and in the early 19th century medals were pursued with passion, while contemporary tokens were more or less ignored (as were, for that matter, federal coins).

The 19th-century issuance of tokens after the Civil War witnessed handsome design concepts relating to the U.S. Centennial Exhibition in

FOREWORD

Philadelphia in 1876 and the World's Columbian Exposition in Chicago in 1893. Some carryover of this type of store card occurred with the Pan-American Exposition in Buffalo in 1901, the St. Louis World's Fair in 1904, and the Century of Progress Exposition in Chicago in 1933.

The last quarter of the 19th century and the first half of the 20th saw huge numbers of tokens of the "good for" type, issued by saloons, billiard parlors, country general stores, coal mines, brothels, lumber operations, and many other entities. These have been out of fashion since 1950, as the value of U.S. legal-tender coinage has dropped dramatically and the U.S. Mint's output of small change is in the billions each year.

We who collect and study American tokens tend to live in bygone days, but we do far more than just enjoy these items. We are recording and preserving the basic economic history of the United States at its corner-store and corner-saloon level. Perhaps readers of this book will discover an ancestor who has been uprooted from some molding city directory and given eternal life through his token issues.

As to the collector, it has been truly said that "once a token collector, always a token collector." To such specialists, these pieces hold far more interest than U.S. coins, are less expensive to collect, are a relatively safe investment, and—most important—avoid that endless hole-filling syndrome associated with acquiring different dates and mintmarks of the same coin. In 1860 tokens were near the top of the numismatic heap and were extensively featured in auction catalogs and elsewhere. By the 1950s tokens were relegated to the sidelines. The late Ralph "Curly" Mitchell said as we formed the Token and Medal Society in 1960, "One man's junk is another man's treasure." This society spurred interest, as did the formation of the Civil War Token Society. Now in the early 21st century we've come full circle: often in auction sales, convention exhibits, and elsewhere, tokens as well as medals take the limelight. Competition in the salesroom for a prized Hard Times token, Civil War token, store card, or encased postage stamp can be fierce—every bit as dramatic as when famous federal coins are sold, but at price levels that are much lower.

No doubt *100 Greatest American Medals and Tokens* will increase interest even more—showcasing interesting items in an interesting and beautiful book. Readers can look forward to learning about these fascinating pieces of Americana, or appreciating even more the tokens and medals they already own.

GRADES AND ESTIMATED MARKET VALUES

Estimated market values are given for each of the 100 listed items. When an entry represents a whole class, the prices given represent one of the more readily available items in that class; rarities are worth more, often much more. Sales are infrequent for many of the rarer items, with years elapsing between auction offerings. Often when a new offering occurs, earlier prices are exceeded by a large amount.

Numerical grading and certification is widespread in the market for American federal coins (using the 70-point official American Numismatic Association grading system) and is rapidly being adopted into auctions and other offerings of tokens, less so for medals. The ANA numerical system is used here, together with grade descriptions such as Very Fine, Mint State, and Proof. Usually there are several grades for each item. Grading is a matter of opinion, and often two experts' opinions can vary, sometimes considerably. Before making any purchase, verify current market conditions and secure current estimates.

MEDALS

Medals did not circulate, although some of them can be very worn (certain Indian peace medals are examples). Generally, medals in this book are evaluated in these grades:

Choice to gem Uncirculated or Proof, 60 to 65: A medal that has seen little if any handling and has very few contact marks. For many if not most art medals of the 20th century, gem is the rule, not the exception (gem being 65 or finer on the ANA scale).

Mint State or Proof, 60 to 62: Light handling will be evident in the form of marks in the field, some tiny nicks on the rim, or similar.

EF-40 to AU-58: Light wear is evident, but all lettering and most of the elements and details of the design will be clearly evident. Some award medals, museum admission passes, Indian peace medals, and the like are often seen in these grades.

TOKENS

Tokens made for *numismatic purposes* are graded the same as medals, as they exist today in higher grades. Those made for *circulation* are graded as follows, with several of these grades (but not all) selected, depending upon the issue.

Choice to gem Uncirculated or Proof, 63 to 65: Same as for medals.

Basic Uncirculated or Proof, 60 to 62: Same as for medals.

EF-40 to AU-58: Same as for medals.

Very Fine-20 to 35: Medium wear from circulation. Details such as hair strands and leaf veins will be worn away in areas of higher relief. Handling marks, nicks, and the like are to be expected, especially on heavier issues.

Fine-12: Extensive wear, with many details gone. Overall design will be bold. Equivalent to 12 on the ANA scale.

Very Good-8: Well worn. Design is clear but flat and lacks details. Equivalent to 8 on the ANA scale.

Good-4: Heavily worn. Designs and legends are visible, but are faint in areas. Equivalent to 4 on the ANA scale.

INTRODUCTION

Welcome to *100 Greatest American Medals and Tokens*. For both of us the creation of this book has been an incredible journey, leading to many interesting and sometimes obscure paths and byways. The arrangement, in order from No. 1, *the* greatest, to No. 100, which brought up the rear, is the result of an extensive survey taken by Whitman Publishing among collectors, writers, and dealers in the field of tokens and medals—what foreword-writer Russell Rulau many years ago dubbed *exonumia*, a name that has stuck.

What is a medal? What is a token? Kenneth Bressett, longtime editor of *A Guide Book of United States Coins* and always a good source for consultation, suggests that, for starters, *coins* are metal pieces "issued by a government or other authority to serve in commerce as money." *Tokens* are "issued by entities other than governments, but have a value in exchange—for goods or services."

Medals form a separate challenge, and in checking around it seems that definitions suggested by well-known experts can vary widely. Medals and their little cousins, medalets, might be, per our thoughts, created for awards, commemoration, recognition, tradition, and so on, with no exchange value of any kind. Medals did not circulate. They were usually sold as souvenirs or mementos and are usually seen today in Mint State grade, or close, or in Proof format.

The *medalet* or small medal has a rich tradition. Political campaign medalets sized mostly below 29 mm were struck in quantity beginning in the 1830s. In the 1850s, George H. Lovett and Augustus B. Sage called certain of their (approximately) 31 mm pieces medalets, such as in the Masonic Medalets series. Perhaps a medalet should be a medal measuring 32 mm or smaller. We'll leave it up to numismatic lexicographers to decide.

Some contributors suggested that tokens are tokens and medals are medals, and never the twain should meet. This defies tradition, however. For a long time—indeed, going back to the cradle days of numismatic auctions in the 1850s and 1860s—they were usually collected by the same specialists. Someone interested in political medals usually finds Hard Times tokens to be interesting, and whether certain of the issues of the late 1850s should be called tokens, medals, or medalets admits of various opinions. Perhaps the name of the Token and Medal Society says it all.

Now, on to the voting results. To have suggested that the greatest tokens and medals are those with the highest market values would have been an insult to history and art, simply a nod to the commercial arena of the moment, which may be different a generation from now. To have suggested that the greatest pieces are the rarest would have been a similar discredit—rarity really says little about the importance of a token or medal. Instead, voters determined the greatest based upon their own opinions of combined historical importance, numismatic tradition, artistry, utility, and other aspects. Certainly, rarity and value attract a lot of attention as part of numismatic tradition, yet the voting tally yielded an incredible spectrum of diverse issues. Indeed, diversity defines tokens and medals. An 1800 Washington funeral medal with the legend HE IS IN GLORY, THE WORLD IN TEARS (No. 11) bears little relation to a token showing a horse-drawn car on the New York and Harlaem Rail Road (No. 85), or the elegant Winfield Scott medal by Charles Cushing Wright, featuring on the reverse several dioramas of battles of the War with Mexico (No. 62). The unique *gold* medal by Wright, presented by Congress to President Zachary Taylor, was unknown to numismatists until September 2006, by which time the voting had been concluded. We can readily imagine that it would have placed high in the voting otherwise.

The writers guessed that the Libertas Americana medal might land in the No. 1 spot, and it did. We thought that the Washington Before Boston medal, if shooed out of first place, would capture No. 2, and it did. Beyond that, there were many surprises. Some favorites were left at the starting gate but are listed in the "What Might Have Been" appendix. Others were numismatic dark horses, at least to us, that finished in the money—this list is a long one and includes, of all things, 1944 OPA ration tokens (No. 81) and an elongated nickel from the World's Columbian Exposition (No. 94).

While most of the 100 finalists are well known, some required some looking up to learn the basics—such as the "1776" Washington / Column Indian peace medal (No. 95) and several of the Betts-listed issues, such as the 1746 Annapolis Tuesday Club medal (No. 80) and the Sir Francis Drake medal commemorating his circumnavigation of the globe (No. 99). The appearance on the auction market of the Lucien LaRiviere Collection of early medals a few years ago (cataloged mostly by John Kraljevich) and of the more recent and incredible cabinet of John J. Ford Jr. (cataloged mostly by Michael Hodder), as well as other significant properties, has focused a lot of attention on early Betts medals as well as other pieces that have been numismatic esoterica for a long time— the 1817 Amelia Island "Green Cross" medal (No. 76) is but one of many examples.

The listing of certain pieces in the *Guide Book of United States Coins* has no doubt greatly aided the popularity and recognition of certain issues. We surmise that otherwise the North West Company beaver token (No. 12), Lesher "dollars" (No. 18), and the Albany Church penny (No. 37) might not have made it into the winners' circle. Who knows?

Likely, *American Numismatics Before the Civil War* (Bowers, 1998), growing interest in the history of our hobby by members of the Numismatic Bibliomania Society (NBS), and the ANS-sponsored Augustus B. Sage Society (2005, sponsored by the American Numismatic Society, or ANS) resulted in many votes for Sage's token depicting early numismatist Charles I. Bushnell (No. 58) and for Sage's own store cards (No. 98).

The TAMS, CWTS, MCA, and for transportation token collectors, the American Vecturist Association (AVA), have provided venues for discussion of current events, sharing of research, and simple old-fashioned camaraderie, making the study and acquisition of such pieces more fun than ever. Specialized reference books have aided the hobby, as have computer databases and instant Internet searches and communications.

Like the selections published in *100 Greatest American Currency Notes* (Bowers and Sundman, 2006), the winners in *100 Greatest American Medals and Tokens* include many pieces that are available to collectors with modest budgets. Part of this is due to this field's being a numismatic byway, rather than the road most often taken. It takes some connoisseurship and knowledge to buy a Hard Times token, or a Civil War cent, or a Theodor Bollenhagen game counter—quite unlike the scenario for federal coins, in which much buying and selling is done by people who have little knowledge beyond current market price and certified grade.

Rarity is a key word for most of the 100 Greatest, even for the majority of inexpensive issues—not rarity in the sense that only a handful are known, but rarity in comparison to federal coins. A Wealth of the South token in Mint State is rare, with fewer than a hundred or so Mint State examples existing of any variety. A population in the dozens is more likely. Such a token might command the best part of $1,000 if a gem. An 1893-S Morgan silver dollar, of which perhaps 50 to 75 Mint State examples exist (plus 10,000 or so worn pieces), would bring perhaps $500,000

INTRODUCTION

at auction if it were a gem. Morgan dollars are more popular than Wealth of the South tokens, of course, but still it is evident that these tokens as well as many others offer much numismatic value for the prices paid. In recent years, more than just a few *unique* Civil War token varieties have traded for $500 to $1,000, although, of course, some with especially interesting characteristics have sold for far more.

Although each of the authors has a good background in history and research, while writing this book we learned many things. In some cases, conventional numismatic wisdom yielded to new information, as with the Manly medal (No. 17), whose portrait attribution has been incorrectly stated for many years, and the Truxtun medal (No. 91). For many others, mysteries remain. We don't know who coined the Feuchtwanger cents (No. 4), whether the 1793–1795 Ricketts's Circus token (No. 23) was struck at the Philadelphia Mint (where the dies were found some years later), or how the Carolina and New England Elephant coppers (No. 30) were distributed. The backgrounds and histories of the New Yorke in America token (No. 25), Gloucester token (No. 33), circa 1785 Bar copper (No. 39), and 1778–1779 Rhode Island ship token (No. 50) are shrouded in mystery, perhaps adding to their appeal. No. 95 (look it up!) has never been illustrated before, to our knowledge, but not much is known about it, including the identity of its engraver.

Historically, enthusiasts have found that a *cabinet* of tokens and medals, as it used to be called—or, today, a *collection*—can be a joy and comfort, readily turned to in an idle moment, to recapture the spirit it represents. America's greatest numismatic authorities saw the inherent value of medals and tokens. William Elliot Woodward, active from the 1860s through the 1880s, presented the J.N.T. Levick Collection of tokens and medals at auction on May 26 through 29, 1884, and included this comment:

> Many of these cards and tokens are amongst the very rarest of all American issues, and if the word rare with its superlatives is thought to occur too frequently, let it be attributed to the fact mentioned, which every collector knows is perfectly correct. The 1804 dollar and the 1802 half dime are actually common in comparison with many of these pieces, and I confess, that apart from their money value, I regard them as much less interesting. These pieces and the political series, now so much neglected, are an epitome of the political and business history of the country, while the Mint series is money—that's all.

In the preface to C. Wyllys Betts's study, *American Colonial History Illustrated by Contemporary Medals*, 1894, Frederic H. Betts gave this rationale for the desirability of medals:

> Medals are original documents in metal. . . . As contributions to the knowledge of the history of portraiture, dress, and habits, as indices of then existing information in architecture, geography, and the natural sciences, and as means of restoring the knowledge of structures long destroyed, medals are not to be underestimated. . . . One is to look upon a cabinet of medals as a treasure, not of money, but of knowledge. . . . "It is safer," it has been said, "to quote a medal than a historian."[1]

Lyman H. Low, one of the most highly respected dealers and numismatic scholars of his era, wrote in the preface to his *Hard Times Tokens* book in 1899:

> By reason of their sarcastic devices, their satirical quips, and the political war cries—humorous, scornful, and sometimes triumphant—which distinguished them, [these issues] have won a well recognized place in the cabinets of collectors of Americana. Indeed, the interest in them seems to be increasing rather than diminishing, especially as the difficulty of obtaining complete sets is found to grow greater and greater as time goes on.

In a live ANA presentation, "Frontiers in Numismatics," in August 1991, John J. Ford stated:

> The rarest, sexiest Civil War congressional medal of honor with documentation "that thick" about how the guy won it, might cost you 6,000 bucks. Compare that to a high-grade Monroe Doctrine half dollar for 30,000 bucks! With medals, you are buying history, not hype.

MEDALS AND TOKENS IN AMERICA
MEDALS RELATED TO EARLY AMERICA
INTRODUCTION

The following pages describe in approximate chronological order the making and use of tokens and medals in America. Included as they appear on the numismatic stage are histories of different engravers and minters and of the development of numismatic interest in their work.

PIERRE EUGÈNE DU SIMITIÈRE

The earliest numismatically inclined person in America for whom we have a fairly detailed biographical record was Swiss-born Pierre Eugène du Simitière (1737–1784), who had settled in Philadelphia by 1774.[2] Although he has no entry in the 100 Greatest, a mention of him here is essential to American medallic history. Not only did Du Simitière collect medals, but he was also involved in their production. On March 25, 1776, the Continental Congress passed this resolution:

> That the thanks of this Congress in their own name and in the name of the thirteen united colonies whom they represent, be presented to his Excellency Gen. Washington and the officers and soldiers under his command for their wise and spirited conduct in the siege and acquisition of Boston; that a medal of gold be struck in commemoration of this great event and presented to his Excellency; and that a committee of three be appointed to prepare a letter of thanks, and a proper device for the medal.

Accordingly, Du Simitière prepared a sketch depicting Washington standing with a figure of the goddess Liberty or Columbia, overlooking Boston Harbor.[3] On November 29, 1776, Congress "[p]aid P.E. DuSim-

INTRODUCTION

itiere for designing, making and drawing a medal for General Washington, $32." It was never used. Congress finally implemented the resolution in 1786, by placing an order for medals with the Paris Mint. Ignoring the work that Du Simitière had done, French engraver Pierre Simon Duvivier cut dies from designs provided by the Royal Academy of Inscriptions and Belles Lettres. He adapted his portrait of Washington from the well-known bust from life by Jean Antoine Houdon, made at Mount Vernon in October 1785. This is the famous Washington Before Boston medal (No. 2).

Although his Washington-Boston medal was not to be, Du Simitière seems to have designed and made a medal that was actually used in the Revolutionary War. A newspaper account related on August 12, 1776:

> The Congress have struck a number of silver and copper medals, which are distributed among the officers of the army, who wear them constantly. On one side are two vases swimming on the water, with the motto "Frangimur si collidimur"; on the other is an emblematical device; four hands clinched together and a dove over them, beneath them is a serpent cut in pieces. These medals were designed or executed by P.E. DuSimitiere.[4]

Perhaps with the hope that an example would come to light someday, Betts assigned 550 as the number for this medal. Should one ever be found, it would create a numismatic sensation. Surely, if it existed now it would be honored among the 100 Greatest.

From this beginning arose many illustrious medals. To honor and commemorate the heroes and triumphs of the Revolutionary War, Congress authorized a dozen medals to be struck—the Comitia Americana ("American Congress") series, which is a focal point of numismatic interest today (Nos. 35 and 56). Commissions for most of these were placed with and executed at the Paris Mint. In 1800, the victory of USS *Constellation* captain Thomas Truxtun highlighted the undeclared war with France, and resulted in a fine medal (No. 91). The War of 1812 medals, struck at the Philadelphia Mint from dies by John Reich and Moritz Fürst, are another impressive series (No. 43).

EARLY COLLECTIONS AND DISPLAYS

THE SCENE IN EUROPE

Americans were latecomers as collectors of tokens and medals. By 1858 (the year generally regarded as the beginning of widespread interest in numismatics in the United States), in the cultured cities of London, Paris, Rome, Vienna, and Leipzig, medal collecting had been popular since the Renaissance. In England, the collecting of tokens and medals was deeply rooted. Many if not most museums had exhibits of coins and medals, and it was a reflection of the taste of a gentleman to have a cabinet of such pieces in a drawing room or parlor. In the 1780s hundreds of varieties of privately minted copper halfpenny tokens were used in commerce. Made in Birmingham, London, and elsewhere, these tokens featured a wonderful diversity of motifs, ranging from royalty to castles and abbeys, exotic animals, commercial services and products, political satire—and more. These ignited a fad and attracted the attention of many people who set about collecting them.

Soon, diesinkers vastly expanded the panorama by striking pieces especially for the numismatic trade. They muled dies for commercial tokens with unrelated dies made for other series, to create illogical com-

Mulings (or mules), illogical combinations of dies, formed a particularly popular specialty within the Conder token series. The 1794 and 1795 Talbot, Allum & Lee token obverses were combined with several irrelevant reverse dies. Above is a 1794 Talbot, Allum & Lee obverse with a 1793 Promissory Halfpenny reverse (Breen-1043; shown actual size 28.6 mm).

binations that were interesting to collect. Books were published to aid the enthusiast, including *An Arrangement of Provincial Coins, Tokens, and Medalets, Issued in Great Britain, Ireland and the Colonies, within the last 20 years, from the farthing to the penny size*, by James Conder, which gave rise to the term "Conder tokens," still in use today. More than a few Conder tokens depicted American motifs, including the Theatre at New York issue, which depicted the Park Theatre (No. 89); one with the portrait of Washington as a Roman emperor (No. 98); several with ships in the maritime trade for the New York City importing firm of Talbot, Allum & Lee (No. 36); and the P.P.P. Myddelton token (No. 20).

At the same time in Paris, medal makers had attained a high degree of artistry, with the designs and engravings of Pierre Simon Duvivier, Augustin Dupré, and others gaining worldwide recognition. These men produced the fledgling American government's congressional award (Comitia Americana) and exhibit medals, including the Libertas Americana (No. 1) and Washington Before Boston (No. 2), among others. Europe also gave birth to special medals for collectors illustrating such diverse subjects as scenes from the Bible, the wonders of nature, the abolition of slavery, and various monarchs. In 1820 in England, James Mudie published by subscription a set of National Medals created by diesinker Edward Thomason, who later turned out other extensive series of large-diameter medals mounted in velvet trays and enclosed in special cases.

In Paris, the Series Numismatica suite of medals included portraits of Benjamin Franklin and Washington, one of the latter having the inscription misspelled as WASINGTON. Completed circa 1830 during the reign of Louis Philippe I, the Gallery of the Kings of France series commemorated every reign since Pharamond in 417 A.D.

JOHN ALLAN: EARLY COLLECTOR AND DEALER

There were three buyers in the United States for Mudie's series, one of whom was John Allan of New York City. Today, Allan is remembered as America's first professional numismatist. His main activity was bookkeeping and the administration of estates from his Pearl Street office in New York, where he maintained an inventory of world coins and medals—American coins being "but little sought for at that time."[5] His customers included Philip Hone, James Thornton, Pierre Flandin, A.D. Moore, and Michael Moore. Hone, who served a term as mayor of New York (1825–1826), assembled an important cabinet.[6] E.H. Ludlow sold Hone's collection on April 28, 1852, the first significant auction offering of numismatic items in New York City.

In 1859, New York City diesinker and engraver George H. Lovett made a token honoring Allan. The subject's name was Latinized as JOHANNES ALLAN, and the reverse illustrated him as an antiquarian examining a coin. Allan died in New York City on November 19, 1863.

INTRODUCTION

Other Pioneers

In 1787, William Bentley of Salem, Massachusetts, entered in his diary some interesting observations of coins then in circulation, creating one of the earliest records of this type known to exist, and including comments on halfpennies imported from Birmingham, England, and the various state copper coins then in circulation.[7] The July 20, 1791, entry included this:

> Being commencement at Cambridge [Harvard College], I set out for Cambridge from Deacon Ridgeway's and in a chaise went to Judge Winthrop's[8] with whom I spent the day. In the morning I entertained myself with his curious cabinet of coins and medals. It was large and not with any antiques, but it had a great variety of small pieces and may be deemed the best we have in this part of the country.

In the same era several museums and libraries added coins to their collections. The Philadelphia Museum, established by artist and naturalist Charles Willson Peale in 1784, had a cabinet of coins and medals, which it sold to P.T. Barnum in the mid-1840s. Peale issued an admission token dated 1821 (No. 55).

Dr. James Mease (1771–1846), a physician, philanthropist, and prominent citizen of Philadelphia, was an early student of medals. Like most other numismatists of the early 19th century, he also collected books, autographs, and artifacts. In 1821, his brief article "Description of Some of the Medals Struck in Relation to Important Events in North America" became the earliest known numismatic article to be published in the United States. In one of the first magazines with significant numismatic content, *Norton's Literary Letter* (No. 3, 1859), Mease was mentioned as one of three early numismatists whose research had been published in journals of historical societies. The other two were Dr. J.B. Felt of Salem, Massachusetts, and J. Francis Fisher of Baltimore, Maryland.

Robert Gilmor Jr., born in 1774 to a wealthy family in the mercantile trade, became an enthusiastic collector of coins, medals, art, autographs, and other historical items.[9] From May 16, 1799, to October 1, 1801, he went on a grand tour of Europe, visiting spots of cultural interest, including museums. While at the Imperial Cabinet of Natural History in Vienna, he saw several impressive numismatic items, including a gold medal that weighed 12 pounds and was said to be worth 1,500 guineas.[10] In 1821, Gilmor commissioned Englishman B. Faulkner to create a medal observing the 50th wedding anniversary of his parents. In his 69th sale, October 13–18, 1884, W.E. Woodward offered this:

> Lot 1221: "Medal of the Golden Wedding of Robert and Louisa Gilmore [sic]. Their busts joined; rev., Cupid with torch of Hymen. This medal is from the private collection formed by President Madison, and was purchased by Mr. [Herman] Ely of Charles H. Parsons, of Washington, D.C. . . . Tin, surface oxidized. Size 24.

This brings up the name of James Madison as a collector of medals—but the details of his cabinet are not known today. Andrew Jackson had a display that included tokens, medals, and coins. His large gold congressional medal in commemoration of the Battle of New Orleans was sold by a family member to a "prominent coin collector in New York City, and it is now in one of the large collections there."[11] Similarly, Jackson's gold 1826 Erie Canal medal (No. 8) was by 1891 in the cabinet of G.P. Thruston of Nashville, and now resides at the New-York Historical Society.[12] Not all pieces were dispersed, however. In 1891 an attractive group of medals still remained at Jackson's ancestral home in Tennessee, the Hermitage, and was prized by its caretakers.[13]

William Gordon Stearns (1804–1872) was a lawyer who in 1824 became steward at Harvard, helping to manage the institution's finances. When the Boston Numismatic Society was formed in 1860, he had been collecting for a longer time than any other of its founding members and had assembled "a somewhat extensive cabinet of coins and medals."[14]

In 1843, William E. Dubois, curator of the Mint Cabinet in Philadelphia, compiled a listing of amateur coin collectors known to him: Dr. Lewis Roper, Jacob G. Morris, Richard W. Davids (nephew of Morris), W.G. Mason, C.C. Ashmead, John Reeve, Mr. Cooper (of Camden, New Jersey), the Hon. Henry A. Muhlenberg (of Reading, Pennsylvania), Rev. Dr. Robbins (of Hartford, Connecticut; an uncle of Matthew A. Stickney), and Edmund B. Wynn (of Hamilton, New York). For some reason, well-known Philadelphia collector Joseph J. Mickley was not mentioned. Likely, by 1843 there were close to 100 dedicated numismatists in America.

Museum and Library Collections

By 1764 the Library Company of Philadelphia had a valuable collection of ancient coins and medals, some of which were the gift of Thomas Penn of England.[15] Quite possibly, this was the first American numismatic cabinet of importance. The collection of the American Museum, (a.k.a. Tammany Museum) established in New York City in June 1790 included at least a few medals, that wound up in 1842 with P.T. Barnum at his American Museum on lower Broadway, which may have been lost when Barnum's museum burned on July 13, 1865. It was said that among the items saved was a small box of coins.

Medal issued by P.T. Barnum for the American Museum in the 1850s. Among the attractions listed on the reverse are coins and medals. White metal; actual size 38.6 mm. Struck by Allen & Moore, Birmingham, England.

Founded in Salem, Massachusetts, in 1799 and incorporated in 1801, the East India Marine Society included prominent seamen, merchants, and traders among its members. Its library and collections were augmented by gifts from all over the world. In 1823, Admiral Sir Isaac Coffin presented a case of 111 medals to the society.[16] In 1846, the New York State Library had eight medals in its collection, and by 1853, when Richard W. Davids of Philadelphia, described its holdings, 58 pages were required in the catalog.[17]

INTRODUCTION

In June 1838 the Mint Cabinet was formally organized at the Philadelphia Mint, and on March 3, 1839, Congress voted an annual appropriation for its maintenance. An 1846 catalog of the holdings included some medals. Many other libraries, historical societies and museums displayed medallic selections through the 19th century.

EARLY ENGRAVERS AND MINTERS

English Coiners and Their Products

The Soho Manufactory, later sometimes known as the Birmingham Mint, was important in the making of certain tokens among the 100 Greatest: the Seasons medals (No. 6) and the P.P.P. Myddelton token (No. 20). Started in 1759 under the direction of Matthew Boulton Jr. of Birmingham, England, and later in partnership with James Watt, the manufactory produced metal utensils and accessories, industrial machines and devices, coins, and medals, and hundreds of varieties of Conder tokens. Talented engraver Conrad Heinrich Küchler cut the dies for the Seasons medals and the P.P.P. Myddelton token, both dated 1796.

Peter Kempson & Co., located in the same city, made the Talbot, Allum & Lee tokens (No. 36). Also in Birmingham, John Gregory Hancock produced the Washington "Roman Head" cent or token (No. 92). Birmingham coiner John Walker & Co. produced the 1820 North West Company beaver token (No. 12). B. Jacobs cut the dies for the Theatre at New York token (No. 89), struck in London by Peter Skidmore's token manufactory in High Holborn Street. This was the only American subject in an entire series featuring famous buildings. The Eccleston medal (No. 24), from dies by Thomas Webb, was also struck in England, as were the Elephant coppers (No. 30), Pitt token (No. 32), Bar copper (39), Felicitas Britannia and America medal (No. 42), and Admiral Vernon medals (70). The New Yorke in America token (No. 25) and the Washington "Born Virginia" medal (No. 72) are attributed to that country as well.

Getz and Perkins

Peter Getz, maker of the Washington Masonic medal (No. 45), is associated with several other early issues not in the 100 Greatest, notably the "Washington President I" pieces. Montroville W. Dickeson provided a sketch of his life in the *American Numismatical Manual* (1859):

> Mr. Peter Getz was born in Lancaster, Pa.; his occupation was that of a silversmith; but he was, otherwise, a very skillful mechanic and remarkable for his ingenuity. He excelled as a seal-engraver, and an engraver on steel, and was the inventor of a very ingenious hand-vise. He built the three first fire-engines for his native town, the Active, Sun, and another, which is still in existence in the county, and invented an improved printing press—noticed in the *Lancaster Journal*, January 8, 1810—worked by rollers instead of the screw, which, by printers was considered a great improvement. . . . Mr. Getz was personally complimented by Washington for his artistic skill in producing the die for what is called the "Washington Cent," and it was also officially recognized by the government.

Jacob Perkins of Newburyport, Massachusetts, one of the most famous figures in American numismatic history, is noticed here for his sentimental 1800 Washington funeral medal (No. 11). Born in 1766, he showed an early aptitude for art and mechanics, and apprenticed to a goldsmith and jeweler in 1779. In business on his own account by 1783, he engraved dies for Massachusetts copper one-cent pieces in 1788. In the next decade he created innovations in the manufacturing of nails and the printing of bank notes, among other activities. In 1792 he sought but failed to get a position at the new U.S. Mint.

After 1800 he introduced the patented stereotype steel plate, which became widely used to print bank notes, and the siderographic process of transferring bank-note vignettes to printing plates. His other inventions ranged from ship navigation devices, to a steam-powered gun, to fire engines. Perkins moved to England in 1818, where he remained for the rest of his life. There he printed the first postage stamps in the world, the British "penny black" issues, with plates made by the siderographic process.

MEDAL ILLUSTRATIONS OF THE 1830S AND 1840S

Jacob R. Eckfeldt and William E. Dubois, officers of the U.S. Mint who were also curators of the Mint Cabinet, formed the collection beginning in June 1838. In 1842 the Assay Office published *A Manual of Gold and Silver Coins of All Nations*, illustrated with numerous engravings of coins of the Mint Cabinet, using a medal-ruling machine. In the coming years, this innovative device would be exceedingly popular for illustrating medals and converting images of coins, medals, and plaques for use as illustrations on bank notes. The book gave an overview:

> It is not difficult to imagine an arrangement of machinery such that while one point is tracing a line across the face of a medal, rising and falling according to the elevations and depressions over which it passes, another point shall draw, on a flat surface, a profile of this line. If now the tracer be made to move successively in a series of parallel and equidistant planes, over the whole surface of the medal, there will be thus drawn a series of profiles corresponding to the sections of these planes with the surface of the medal, and these lines will together form a drawing or engraving of the medal itself.
>
> Such an instrument was invented and executed, in 1817, by Mr. Christian Gobrecht, a native of Pennsylvania, now engraver of the Mint of the United States. In this instrument the "tracing point" moved across the medal in parallel planes perpendicular to the flat surface or "table" of the medal, and the profile lines were drawn on an etching ground laid on copper or steel, by the "etching point."

Asa Spencer, American mechanic and bank-note engraver, took one of Gobrecht's devices to London in 1819 and exhibited it widely. Joseph Saxton of the Mint improved Gobrecht's machine with a device powered by steam that took about a half hour to copy a coin or medal of about an inch in diameter.

INTRODUCTION

The famous Washington Before Boston medal as illustrated on the frontispiece of Thomas Wyatt's *Memoirs of the Generals . . .*, with medals illustrated via the medal-ruling machine.

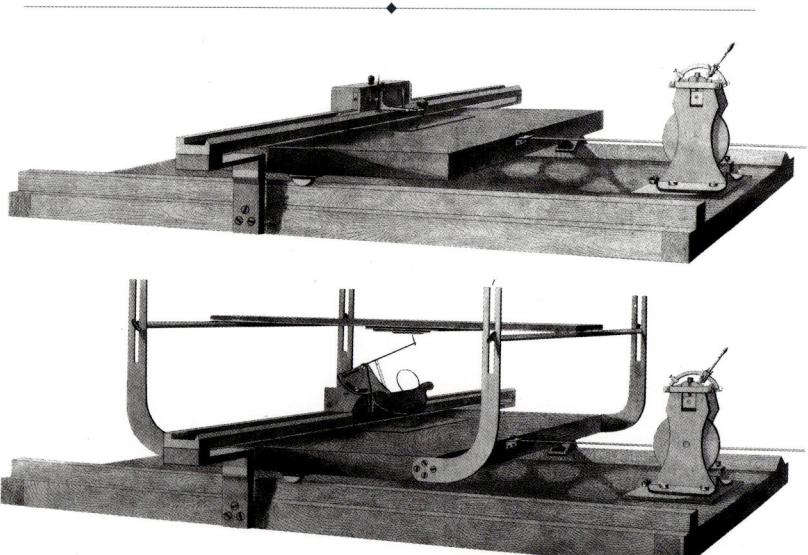

A medal-ruling machine (top) and a medal-copying machine made by W.L. Ormsby. The medal-ruling machine permitted coins, tokens, and medals to be copied with precision to make printing plates. (Illustrated in *Bank Note Engraving*, Ormsby, 1852)

In 1848, Philadelphia publishers Carey & Hart issued Thomas Wyatt's 315-page, extensively illustrated book, *Memoirs of the Generals, Commodores, and Other Commanders, Who Distinguished Themselves in the American Army and Navy During the War of the Revolution.* Engraver W.L. Ormsby prepared 14 of its plates using a medal-ruling machine of his own make.

TOKENS AND MEDALS TO THE FORE: 1858 THROUGH THE 1860S

THE MEDALET PASSION OF 1858 AND 1859

In the summer of 1858, several elements came together to initiate what became a passion for collecting newly minted medals. The successful laying of the Atlantic Cable, completed on August 5, 1858, spurred George H. Lovett to create a commemorative medalet for general sale to the public. The obverse depicted a stylized view, as seen from the north looking south, of John Bull on the left, representing England, exchanging electrical sparks with Brother Jonathan, representing America. Although details are scarce today, these medals probably proved to be popular with souvenir hunters as well as numismatists.

In 1858 the coin hobby was just beginning to spread, fueled by the rapid disappearance of "large" copper cents and the advent of the small Flying Eagle cents, launched on May 25, 1857. More than a dozen coin dealers were active in New York City, Philadelphia, Boston, Baltimore, and elsewhere, handling items such as popular prints, books, and antiques. New York City dealers Augustus B. Sage, Ezra Hill, and John Curtis were enjoying a lively trade. In Philadelphia, William K. Idler and Edward Cogan entered the business, and in Boston was Henry Cook, who also operated a shoe sale and repair shop.

Joseph Merriam of Boston was one of America's most highly talented engravers in the 1860s when he issued an illustrious series of medalets for the numismatic trade. This one (shown actual size, 27 mm) combines the obverse of a store card for the Apollo Gardens, a Boston watering hole, with an irrelevant reverse die stating that the medalet was struck from copper taken from the ruins of the turpentine works in New Bern, North Carolina, destroyed by the rebels on March 14, 1862. These and other Merriam medalets are eagerly sought by numismatists today.

Supplying the dealers were medalists in New York and Philadelphia—the sons of Robert Lovett (George H., John D., and Robert Jr.), William Bridgens, F.B. Smith & Hartmann, and F.C. Key & Sons—while Joseph H. Merriam was at work in Boston, and Benjamin True in Cincinnati. Each of these and many more tapped into the growing numismatic market to create medalets and tokens depicting people and events from the past as well as current events. Most of these ranged from 28 mm to 31 mm and came in copper, brass, and white metal. Sometimes silver strikings were produced on special order. As with the Conder series, "rarities" were concocted by mixing dies in combinations never intended to be mated with each other. (Most were made in very small numbers, some as restrikes years after the original issues.) Today these illogical pieces are highly prized by collectors. Some even combined dies from different makers, such as Lovett dies coupled with those of Merriam, Bridgens, or Key. Hundreds of medalets from the late 1850s are described and priced in Rulau's *Standard Catalog of United States Tokens 1700–1900.*

ISSUES OF 1860 AND 1861

Political-themed medalets had been popular ever since the Hard Times era, and the elections of 1860 spawned many medalets. Slavery was the main campaign issue. Candidate Abraham Lincoln was against it, while his opponents either opposed it mildly or were content to let the institution remain in place, so as not to worsen the greatly strained relations between the North and the South. Playing into this scenario, Cincinnati diecutter Benjamin C. True created the Wealth of the South tokens (No. 64) with the inscription NO SUBMISSION TO THE NORTH. From 1860, these enjoyed a wide sale in the South, but numismatists acquired them as well. Meanwhile, William Leggett Bramhall, a New York City numismatist and early member of the ANS, issued an extensive series of political medalets for the numismatic trade bearing portraits of Lincoln and Washington.

INTRODUCTION

The Crystal Palace token (shown actual size, 32 mm) was engraved and struck by George H. Lovett and marketed by Augustus B. Sage in autumn 1858, the first issue in his Odds and Ends series.

Since the late 1850s, politician and orator Edward Everett gave over 200 speeches telling of the life of our first president, to encourage citizens to support a restoration of Mount Vernon. At the same time, Mint director James Ross Snowden was working to expand the nation's Washington Cabinet (see No. 75). These events sparked a great demand for Washington items. Collectors scrambled to buy them in competition with Snowden, prices multiplied, and engravers worked to supply numerous new issues.

By 1861, the Civil War with its coin shortages occupied everyone's attention, and the creation of numismatic novelties slowed to a trickle, although Alfred S. Robinson of Hartford, Connecticut, endeavored to launch a new series with historical motifs.

Civil War Tokens

What is a Civil War token and what is not has eluded precise definition. Today it seems to be the case that if a token is listed in either of the two books by Melvin and George Fuld on Civil War tokens—patriotic issues and store cards—it is a Civil War token, or at least is collected as such. The Civil War began on April 12–13, 1861, with the bombardment of Fort Sumter, and ended on April 9, 1865, with the signing of the peace treaty at Appomattox, Virginia. During that period, numismatic items struck from dies proliferated, including the following:

Patriotic tokens. These bore patriotic inscriptions relating to the flag, the Union, the army and/or navy, and so on, with no merchant or town

Bronze medal (shown actual size, 38.6 mm) from dies by Robert Lovett Jr. of Philadelphia for the Washington Light Infantry (WLI) of Charleston, South Carolina, July 4, 1860. The reverse shows Fame painting Washington's name on a cloud. The state seceded from the Union on December 20, 1860, after which Captain Simonton and his company patrolled the harbor in an effort to persuade Major Robert Anderson and his federal troops to evacuate Fort Sumter (see No. 100).

listed. Most were about the size of a federal cent (19 mm), but there were exceptions (see No. 15).

Store cards. These bore commercial messages, including the name or other indication of the issuer and, sometimes, the product or service. Often the location of the issuer was given as well. Most were the approximate size of a federal cent, but there were exceptions (No. 16).

Political tokens and medals. These were issued for the presidential election of 1864 and were of small size, approximating the federal cent. Lincoln and McClellan were the candidates.

Sutlers' tokens. These were issued by camp suppliers in the Civil War. Sutlers were authorized merchants who traveled with military units and sold products such as writing paper, magazines, books, patent medicines, clothing, and other items. Certain of these tokens use Civil War token dies for one side and bear sutlers' names and affiliations on the other (No. 54).

(Left) A coining press of the type used to strike Civil War tokens, as depicted on such a token (reverse of Fuld NY-630-AJ-1a). (Right) The Civil War token die (Fuld-1069) depicting an Indian head with the inscription THE PRAIRIE FLOWER has been a collectors' favorite for many years. Several dozen different varieties were made, the illustrated example being Fuld OH-165-DY-4a. Civil War tokens vary in size, usually about 19 mm.

Also made during this era were military badges, military medals, "dog tags" (soldiers' identification medals with a space for a stamped or engraved inscription), award medals, numismatic medalets, and other struck items, usually of size larger than a cent, often much larger. These are not considered Civil War tokens but are widely collected in their own right. The Wealth of the South tokens of 1860 are listed in the Fuld book and are often collected with that series.

Few large medals were issued to commemorate Civil War generals, battles, and related events—in contrast with, for example, the War of 1812. A fine selection was voted into the present listing: the Fort Sumter medal (No. 100), the Abraham Lincoln Indian peace medal (No. 57), the Stonewall Jackson medal (No. 74), and the Congressional Medal of Honor for the Civil War (No. 61).

Societies

On December 28, 1857, John Bohlen, Arthur G. Coffin, Mark Wilkes Collet, Samuel H. Fulton, Montgomery L. Frederick, J. Ledyard Hodge, Joseph J. Mickley, Alfred Bates Taylor, and William S. Vaux met in Philadelphia to organize a club for coin and medal collectors, the Philadelphia Numismatic Society.[18] By January 1859 there were 25 members.

On March 8, 1858, New York numismatists Augustus B. Sage, Henry O. Hart, James D. Foskett, Edward Groh, and James Olive affixed their names to a circular letter inviting interested collectors to meet at Sage's family residence to establish what became the American Numismatic Society (ANS). They formed a small collection of coins, tokens, and medals through donations. The society lapsed until 1864, when

INTRODUCTION

Robert Hewitt Jr. and George H. Perine revived it as the American Numismatic and Archaeological Society.[19]

IN THE AUCTION GALLERY

Sales of estates, artworks, books, and other items held in early 19th century cities occasionally included coins, tokens, and medals, but these items were not highlighted. Then in 1859, five sales were cataloged in New York City. The venue was typically the salesroom of auctioneers Bangs, Merwin & Co. The most honored cataloger of the 1860s was W.E. Woodward, who added detailed historical and numismatic descriptions to many of his listings. His sales, which continued through the early 1890s, were rich with tokens and medals, including great rarities. Edward D. Cogan, who began with a mail-bid sale of old copper cents in 1858, was the second most prominent cataloger of the decade. Several others conducted sales as well.

For the serious collector of tokens and medals, purchases at auction provided the main source for acquisitions. There were no generally agreed-upon grading standards. Most numismatists either attended sales in person or paid a small commission to a dealer who would examine the lots and bid accordingly.

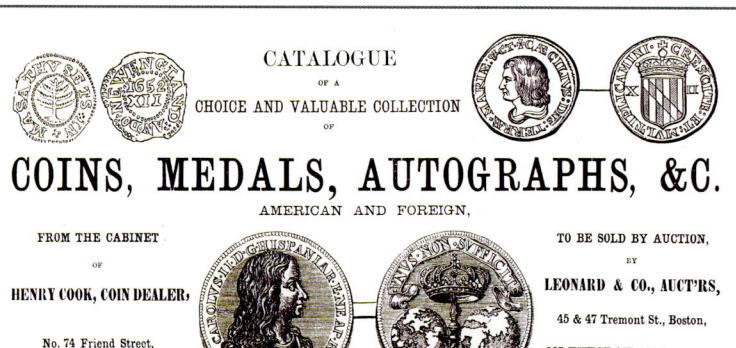

The cover of a four-page listing of 422 lots sold by Leonard and Company auctioneers in Boston in November 1863, with pieces consigned by well-known local dealer Henry Cook. Many interesting tokens and medals were offered, several of which were voted into the present 100 Greatest (see lots 28, 29, 30, 40, and 45 in the 1863 catalog).

BOOKS AND PERIODICALS OF THE 1850S AND 1860S

January 1857 saw the first issue of *Historical Magazine*. This monthly periodical would become a focal point for inquiries, news, and articles on many subjects, including coins and medals, in an era in which no magazine was exclusively devoted to numismatics.

Norton's Literary Letter, published by Charles B. Norton—New York City bookseller and dealer in autographs, coins, and other collectors' items—also premiered in 1857. Coins and medals were among the topics featured. The famous 1778 Non Dependens Status token, whose origins are still a puzzle to scholars today, was described in the second issue. Also in 1858, in *An Historical Account of American Coinage*, John Hickcox made note of the token:

> 1778. A copper piece, size of a cent. Obverse, a bust; legend, NON. DEPEN-DENS STATUS: reverse, a full length figure of an Indian seated on a globe, with a girdle about his loins. In his right hand, which is extended, he holds a branch of tobacco; his left hand rests on a shield, on which is the American flag and sword, crossed, and the fleur de lis of France; legend, AMERICA. Exergue, 1778.

It seems to have created quite a stir—so much so that Connecticut numismatist and banker Alfred S. Robinson had copy dies made of it, probably by George H. Lovett, and issued examples in copper and silver. Sylvester S. Crosby added an engraving of it to his *Early American Coins* (1875). This was picked up by Lyman H. Low, as part of the description of Lot 25 in his sale of September 25, 1918:

> This interesting piece entered the numismatic arena quite in the same manner as its many companions, though not contemporary. It has strangely wandered incognito, through catalogues and collections, for upwards of 50 years, carrying a total absence of origin, issuer or publisher.

In 1858, Charles I. Bushnell, prominent New York City collector and scholar, published *An Historical Account of the First Three Business Tokens Issued in the City of New York*. Featured were the 1789-dated Mott token and both dates of Talbot, Allum & Lee tokens, 1794 and 1795 (No. 36). In the same year appeared his far more important work, *An Arrangement of Tradesmen's Cards, Political Tokens, Also, Election Medals, Medalets, etc. Current in the United States of America for the Last Sixty Years, Described From the Originals, Chiefly in the Collection of the Author, With Engravings*.[20] Listed were many pieces now among the 100 Greatest.

In January 1860, Mark W. Collet, J. Ledyard Hodge, and Alfred B. Taylor described 423 pieces as the *Catalogue of American Store Cards &c., With Space for Marking the Condition, Price, Rarity, &c., of Each Piece, Designed for the Use and Convenience of Collectors*, the result of a study by members of the Philadelphia Numismatic Society. In 1862, Alfred H. Satterlee published his *Arrangement of Medals and Tokens, Struck in Honor of the Presidents of the United States, and of the Presidential Candidates, From the Administration of John Adams to That of Abraham Lincoln, Inclusive*. Although copies were never plentiful, this served as the standard reference on political tokens and medals for many years.

At the ANS meeting of March 1866, J.N.T. Levick (issuer of No. 63) proposed that a monthly journal be published, and in May 1866 the

INTRODUCTION

American Journal of Numismatics made its debut. From the outset it carried extensive coverage of tokens and medals, including important studies of Civil War issues. After the advent of the *Journal*, numismatic contributions to *Historical Magazine* dropped precipitately.

In 1867 Ebenezer Locke Mason Jr. launched *Mason's Coin and Stamp Collectors' Magazine*, the first house organ published by a rare coin dealer, continuing through 1872. His February 1869 issue contained a pasted-in sheet titled "Mason's Photographic Gallery of Coin Collectors of the United States, No. 1," showing portraits of 48 numismatists. There never was a number 2.

There were no general reference books on American tokens and medals in print, except for limited coverage in William C. Prime's 1861 *Coins, Medals and Seals*. In 1859, Montroville Dickeson's *American Numismatical Manual* emphasized federal coins, but included a few tokens and medals. A great specialized text by Mint director James Ross Snowden, *A Description of the Medals of Washington*, appeared in 1861.

DIESINKERS AND MEDALISTS OF THE 19TH CENTURY

Many of the issues highlighted in Andrew C. Zabriskie's "Reminiscences of Some Old New York Die Sinkers" (*Proceedings of the American Numismatic and Archaeological Society*, 1887) are enshrined in the 100 Greatest. Zabriskie recounted the elegant medallic productions of diesinkers linked to the earliest New York diesinkers, Richard Trested and C.C. Wright—Frederick B. Smith, James Bale, and Herman Hartmann—saying:

> Superb as are these works, it is my opinion nevertheless that to the New Yorker the most interesting products of Mr. Wright and his partners are the somewhat despised store cards. It is greatly to be regretted that many cards, although bearing in their workmanship strong proof that they were made by Messrs. Wright and Bale, have yet nothing to identify them as such; and as no record of the emissions from the workshop of this firm seems to have been preserved, it is extremely doubtful whether any light can be thrown upon the subject. One series, however, can be verified as the work of these men, viz:—the cards of the well known dry goods firm of Doremus, Suydam & Nixon.

Further regarding Charles Cushing Wright, it is not widely known that he was also a numismatist. In 1831 he gave lectures on classical coins and medals at the National Academy of Design, and exhibited there a medal he had made of DeWitt Clinton. Today, Wright is remembered as America's preeminent medalist from the mid-1820s until his death in 1854. Any important collection of American medals, whether formed in the 19th century or the present era, includes examples of his work.

OTHER MAKERS OF MEDALS AND TOKENS

In addition to the artists mentioned by Zabriskie, others are worth noting. The Scovill Manufacturing Company of Waterbury, Connecticut, was important in the 19th century and continues in business today. Its circa 1855 store card, the inscriptions of which describe its services, was voted as No. 87 in the 100 Greatest, and its encased postage stamps landed in the No. 14 spot. Scovill was also an important maker of patriotic Civil War tokens (No. 15) and store cards (No. 16).

There were numerous other important makers of these Civil War issues. Some also made sutlers' tokens (No. 54). In Cincinnati, John Stanton had a large token-making business, as did William K. Lanphear. Milwaukee businesses were featured on tokens by the talented duo Mossin and Marr. In New York City, William Bridgens produced many interesting motifs, as did Emil Sigel and others. The talented Joseph Merriam of Boston issued the "Good for a Scent" token (No. 83). John A. Bolen, of Springfield, Massachusetts, turned out the Pioneer Base Ball Club medal (No. 84), the first numismatic item dedicated to the "American game."

LATER YEARS OF THE 19TH CENTURY
THE 1870s

The decade of the 1870s was dynamic for collectors of tokens and medals. Auction catalogs proliferated as more dealers entered the field—including S.H. and Henry Chapman (the Chapman brothers), John W. Haseltine, J.W. Scott & Co., and Édouard Frossard, among others. In the absence of any generally available standard reference books on tokens and medals, catalogers such as W.E. Woodward furnished detailed descriptions of their designs, rarity, and other information—this in sharp contrast to listings of U.S. coins, which were apt to contain simply date and grade.

The *American Journal of Numismatics*, which became a quarterly and shifted its publication location to W.T.R. Marvin in Boston, served as a forum for information on tokens and medals. Frossard worked for Scott, and in December 1875 was editor of the first issue of *The Coin Collector's Journal*, a useful magazine that endured to January 1888. Alienated from Scott, Frossard started his own magazine, *Numisma*, in January 1877, continuing it through December 1891. In Philadelphia, E.B. Mason Jr. continued his magazine, which was started in 1867. All of these publications contained useful information on tokens and medals.

Engravers and medal shops continued to turn out pieces for the numismatic trade. Isaac F. Wood promoted his Wood's Memorial Series of medalets, from dies by George H. Lovett. Seemingly lacking a sense of marketing, Wood selected obscure topics with limited appeal. Accordingly, sales were slow, and such specimens are rare today. Lovett retained certain dies that he had made for Augustus B. Sage in 1859 and used these together with Wood dies and others to create nonsensical mulings—likewise rarities today. In the late 1870s Wood operated the New York Medal Club as a business enterprise at 64 Madison Avenue (styling himself as the "actuary" of the club) and advertised as a publisher of tokens and medals and a dealer in numismatic items.

Sylvester Sage Crosby, a native of Charlestown, New Hampshire, began collecting coins in 1857—the pivotal year in which large copper cents were discontinued. He was a watchmaker by trade, and conducted his business in Boston. On April 6, 1866, Crosby was named curator of the newly formed New England Numismatic and Archaeological Society. An account of the August 15 meeting the same year noted:

> Mr. Crosby produced, for examination, a Washington medal in bronze, having for an inscription on the reverse, "Presented to Cadet Palfrey, 1866." It is said that only 15 of these medals were struck. He also exhibited a set, in silver and bronze, of the rare pieces known as the "Season Medals," one of which derives additional interest from the fact of its having been for many years in the possession of the late Governor Eustis of Massachusetts. [See No. 6][21]

INTRODUCTION

Crosby's claim to enduring numismatic fame is his 1875 study, *The Early Coins of America and the Laws Governing Their Issue Comprising Also Descriptions of the Washington Pieces, the Anglo-American Tokens, Many Pieces of Unknown Origin, of the Seventeenth and Eighteenth Centuries, and the First Patterns of the United States Mint*. Comprising 381 pages with 10 heliotype plates and 110 wood engravings, this work is still a viable standard reference, and illustrates many items among the 100 Greatest: the Gloucester Court House token (No. 33); Higley coppers (No. 7); the Bar copper (No. 39); Talbot, Allum & Lee tokens (No. 36); Elephant coppers (No. 30); the Myddelton token (No. 29); and the New Yorke in America token (No. 25). In his chapter "The Washington Pieces," Crosby describes smaller-diameter tokens and medalets of the 18th century, including the 1792 Roman Head (No. 92) and Washington "Born Virginia" (No. 72).

The Centennial

Fairmount Park in Philadelphia was the scene of the 1876 Centennial Exhibition celebrating the first century of American independence. It was the United States' first world's fair, emulating the great fairs of London and Paris beginning in 1861. Crowds thronged the park and its elegant buildings, which included exhibition halls erected by many different states and countries. Scores of tokens and medals were issued in connection with the event, including the official centennial medal struck at the Mint (No. 52). The first steam-coining press used at the Philadelphia Mint in 1836 (see No. 44) was set up at the fair and used to stamp out tiny brass medalets for sale to the public. In connection with the tourist bonanza, Philadelphia merchants issued hundreds of tokens and medals as souvenirs and advertising pieces. Many bore historical motifs, including the Libertas Americana portrait, Independence Hall, and the Liberty Bell.

In 1878, Jacques Florimond Loubat celebrated the centennial with an impressive two-volume work, *The Medallic History of the United States of America, 1776–1876 with 170 Etchings by Jules Jacquemart*. Loubat surveyed the panorama of American medals and selected 86 describing aspects of the progress of the United States, favoring early medals struck in Paris and later issues made at the Philadelphia Mint. Today most remain important, but the last of his favorites, an 1874 medal awarded to John Horn Jr. by act of Congress "in recognition of his heroic exploits in rescuing men women & children from drowning in the Detroit River," is little remembered. Loubat did his homework in history, however, and nearly every medal description reproduces original correspondence and legislation leading up to its issue.

The 1880s

The numismatic activity of the 1880s had no precedent, and when it was over, the coin market would not see comparable enthusiasm until the 1930s. Several influences came together to create a frenetic scene, with coin auctions for some years held at a rate of more than one a week, with record production of Proof coins (especially cents, three-cent pieces, and nickel five-cent pieces), and many new issues of tokens and medals. Economic times were good, and there was a great boom in the prairie states, where entire new towns often sprang up overnight. There was a new wave of interest in the traditions of America, and in this decade more lavish histories were published of cities and counties than at any time before or since. Elegant maps and prints also found many buyers. It was a time to sit down, relax, and enjoy the pleasures of life.

The 1882 sale of the Charles I. Bushnell Collection by the Chapman brothers was the auction sensation of the decade. The cabinet consisted almost entirely of colonial issues, tokens, and medals, with scarcely any coins. This single event propelled S.H. and Henry Chapman, both in their 20s, into the front rank of catalogers, amid many sour-grapes complaints from gray-bearded old-timers of the trade. Continuing their partnership until 1906, then conducting auctions separately into the 1920s, the Chapmans produced catalogs that today are an especially rich source of information about tokens and medals.

In the same decade, T. Harrison Garrett, whose family controlled the Baltimore and Ohio Railroad, expanded his interest and added many rarities to his collection, including highly important tokens and medals. By the time of his death in a boating accident on Chesapeake Bay in 1886, he had the most important private cabinet in America. Also in the 1880s, Virgil M. Brand, son of an important Chicago brewer, entered numismatics—eventually building the largest collection ever assembled, comprising some 350,000 pieces, including countless tokens and medals, by the time of his passing in 1926.

This was a decade of expansion in other hobbies, including collecting birds' eggs, Indian relics, stamps, autographs, and artifacts. Over a dozen new periodicals were launched, most containing a column or some information on coins. *The American Numismatist*, edited by George F. Heath, was published in Monroe, Michigan, beginning in 1888. After the first issue, the word *American* was dropped from the title. *The Numismatist* went on to serve the hobby well, in the 1890s becoming the official magazine of the newly formed (1891) American Numismatic Association, in which position it remains today.

In 1885, W.S. Baker's *Medallic Portraits of Washington* became the second major book published on numismatic Washingtonia (after James Ross Snowden's 1861 effort). An annotated 1967 reprint by George Fuld made Baker numbers the standard for all catalogers. Still later, Fuld and Rulau created a similarly titled expansion of the subject for Krause Publications.

The 1889 centennial of Washington's inauguration produced several dozen medals of scattered sizes and styles issued by different merchants, societies, and engravers. George H. Lovett and Peter L. Krider issued new medals, as did the Philadelphia Mint, Gorham Manufacturing Co. (silversmiths), and the venerable Chicago firm of Childs & Co., active since the Civil War. None were considered sufficiently popular or important by our voters to gain entry among the 100 Greatest.

Medallic Awards and Recognitions

The second half of the 19th century saw the rise in popularity of medals used in advertising. Beginning in the 1820s, various learned societies, farm and factory exhibition hosts, and competition sponsors awarded medals to artists, inventors, and industrial innovators to encourage excellence in American production. The American Institute, the Franklin Institute, the Massachusetts Charitable Mechanic Association, and other groups judged the exhibits and awarded medals. Moritz Fürst cut the original dies for the American Institute medals, while Christian Gobrecht created the Franklin Institute (No. 65) and Massachusetts Charitable Mechanic awards. Charles C. Wright, F.B. Smith, William Barber, and others created award medals ranked among the most beautiful produced in this country.

After the success of the 1876 Centennial Exhibition, those who staged prize fairs quickly learned that it was good business to "award" medals to any person or company who signed up for exhibit space. The exhibitors reproduced these medals in advertising, on bottle labels, on a panel above the keyboard of a piano or organ, or elsewhere—implying that the product so labeled had great merit and had been judged to be first class. The Louisiana Purchase Exposition (St. Louis World's Fair of 1904) gave medals inscribed GOLD MEDAL to many of those who showed up, and to others a SILVER MEDAL, but to save money these were struck in bronze! Today, whether truly honorific or meaningless, fair medals are eagerly sought by numismatists. Most seen in the marketplace are in copper or silver, rarely gold. The typical award has an artistic obverse of a standard design, while on the reverse, the name and product of the recipient is inscribed on a blank space, sometimes surrounded by a wreath.

THE 1890s

By 1890 the numismatic hobby was suffering from fatigue. The economy was experiencing a chill, and many high-interest bonds issued in the Midwest to build towns, make civic improvements, and construct railroads were in default. The situation would culminate in the Panic of 1893, and good times would not return until about 1898.

Existing dealers continued their business, but trade dropped off sharply. Among the leaders were the Chapman brothers, J.W. Scott, W.E. Woodward (in the twilight of his life and career), David U. Proskey, John Haseltine, Lyman H. Low, Ed. Frossard, Charles Steigerwalt, and the auction firm of Bangs, Merwin & Co. Centers of activity remained in Philadelphia, New York, and Boston, but several professionals enjoyed good business in Chicago, Los Angeles, San Francisco, and other western cities.

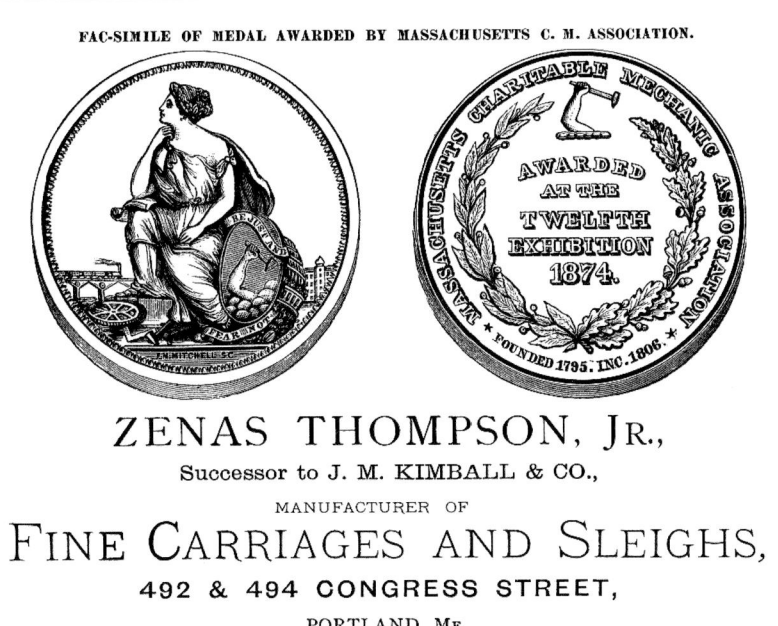

Carriage maker Zenas Thompson Jr. illustrated an award medal to reflect the quality of his product. (*Portland and Vicinity*, 1876)

In Chicago in November 1891, the American Numismatic Association (ANA) was formed. Its first decade was fraught with difficulties. Members signed up but did not renew; officers would not answer correspondence. Most members received *The Numismatist*, which later in the decade would become the ANA's official journal. Editor George F. Heath viewed the ANA as moribund, if not completely dead. Lo and behold, by the end of the decade the spirit had been rekindled, growth resumed, responsible officers were in place, and the ANA embarked on a course of progress.

In the 1890s the *American Journal of Numismatics*, still published four times a year, was the main forum for the more scholarly side of the hobby, including tokens and medals. *The Numismatist* contained lighter fare, but was still important.

To observe the 400th anniversary of Christopher Columbus's "discovery" of America, a world's fair was planned for Chicago, to open in 1892. It was not until the summer of 1893 that the gates were thrown open to the public. The fabulous World's Columbian Exposition was a smash success. The Mint had a display featuring parts of the Mint Cabinet, by now often called the Mint Collection, and the private sector issued hundreds of different souvenir tokens and commemorative medals. By now it had become a tradition to issue an official exposition medal, and the Columbian Exposition medal with obverse by sculptor Augustus Saint-Gaudens and reverse by Charles E. Barber is our No. 53.

In the presidential contest of 1896, the "silver issue" reached a climax. William McKinley, a Republican of the old school who felt that gold was a fine basis for coinage value and that illogical purchases of silver were wasteful, headed one ticket. On the Democratic side, William Jennings Bryan, the "silver-tongued orator of the Platte," carried the banner. The election was enlivened by quantities of "Bryan money," including "dollars" illustrating that if a dollar-size coin were to actually contain full value in metal, it would be more than twice regular size. An example of such a medal here holds position No. 22.

A classic medal collectors' reference is *American Colonial History Illustrated by Contemporary Medals*, by C. Wyllys Betts, published posthumously in 1894. Betts was born on August 13, 1845, in Newburgh, New York. By his teens he was a knowledgeable numismatist, and in 1862 he made some fantasy tokens and medals, drawing upon his knowledge of history to create pieces that *might* have existed had someone thought to make them. One of these became very famous: the Novum Belgium token dated 1623. This piece slipped into a W.E. Woodward auction in an obscure addendum listing in 1864, then in the late 1870s was "discovered" by highly esteemed dealer and author Édouard Frossard and published in *Numisma* as a marvelous new find. When the truth was learned, Frossard's competitors reacted with glee.

Later, Betts expressed slight remorse:

> Unfortunately, someone about 1862 presented me with a set of letters and several engraving tools, and in learning the use of them I made a great number of store cards and medalets, most of which are unique, and all, I think, in the Yale College cabinet. The earlier ones I look upon with some interest because they used to afford me a great deal of amusement, not only in the making, but in the astonishment of collectors when looking over my cabinet.

After a week's bout with pneumonia in 1887, Betts died at his home in New York City. Lyman H. Low and William T.R. Marvin completed his masterwork on colonial medals. Today, the work stands tall as the major source for information on the subject. A number of scholars (Michael Hodder, John W. Adams, and John Kraljevich among them) have added to and revised its information. Betts medals among the 100 Greatest include Nos. 1, 9, 32, 35, 42, 59, 69, 70, and 99.

In 1899 Lyman H. Low published his monograph, *Hard Times Tokens*, generating further interest in an already popular series. This book was likely a major element in lifting the ANA out of its comatose state

INTRODUCTION

and spurring a long run of years in which tokens and medals would come to the fore, becoming hot tickets in the market. Today Low is remembered as one of the finest numismatic scholars of his time, a key figure in numismatic research. He died on February 10, 1924, at the age of 79.

INTO THE 20TH CENTURY
MEDALS AND TOKENS ON PARADE

The power of the printed word cannot be overestimated. Low's *Hard Times Tokens* had achieved good sales, and others published supplements and photographic plates to accompany it. In *The Numismatist* of January 1898, Benjamin P. Wright contributed the first installment of what would become an extensive series, "The American Store or Business Cards," which continued into 1901, the year that Wright was elected president of the ANA, further broadening the interest created by Low. Soon the collecting of tokens, political medals, and related items was the most active area in American numismatics.

In 1902 *The Numismatist* announced a fad for collecting encased postage stamps and listed known varieties and their auction records. In the June issue appeared the following lines: "According to reports there is an effort being made to corner the market on encased postage stamps. Many will remember, no doubt, a similar effort made about a year ago on the 1856 Flying Eagle cent, and we think this should be a warning." Of course, today all encased postage stamps (No. 14) are worth many times their 1902 values.

In 1900 and 1901 in Victor, Colorado, which styled itself as the "City of Gold," Joseph Lesher sought to promote the use of silver metal, the value of which had been in a market slump ever since the early 1870s. He designed and had struck (in Denver) octagonal silver Referendum Souvenir medals, typically denominated as worth $1.25 "at any bank," later in exchange for merchandise. These were popular in their time, but quickly disappeared. Within a generation they became eagerly sought by numismatists. These interesting pieces landed in our No. 18 spot.

In 1904 everyone was singing or humming, "Meet me in St. Louis, Louis; meet me at the fair." The Louisiana Purchase Exposition, dazzlingly illuminated by electricity, was the greatest event since the World's Columbian Exposition of 1893. Many tokens and medals were issued, including an impressive award medal designed by Adolph A. Weinman (No. 106 in our appendix of also-rans; it did not make it into the 100 Greatest).

In the same year Albert R. Frey's *Numismatist* series, "The Tokens and Medals Relating to Numismatists and Coin Dealers," attracted attention and spurred the desire to acquire such pieces, many of which dated back to the medalet craze of the 1859 era. A rash of new tokens and medalets appeared, the issues of current collectors who created their own store cards (usually of brass, less often of aluminum) through one or another of the Chicago token producers. Up-and-coming dealer Thomas L. Elder ordered 1,000 store cards comprising two varieties, one with an error in the inscription. Elder would go on to be a leading advocate and publicist for collecting tokens.

George H. Burfeind, of 1003 G Street N.W., Washington, DC, sent to the publisher of *The Numismatist* two of his tokens in brass and copper. "The workmanship on them is very fine," the editor noted in the March 1904 issue, "and Mr. Burfeind would be glad to hear from any others who are contemplating the issues of cards and thinks he can give them some pointers." Mostly made in Chicago, similar pieces, often nickel-size, were sold widely to gambling parlors, saloons, and other businesses. Imprinted "Good for 5¢ in trade," "Good for one tune," and the like, these were fed into slot machines and paid out as winnings—in areas in which paying out coins was illegal. Such makers of gambling machines as the Mills Novelty Company (Chicago) and Caille Brothers (Detroit) circulated millions of what collectors now call "good-fors."

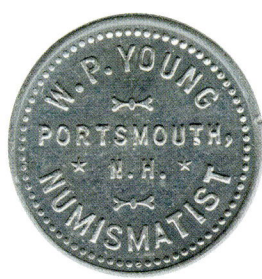

Many numismatists issued their own tokens in brass, copper, or aluminum in the early 20th century, such as this one by W.P. Young, who listed his collecting specialties (actual size 25 mm).

By the end of the decade, focus had shifted away from tokens and medals somewhat, and increased attention was paid to rarities in the federal coin series, such as those showcased in several important auction sales of old-time cabinets.

THE MEDALLIC ART COMPANY

Founded in New York City in 1907 by French sculptors and entrepreneurs Felix and Henri Weil, using equipment owned by the Deitsch brothers (American sales agent for the Janvier portrait or medallic-transfer lathe), the Medallic Art Company (MACo) grew to become America's preeminent maker of medals.

MACo was the brainchild of New York numismatist Robert Hewitt Jr. A passionate fan of art medals, he encouraged the Weils to form a new company to strike medals for clients. In 1909, Hewitt sponsored two Lincoln birth-year centennial medals sculpted by Jules Édouard Roine, a French artist living in the United States. With Charles Augustus de Kay, he embarked on the Circle of Friends of the Medallion series. The last of its 12 issues, in editions of 500 pieces in bronze, was struck in 1915, and then the circle expired as the nation turned its thoughts to world war. MACo, however, prospered and became the first choice for most American societies, organizations, and businesses desiring artistic medals.

The Bohemian Beer Garden in Willard, Ohio, issued this "good-for" token in the early 20th century (shown actual size, 21.4 mm). Likely, the establishment had gambling machines on the premises that paid off in tokens, rather than in coins, to evade laws against such devices. This token could be dropped in a piano, perhaps made by Seeburg or Wurlitzer, which would then automatically play a two-minute tune. Such tokens could also be redeemed for cash at the bar. Part of the enjoyment of collecting "good-fors" is learning about the establishments that issued them—through old advertisements, postcards, historical societies, and other sources.

INTRODUCTION

The unique striking in gold of Charles Cushing Wright's medal presented by Congress, per a resolution of 1848, to Zachary Taylor (Julian MI-24) was not publicly revealed to the numismatic community until September 2006, after the voting for the 100 Greatest had taken place, although the copper version landed in the 114th position in the appendix of runners-up. Commemorated is Taylor's valor in the February 1847 Battle of Buena Vista in the war with Mexico. The medal, shown here at its actual size of 90 mm, was struck on July 4, 1849.

A Most Remarkable Medal Is Found

Zachary Taylor was the victorious general in the February 1847 Battle of Buena Vista, which paved the way to the American forces' taking of Mexico City and ultimate success in the war with Mexico. The prizes included the annexation by the United States of all of California and Arizona as well as certain other areas in the Southwest, delineated in the February 1848 Treaty of Guadeloupe Hidalgo. Three months later, the U.S. Congress voted that two large gold medals be given to the victorious generals, namely Major General Zachary Taylor and Major General Winfield Scott (No. 62). For Taylor, it would be the third time he would be honored with a congressional gold medal—more than any other American before or since. The Buena Vista Taylor medal was awarded for his defeat of "a Mexican army of more than four times their number, consisting of chosen troops, under their favorite commander, General Santa Anna," according to the original joint resolution.

Between the 1847 victory and the 1848 resolution to recognize that accomplishment with a gold medal, the world was gripped by news from a territory claimed by both warring parties: the discovery of gold at Sutter's Mill on the American River in California on January 24, 1848. A gold rush soon followed, and thousands of American settlers poured into the territory.

The largest early deposit of metal from the gold rush was delivered to the Philadelphia Mint by David Carter on December 8, 1848, and consisted of 1,804 ounces of gold from near Sutter's Mill. From this deposit the Mint struck the Taylor medal and one for Major General Winfield Scott, and these stand today as the only numismatic items remaining from this historic event. A day later, on December 9, additional gold was deposited at the Mint from another California shipment, from which 1,839 quarter eagles were struck with CAL. counterstamped on the reverse.

A letter from Mint director Robert L. Patterson to Secretary of War George W. Crawford of July 5, 1849, confirms that the Buena Vista medal "contains twenty ounces of California gold—the silver combined with it having been previously separated. It was struck at the Mint yesterday, the 4th of July."

This medal was obtained from the Taylor family in 2006. The news of its appearance in the autumn of that year was exciting to the numismatic community.

In 1937, the Weil brothers added Clyde C. Trees, an Indiana businessman, to the company. The Trees family owned and operated the company for many years afterward. William Trees Louth was president beginning in 1961, and was well known to the numismatic community; he was a frequent attendee of events, especially those held in and near New York City. D. Wayne ("Dick") Johnson, a well-known numismatist who was a founder of the Rittenhouse Society and in 1960 became the first editor of *Coin World*, was named sales promotion research director for MACo in 1967. Now retired, he is still considered the world authority on the company's products and history.

From 1910 Through the Great War

In his article "Fine Art in Medals" in *Harper's Weekly* of April 22, 1911, Charles de Kay wrote, "Last spring's international show of medals under the management of Archer Huntington did much to open the eyes of American amateurs to the beauty and diversity possible to small sculpture in relief." He was referring to the ANS's New York exhibition of 1910, a competition thrown open to every medal sculptor in the world. Belgian Godefroid DeVreese, a master in the Art Nouveau and Beaux Arts styles that had flowered in Europe over the preceding two decades, claimed the $10,000 grand prize. Many of the 53 Americans who exhibited had been

INTRODUCTION

Dollar-size nickel alloy token (actual size 34 mm) issued for use in an Ingle System dispenser in the store of E.T. Burke in Junction City, Kentucky. A few years ago the countertop dispenser was found, with 281 tokens still in it, of which 250 were of the $1 denomination. Patented in 1909 by a Dayton, Ohio, entrepreneur, this was a series of tokens ranging in value from 1¢ to $1. These were issued by coal-mining companies, farms, and other businesses and were paid to workers, who could then spend them at—where else?—the company store. The Orco (Osborne Register Co.) tokens, also made by a Dayton firm, were similar.

Aluminum "good-for" token issued by Miss M.J. Drury of Williamstown, Vermont, circa 1910. When a small cache of these was found in a Vermont estate in 1996 and acquired by Littleton Coin Co., token chronicler Russell Rulau commented that this was the only token he knew of with "Miss" in the inscription.

schooled in France, like their mentor Augustus Saint-Gaudens, who trained at the Parisian École des Beaux-Arts. The master's later accomplishments in both monumental and medallic sculpture, and his stature as Theodore Roosevelt's preferred coin designer, made it almost compulsory for aspiring American sculptors to do the same. Chester Beach, John Gutzon Borglum, Victor David Brenner, Edward Sawyer, John Flanagan, Frederic MacMonnies, Janet Scudder, and many others studied in Paris, and brought the Beaux Arts influence home with them.

Yet interest in exonumia as a whole was lagging. In *The Numismatist* of March 1915, Thomas L. Elder commented:

> There are comparatively few collectors of another most interesting series, the medals relating to the colonial and continental period of America's history. . . . It is to be regretted that collectors should so lightly regard this very important subject, for there is no excuse for slighting it. . . .
>
> The subject of publication is so important that I have taken it upon myself to make some suggestions in regard to it. I find that when medals and tokens are not published, or illustrated, the American collectors do not, for several reasons, regard them of special interest or value—hence, partly true to his commercial instinct—he does not collect them.

In the next issue, Elder discussed a wide variety of pieces ranging from the Gloucester token of 1714 through the Higley issues, Hard Times tokens, political items, pieces pertaining to Lafayette, and Civil War tokens.

Number 9 in the Circle of Friends of the Medallion series featured John C. Fremont, "The Great Pathfinder," who was also the first Republican candidate for president in 1856 (he lost to James Buchanan). René de Quelin created the motifs. Shown actual size, 57 mm high by 76 mm wide.

In April 1915, "Civil War Tokens of Tennessee" by Edgar H. Adams appeared, followed by Farran Zerbe's illustration and description of the official medal of the Panama-Pacific Exposition (our No. 79). The world war raging in Europe from 1914 to 1918 furnished the topic for many medals, most issued overseas and not relating to America. There were exceptions, including a well-known issue by Karl Goetz showing a skeleton buying a ticket to cruise on the ill-fated *Lusitania*. The ANS in cooperation with the Medallic Art Company issued many medals showcasing the work of well-known artists and sculptors.

The July 1919 issue of *The Numismatist* commenced with "A Trial List of the Countermarked Modern Coins of the World," by Frank G. Duffield, the first in a continuing series that was to become the standard reference on the subject until superseded by Gregory G. Brunk's *American and Canadian Countermarked Coins* in 1987. Included were Nos. 48, 60, 68, and 77 of the 100 Greatest.

THE 1920s

Elder kept up his call for new publications into the next decade. In 1924, he wrote:

> Badly we need books on American numismatics and paper money, especially books on our political medals and tokens. . . . There are

INTRODUCTION

plenty of neglected subjects in American numismatics . . . [and] I do not think a country with 113 million people ought to neglect its own numismatics.

Elder's comments reflected that by this time the ANS had lost sight of the *American* part of its name and devoted the majority of its curatorial, publication, and exhibit efforts to ancient coins—a matter of practicality, perhaps, as the main donor for their new 1908 building, Archer Huntington, had ancients as a specialty. It was not until the late 20th century that the efforts of Margo Russell, Harry W. Bass Jr., Donald G. Partrick, and others set the society back on track. Since then American coins have had their due.

J. Sanford Saltus, an ANS benefactor for many years, died in his room at the Hotel Metropole in London on June 24, 1922, while cleaning coins with potassium cyanide. He took a drink from a glass of the deadly poison, mistaking it for ginger ale. He is remembered today for establishing and endowing the J. Sanford Saltus medal (No. 97) "for distinguished achievement in the field of the art of the medal." In the years since its establishment it has been awarded to many famous sculptors and artists and is considered to be the preeminent honor in the field.

The auction of the decade was held in three parts in 1925, 1926, and 1927 at the Anderson Galleries in New York City. Cataloged by Wayte Raymond as *The Important Numismatic Collection Formed by the Late W.W.C. Wilson, Montreal, Canada. United States and Canadian Coins, Early American and Canadian Historical Medals, Medals Presented to North American Indian Chiefs, Foreign Coins and Medals*. Indeed, this offering was one of the finest ever.

In 1925 the Norse-American Centennial Committee desired to have its own commemorative half dollar, but Congress allowed a medal instead. Designed by James Earle Fraser, this is No. 38 of the 100 Greatest.

In 1926 longtime collector Virgil Brand died, leaving behind an immense collection, including tokens and medals in quantity. Years later these were filtered into the market by his heirs.

LATER TIMES

Under the auspices of the American Federation of Arts, the Society of Medalists formed in 1928, with the purpose of encouraging interest in medallic art. Subscribing members were to receive two medals each year, designed by artists and sculptors of high rank and reputation. The first medals were issued in 1930 to great acclaim, and the 129-medal series (recognized as a class at No. 19) endured until 1995. A decade later, interest has gained momentum, and several of the varieties are now quite difficult to obtain.

There were changes in the wind. In the mid-1960s, much new business in the commercial sector was captured by Joseph Segel's Franklin Mint, which marketed its coin-medals and related products worldwide through innovative advertising and promotion. Its metallic casino "dollars," extensive commemorative-medal series, and other items propelled the Franklin Mint into the position of the best-performing stock on the New York Stock Exchange. In the late 1970s, there was a sharp run-up in the price of silver and gold, with silver at one point crossing the $40-per-ounce level and gold testing the $900 mark, making these metals impractical for medallic use. Meanwhile, the Franklin Mint was the subject of a negative program on CBS's *60 Minutes*, which ridiculed the buying of medals as an investment. After the market prices of silver and gold crashed in January 1980, the momentum was never recovered. Just as it was said in biblical times that prophets are without honor in their own country, modern medals such as Franklin Mint issues are generally ignored by present-day collectors. Perhaps an edition of the 100 Greatest published a century hence, with new nominees and voters, will include some issues of this private mint, many of which are of remarkable quality and beauty.

FIDEM, or the International Medal Federation, established in 1937, holds biennial meetings in various countries. Its aims are "to promote and diffuse the art of medals at the international level . . . and to make the art known and to guarantee recognition of its place among other arts by increasing awareness of the art, history, and technology of medals." The society is composed mostly of artists rather than numismatists.

Much more could be said about the making of tokens and medals from 1930 to date, but it would be largely irrelevant to the 100 Greatest. Apart from the SOM issues, only two later issues made the cut: No. 81, the 1944 OPA red point ration token, and No. 82, sales-tax tokens.

Today tokens are still in wide use, often, produced by computer designs with photographic etching of dies that long since outmoded the painstaking art of hand engraving. Present-day venues for tokens include turnpike toll booths (but these are rapidly giving way to electronic scanning devices), amusement arcades, and tourist attractions. Medals still serve for honors and awards, but not as extensively as a generation ago.

In recent decades, more personal tokens and store cards have been minted than ever before—not for distribution in commerce or for use in exchange for goods and services, but as numismatic souvenirs. In the 1970s, the Patrick Mint (Jesse Patrick) produced hundreds of bronze tokens slightly larger than a cent, and other private minting facilities turned out more, including discs and bars of silver (called *art bars*). To preserve the fading era of diecutting, the Gallery Mint Museum was established in 2005 as a nonprofit institution that reenacts traditional engraving methods. Located in Eureka Springs, Arkansas, the museum passed into private hands in 2006 and is now known as the Striker Mint.

Perhaps the greatest advances in tokens and medals have been made on the *collecting* side of the equation. In recent decades, dozens of standard references have been published on every category of exonumia. Tokens and medals are featured in the leading periodicals of our time, including *Coin World*, *Numismatic News*, *COINage*, *Coins*, and *Numismatist*. While these specialties are often in the shadows of a numismatic auction world, in which it is not unusual for a federal-coin rarity to cross the million-dollar mark, offerings are met with enthusiasm, and intense competition. Many participants know this secret that really isn't a secret, that so many interesting and rare tokens and medals can be purchased inexpensively.

UNDERSTANDING AND COLLECTING MEDALS AND TOKENS

THE MAKING AND DISTRIBUTION OF MEDALS AND TOKENS

DIES AND MINTING

Most medals and all tokens under discussion here were struck from engraved dies placed in a coin or medal press. A few medals involved other processes. The "Happy While United" medal (No. 21), made in an era when a coining press was not available to the issuer, was cast in a mold, using liquid metal, and the edges were then trimmed. The Manly medal (No. 17) is believed to have been made on a planchet that was cast, perhaps with many of the features of the finished medal, then given addi-

INTRODUCTION

tional detail in a medal press. The largest-size Jefferson Peace medal (No. 3) was made by joining two thin shells of silver, obverse and reverse, to create the finished medal, again when a coining press of sufficient diameter was not at hand.

In the early days, the striking process involved placing an engraved obverse and reverse die in a medal or coining press, and inserting a blank disk (planchet) between them. By means of arms attached to a screw, the top die would be forced downward to meet the bottom die and impress the appropriate features on the planchet. In time, other types of presses were devised, including the steam-powered knuckle press and the hydraulic press. From the late 19th century onward, the hydraulic press was favored, as it permitted relatively slow striking of medals under very high pressure.

The Philadelphia Mint established in 1792 began making copper half cents and cents for circulation in 1793, using screw presses operated by men pulling on the attached arms. Their power was insufficient for striking larger-diameter pieces. In the summer of 1795, a press was found that could make dollar-size coins. It was not until the early 19th century, however, that presses were strong enough to produce large-diameter medals such as the War of 1812 congressional awards.

Quarter-size token issued by Clark's Trading Post, Lincoln, New Hampshire, in the 1990s. Thousands are bought each year by tourists who desire a memento of the state's largest privately owned attraction. Founded in 1928, Clark's offers a trained-bear show, steam train rides, museums of Americana, shops, and other features. Shown at actual size, 24.4 mm.

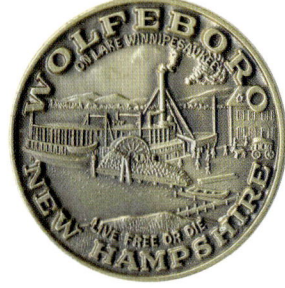

In the 20th century many cities and towns issued medals to celebrate various anniversaries, as Wolfeboro, New Hampshire, did in 1970. Shown at actual size, about 38mm.

In the meantime, in France and in England, technology had advanced much further. The Soho Manufactory had steam-operated presses with automatic devices so efficient that even a boy could tend to several presses at a time. It was a simple thing for Soho to strike the large-diameter Seasons Medals (No. 6) on commission from the U.S. government. Similarly, the Paris Mint had extensive equipment to produce large-size medals for the early issues for the United States. The histories of both the Philadelphia and Paris mints are well known and easily obtainable, so the authors have elected to give attention to makers who are not as well known in the mainstream of numismatics.

Over a period of time various diesinkers, medal shops, and manufacturers installed minting equipment. Richard Trested was among the earliest makers of tokens in New York City in the early 1820s, with one or more coining presses of unknown type. Other individuals and partnerships soon went into operation to make tokens (less often medals), including the immense Scovill Manufacturing Company in Waterbury, Connecticut, long known as a maker of buttons and other stamped items. In the 1860s, prominent New York jeweler Louis Comfort Tiffany entered the medals business, contracting the engraving of dies with private diesinkers, as did jeweler Bailey, Banks & Biddle of Philadelphia. By the early 20th century, important firms turning out large medals for awards, expositions, advertising, and societies included MACo, Joseph K. Davison's Sons in Philadelphia, and Whitehead & Hoag in Newark, New Jersey. Since 1968, the Robbins Company of Attleboro, Massachusetts, has struck the mission medals carried on NASA's space flights, and today there are dozens of firms that produce tokens and medals.

Aspects of Design and Arrangement

Each token or medal has a design. For many diesinkers, arrangement on obverse and reverse of letters and motifs was done casually, by picking up a portrait punch—such as an Indian head, a Liberty head, or some other element—punching it into the die, then individually punching letters and numerals for the inscription and date. His merchant patron might specify the nature of the inscriptions or even suggest a motif, such as a ship for someone in the maritime trade, a barrel for a brewer, or a clock face for a watchmaker. Political tokens often depicted the candidate's portrait, with a motto or information about that person's platform or background.

Tokens or medalets made for the numismatic trade were planned more carefully. In Philadelphia in the 1860s, Robert Lovett Jr. created a Washington series, each with the same portrait of Washington on one side but with a different scene on the reverse. Creators of historical series from Augustus B. Sage to the Franklin Mint carefully planned each piece to be interesting to the recipients, so as to encourage collecting as many as possible.

Most if not all medals described here were carefully planned, many with the portraits and inscriptions mandated by an act of Congress. For award medals, similar planning was done by the organizations that intended to present them. In art medals created to showcase the talents of prominent artists and sculptors, every bit of the maker's talent and imagination was unleashed, creating for collectors, in effect, a miniature art museum in their homes.

Techniques for the preparation of designs and dies evolved gradually. Early medals were usually engraved by hand on soft steel dies, with letters punched in, after which the die was hardened, polished, and used for striking. By the 1830s, the Contamin portrait lathe, developed in France, made it possible to create art for a medal in the form of a plaque, wax impression, plaster cast, electrotype (galvano), or other form, and then reduce it by means of a tracer point set against the original art and a tiny rotating cutting die at the other end, to create a hub, master die, or a working die. In the 20th century the Janvier pantograph revolutionized the technology, paving the way for the sculpted medal.

Surfaces and Finishes

Most medals were struck with a special surface, usually mirror Proof in the 19th century and earlier. Copper impressions were sometimes bronzed, giving them a rich chocolate color (in contrast to the bright orange-red of raw metal). Beginning in the late 19th century, the sand-

INTRODUCTION

blasting and acid dipping of presentation medals became popular, the thought being that the artistic features would be enhanced. Some were also "antiqued" to give them a Florentine finish. Most of MACo's impressive output has been of medals with a microscopically porous finish.

Not much attention was paid to the surface or finish of tokens, as they were intended to be utilitarian—to pass in commerce as a medium of exchange, to help push somebody into the office of president, or to serve a related use. Tokens were often passed out to the general public, where they were extensively handled. A new token was apt to have a lustrous or frosty surface, what would be called Mint State today. Tokens made for the numismatic trade, such as during the Washingtonia enthusiasm of circa 1860, tended to have Proof finish.

PRODUCTION QUANTITIES

Medals were usually struck to order, with a certain quantity specified by legislation or by the sponsor. It was common to make a limited number in a precious metal, such as one in gold for the person honored or some other recipient, a few others in silver, and then a larger number in copper or white metal. There were no rules, and practices varied.

In contrast, tokens were usually made in quantities limited only by the demand for them. Accordingly, a small token used to take a ride on the New York and Harlaem Rail Road (No. 85) was produced as the line needed them for use. Similarly, makers of Hard Times and Civil War tokens turned out as many as they could, as long as there was a demand for them. Such pieces were typically sold at a discount, such as $6 per thousand, so those passing them out at 1¢ each could earn a profit. Modern-day tokens, such as those used for turnpike tolls and in arcades, have been produced by the millions.

THE IMPORTANCE OF GRADING

In the field of U.S. coins, the official ANA grading system is almost universally applied in the sale of pieces certified by the leading services and others. This scale ranges from Poor-1, or a coin barely decipherable, to Mint State-70, representing perfection. This system is well known, and detailed discussions of grading-level definitions abound in other publications.

While the ANA system has been applied to many tokens in recent times, most medals are described adjectivally, such as Good, Very Good, Fine, and—in increasing quality—Very Fine, Extremely Fine, About Uncirculated, and Uncirculated (or Mint State). Pieces struck in Proof finish are described in the upper ranges as Extremely Fine, impaired Proof, and Proof. Among Mint State and Proof pieces quality can vary. Some have friction or handling marks, while others are of especially fine quality and may be classified as choice or gem.

As in other areas of numismatics, the higher the grade of a token or medal, the more it is worth in the marketplace. This is especially true in earlier issues that tend to show wear or friction. Accordingly, the interesting three-cent token of Atwood's Hotel (No. 46) is worth much more in Mint State than if well worn and in a grade such as Good or Very Good. For quite a few tokens, the grades of About Uncirculated and Mint State are not known today. Indeed, for the 1714 Gloucester token (No. 33) the striking is so casual and the wear so great that one can hardly make out the inscriptions. The Higley coppers (No. 7) are known only as well circulated.

Study of individual issues is needed to determine the relation of grade to value. For the Talbot, Allum, & Lee tokens (No. 36), generally the regular pieces (not mulings) dated 1794 are found with evidence of significant wear. A Mint State 1794 would be a prize indeed, although not a landmark rarity. In contrast, for tokens dated 1795, most are Mint State, and finding a worn one would be unusual. Most tokens and medalets made for the numismatic trade are seen today in high grades, as these never circulated.

While early medals nearly always show some signs of handling or friction, those made in the 20th century are often seen well preserved. Examples include Assay Commission medals (No. 28), the 1905 Roosevelt Inaugural Medal by Saint-Gaudens (No. 27), and the SOM issues (No. 19), to which can be added any number of such pieces not represented among the 100 Greatest.

It is common for some tokens and medals to be holed or have loops attached for suspension, Indian peace medals being examples. Except for certain matte-finish 20th-century issues and pieces that have been dipped or cleaned, nearly all medals and tokens more than a few decades old will exhibit toning or patination. Neither attribute affects grade.

DETERMINING VALUES

Determining the current market value of a given token or medal requires some research. Even when guides exist for certain series, such as Russell Rulau's *Standard Catalog of United States Tokens 1700–1900*, or the Hibler-Kappen *So-Called Dollars* book, updated editions are done infrequently, if at all, and listed prices can be out of date. Yet if a reference book published 10 years ago lists one token or medal at $100 and another at $500, today the ratios probably still stand, although the prices may be different.

Auction records are also helpful. Although it can often be a sizable stretch of time between presentations of your desired piece, checking prior auction descriptions and the related prices realized affords a basis for comparison.

Dealer price lists can be equally valuable, including Internet listings by leading responsible dealers (such as those who are well known within the special societies or are members of the Professional Numismatists Guild or the International Association of Professional Numismatists). Although a list price does not necessarily represent a selling price, dealers do have reputations to protect, and they realize that the best way to gain continuing business is to give good value for the price paid. It is worthwhile to subscribe to price lists as well as printed auction catalogs: the cost is modest in comparison to the knowledge gained. Likely, if you become a regular buyer, future issues of these publications will come your way free of charge. Such publications are quite expensive, and it is not reasonable to expect a free ride without doing business.

The Internet offers much information, but there are far too many posted prices, auction offerings, and the like from sellers who have little information about what they have for sale or, worse, have criminal intent. Fakes are widespread, and in some specialties, such as Indian peace medals, probably more than 90% of the pieces offered by sellers who are not recognized professional numismatists are outright fakes. Still, hope springs eternal, and transactions take place when naïve buyers think they are getting bargains. In a phrase, the Internet can be useful, but only when postings are by professionals with expertise in tokens or medals—generally the same people who regularly issue printed catalogs.

Simply asking around is another very valuable source of information. By all means, make friends with one or several favorite dealers. Most will be willing to give their estimate of the value of a particular piece that is coming up at auction. In other instances, if a piece hasn't sold recently, they still may be able to give you a ballpark idea based on their professional experience.

INTRODUCTION

CARING FOR MEDALS AND TOKENS

As a general rule, numismatic specimens of all kinds are best not cleaned, unless by an expert. Polishing or dipping a piece to make it bright or brilliant is definitely the wrong way to go, as this is not an easily reversible process. More than a few medals, in particular, have been repeatedly polished, including some in displays as important as the Mint Collection (in the 19th century it was the policy to polish such pieces regularly). Today, the sophisticated owner of such a piece will generally leave it alone.

There are, however, some things that can be done to improve the appearance of a piece. Sometimes dirt, grease, or verdigris can be present on the surface of a token, and these are removable by dissolving with acetone (a substance that is highly inflammable and must be used with care and under well-ventilated conditions) or with soap and water, but without rubbing or applying friction of any kind. While dipping 19th-century coins to make them brilliant has been widely done (otherwise there would be *no* fully brilliant Mint State coins in existence for 19th-century silver pieces, except for some hoarded Morgan dollars and a few others), thankfully this has not been the case for tokens and medals. Here and there a brightened-up Hard Times or Civil War token or other issue can be seen, but to dip or brighten a medal could sharply reduce its value, particularly a bronze or copper piece with chocolate surfaces. With silver medals, including awards, few numismatists want flashy, bright pieces but instead prefer those with attractive toning. If you must try to improve tokens or medals, spend a lot of time experimenting with low-value coins from pocket change. Also, remember that a token or medal not "improved" can always be revisited in the future. The value of a piece improperly cleaned might suffer greatly.

STORAGE AND DISPLAY

Medals and tokens are meant to be enjoyed, and it is nice to be able to view them. Popular albums and holders made for coins may be used for tokens and medals as well. Cent- or nickel-size albums match the size of Civil War tokens. Certified pieces encapsulated in "slabs" are provided with their own storage and display as part of the process. While such pieces are infrequent now among tokens and even more so among medals, this may change. Slabs do have an advantage in that they prevent pieces from being inadvertently damaged by handling, and they also permit viewing of both sides (but often not the edge).

Medals that come in presentation cases or boxes can be left there, to be opened to view when desired. Sometimes holders will cause a medal to darken in an unfavorable manner. A thin coating of clear fingernail polish or Krylon spray, easily removable by dissolving, will serve to protect the surface while you own the piece.

For pieces up to the size of silver dollars, clear circular plastic covers are available that neatly snap over the token or medal. Other commercial products include snap holders and clear plastic flips. The old-time method of storing a collection in trays is interesting, but needs to be viewed with caution. Wooden cabinets, particularly those made in recent years, sometimes impart fumes to the pieces, causing them to tone or discolor. Also, pieces open to the atmosphere, even when the tray is pushed into a cabinet, may discolor if there are contaminants in the air (such as from coal or oil heating or from vehicular traffic).

In addition, in all circumstances it is desirable to store pieces in dry circumstances away from heat or direct sunlight. On balance, keeping your tokens and medals in the condition in which you acquired them should not be much of a problem if some simple precautions are observed.

SHOW, TELL, ENJOY

If you are inclined to share information with others, you will find that members of the various societies will be eager to learn about the specimens you own, and to talk about them at conventions, on the Internet, and elsewhere. The larger coin shows often have areas for educational displays. As every token has a story, even a single piece can attract a lot of attention—as, indeed, did a stand-alone 1820 North West Company beaver token (No. 12), accompanied by a printed commentary, at an ANA convention a few years ago.

Joining a special interest group such as TAMS, the CWTS, AVA, or the MCA will bring to your mailbox newsletters and publications. Both the ANA and the ANS have important tokens and medals in their collections, that of the ANS being almost definitive and cataloged online. Both also hold occasional seminars and discussions relating to such pieces.

While on the following pages a few paragraphs have been allotted to each of the 100 Greatest, this is just the tip of the exonumia iceberg. Virtually any one of these items invites you to learn more about its history, romance, and numismatic tradition. There are many pleasures in life, including, for some, the enjoyment mentioned on No. 63 among the 100 Greatest. The authors hope this book will be a pleasure to own and to read, as it details a fascinating frontier of American numismatics.

Note on the Sizes of the 100 Greatest American Medals and Tokens

The majority of items in the 100 Greatest American Medals and Tokens are shown at a diameter of 60 mm. Actual sizes may be smaller or larger, as indicated in the related text.

100 Greatest American Medals and Tokens

1776 LIBERTAS AMERICANA MEDAL

Betts-615, Loubat-14 • Silver: 30 to 35 known • Copper: 100 to 125 known

When all the votes were counted for the 100 Greatest, the Libertas Americana was elected No. 1, and by a good margin. Its beauty, its rich history, and its inspiration for federal Liberty Cap coinage combine to make this medal an object of desire for many numismatists.

The obverse depicts the goddess of America, a portrait that numismatists call Miss Liberty, facing to the left, with LIBERTAS AMERICANA above and the historical date 4 JUIL 1776 below. Behind her hair is a liberty cap on a pole, the cap being an ancient symbol of freedom.

The dies for this beautiful work of art were engraved in Paris in 1782 at the behest of Benjamin Franklin, who conceived the medal and suggested the mottoes. French artist Esprit-Antoine Gibelin sketched the design, and the dies were made by Augustin Dupré.

Franklin, who was in France at the time, described the medal in a letter to Robert R. Livingston (secretary of foreign affairs under the Confederation) on March 4, 1782:

> This puts me in mind of a medal I have had a mind to strike, since the late great event you gave me an account of, representing the United States by the figure of an infant Hercules in his cradle, strangling the two serpents; and France by that of Minerva, sitting by as his nurse, with her spear and helmet, and her robe specked with a few fleurs de lis.
>
> The extinguishing of two entire armies in one war is what has rarely happened, and it gives a presage of the future force of our growing empire.[22]

On April 15, 1783, Franklin advised Livingston:

> I have caused to be struck here the medal which I formerly mentioned to you, the design of which you seemed to approve. I enclose one of them in silver, for the President of Congress, and one in copper for yourself; the impression in copper is thought to appear best, and you will soon receive a number for the members.
>
> I have presented one to the King, and another to the Queen, both in gold, and one in silver to each of the ministers, as a monumental acknowledgment, which may go down to future ages, of the obligations we are under to this nation. It is mighty well received, and gives general pleasure. If the Congress approve it, as I hope they will, I may add something on the die (for those to be struck hereafter) to show that it was done by their order, which I could not venture to do until I had authority for it.

Time increases its fame, so to speak, and today the appearance of a copper example rates multiple paragraphs in an auction catalog, and for a silver impression a full-page display may be in order.

The obverse of the 1783 Libertas Americana medal became the model for the Liberty Cap, Head Facing Left design of the U.S. half cent of 1793 (actual size about 22 mm), as well as dozens of commemorative medals and tokens struck since then.

Estimated Market Values	
Silver	
PF-63 to 65 (choice to gem):	$60,000 to $100,000 +
PF-60 to 62:	$30,000 to $60,000
PF-50 to 58:	$20,000 to $30,000
Copper	
PF-63 to 65 (choice to gem):	$15,000 to $30,000
PF-60 to 62:	$10,000 to $15,000
PF-50 to 58:	$6,000 to $10,000

Commentary on Value

Commentary: Prices can vary widely at auction; higher-grade coins with superb eye appeal often bring the best prices. Market appearances of copper strikings are frequent, silver impressions less so. Consult an expert when contemplating a purchase. Paris Mint restrikes exist and are worth only nominal sums.

No. 1
THE ICONIC PORTRAIT OF LIBERTY
1776 LIBERTAS AMERICANA MEDAL

Shown Here Actual Size: 47.6 mm

The beautiful Libertas Americana medal, impression in silver from original dies. Two gold impressions were struck, but are unaccounted for today.

IMPORTANT CONGRESSIONAL AWARD
WASHINGTON BEFORE BOSTON MEDAL

Julian MI-1, Baker-47, Loubat-1, Betts-542 • Gold (B-47): 1 known • Silver (B-47A): 5 known • Copper (B-47B): 25 to 40 known

The authors had a hunch our No. 2 item would be the Revolutionary War medal voted to General George Washington for his achievement of routing the British from Boston on March 17, 1776, and our voters confirmed it. As Robert Julian has noted, "There has been more interest in this medal than perhaps any other struck in this country." Washington had already assumed the presidency when he received his French-made gold strike from the hands of Thomas Jefferson on March 21, 1790.

Parisian engraver Pierre Simon Duvivier took his portrait for Washington's award from the only source available to him, the Houdon bust of 1785. This profile was widely copied by dozens of later artists and engravers, including C.C. Wright and the Lovett family. John Flanagan adapted it for use on the Washington quarter dollar in 1932, and a caricature of this portrait, with "improvements" made in modern times by the Mint staff, is currently used. Duvivier's reverse scene showed a realistic portrayal of Washington and his troops overlooking Boston from a cannon emplacement on Dorchester Heights. On March 19, 1776, in a letter to the president of Congress, John Hancock, Washington stated he believed it was the construction and manning of this installation that ultimately frightened the British into evacuating the city after an 11-month occupation.

According to Mark Jones in *The Art of the Medal*, "The American War of Independence provided French medalists with a unique alternative to the normal run of official commissions and the opportunity to evolve a style fit to express [new] ideas." The task placed Duvivier, the favorite engraver of Louis XVI, in the delicate position of having to create Revolution-themed designs while at the same time professing loyalty to his monarch. After France's own revolution came to a head and the "citizens" took over in 1789, they stripped Duvivier of his mint position in spite of his work for the United States. In fact, this happened around the same time his Washington medal dies were completed, since a specimen of this medal was displayed at the Royal Academy of Paris even before presentation to Washington, in late 1789.[23]

Beginning immediately afterward, the Paris Mint made restrikes in silver and copper. The original reverse broke in the 1790s, and its replacement bore a die-cutting error: Roman numerals on the exergue read "1276" instead of "1776." To correct this, the numerals were repunched, creating an overdate. In 1861, the Philadelphia Mint sought and failed to acquire the dies, so in 1863 Mint engraver James B. Longacre hubbed copy dies from a French specimen, from which more pieces were struck.

The gold impression of the medal that Jefferson presented to Washington on March 21, 1790. In 1876, 50 citizens of Boston raised $5,000 to secure the medal for the city, after which it reposed at the Boston Public Library. (Photo courtesy of the trustees of the Boston Public Library)

Estimated Market Values
Silver Striking From Original Dies
PF-40 to 58: .... $40,000 to $70,000
Copper Striking From Original Dies
PF-63 to 65 (choice to gem): .... $4,500 to $5,500
PF-60 to 62: .... $3,500 to $4,500
PF-40 to 58: .... $3,000 to $3,500

Commentary on Value
Commentary: Originals and restrikes from the first die pair are the most desirable and are priced here. Later restrikes and impressions from copy dies are less valuable—often much less. Consult an expert numismatist before making a purchase.

No. 2
IMPORTANT CONGRESSIONAL AWARD
WASHINGTON BEFORE BOSTON MEDAL

Shown Here Actual Size: 68.8 mm

Washington Before Boston medal, copper from original dies (Baker-47B). The unique gold specimen (facing page) is in the Boston Public Library. Copper impressions, as here, are the only generally collectible versions.

No. 3

Peace and Friendship
JEFFERSON INDIAN PEACE MEDAL

Julian IP-2 to 4, Prucha 38 and 39, Loubat-22 • Large size (102 mm, shell): 10 to 15 known
Medium size (76 mm, shell): 5 to 9 known • Small size (53.6 mm, struck): 8 to 12 known

No single American exerted a greater philosophical influence on our nation, or practical influence on its form of government, than did Thomas Jefferson. The third U.S. president attached considerable importance to how the country represented itself to the rest of the world, involving himself with the designs for official seals, medals, and even government buildings. He must have been pleased with the classic reverse design for his 1801 peace medal, with its succinct but warm visual image of cooperation, the handshake. Subsequent presidents retained this reverse on all peace medals struck through 1850. The obverse portrait of a young, vigorous Jefferson, taken from a Houdon bust and similar to the one on his inaugural medal (No. 26), also gratified its subject, who wrote his granddaughter in 1802, "[This artist] lately from Europe appears to be equal to any in the world." Johannes Reich had arrived in Philadelphia from Germany on an indenture that was paid in full by an officer of the U.S. Mint. As discovered by late researcher Stewart Witham, Mint director Elias Boudinot personally instructed Chief Engraver Robert Scot to employ Reich for the peace-medal work.

Lewis and Clark distributed Jefferson peace medals to smooth their way through various tribal territories on their explorations of the Missouri River Valley. According to William Clark's 1803 list of articles intended as presents for Indians, they carried three large, 13 medium, and 16 small silver medals. Undoubtedly Zebulon Pike *wished* he had carried Jefferson peace medals on his tour of the upper Mississippi. As the first U.S. emissary to the region, the empty-handed Pike had the awkward task of demanding old English peace medals from all the chiefs who held them, on a promise that U.S. medals would be provided in the future. Large lots of Jefferson medals were struck through 1810 to meet this and other needs, and some did eventually reach the chiefs Pike had designated.

As the peace-medal series progressed through the 19th century, with a new obverse design and issue for each president, interest rose among antiquarians and collectors. In 1841 the U.S. Mint began making bronze restrikes of the Jefferson medals from the original dies, and continued to restrike them occasionally, in silver and bronze, through the end of the century. It is easy to distinguish the solid metal restrikes from the originals, which were made from paired uniface strikes on thin sheets of silver, joined back to back by an encircling rim, like a shell.

2004 Obverse — Peace Medal Reverse — Keelboat Reverse — 2005 Obverse — American Bison Reverse — Ocean in View Reverse

2006 Obverse — Monticello Reverse

The historic Jefferson peace medal design was revisited at the start of the Mint's program commemorating the bicentennial of Lewis and Clark's expedition. The peace medal appeared on the reverse of the first issue in the series, in 2004. It was followed by designs symbolizing different stages of the journey: the keelboat that carried the explorers through the Louisiana Territory; a bison like the ones encountered in the crossing of the Great Plains; and a view of the Pacific Coast, with the inscription "Ocean in View! O! The joy!" (from Clark's journal). The series culminated with the Monticello reverse design; its title, "Return to Monticello," is meaningful both literally and figuratively, as both the design and the explorers returned to their origins at the end of their respective journeys.

Estimated Market Values	Commentary on Value
Silver Originals	*Commentary:* All examples are highly prized rarities. Buy only from an expert numismatist. Indian peace medals of all kinds on the Internet, if not offered by credentialed professionals, are apt to be modern copies or restrikes; fewer than 1 out of 1,000 new-to-the-market early peace medals is original and valuable. *Caveat emptor.*
EF-40 to AU-58:	
102 mm (approximate), shell .... $100,000 to $200,000	
76 mm, shell .... $100,000 to $200,000	
53.6 mm, struck .... $75,000 to $175,000	

No. 3
PEACE AND FRIENDSHIP
JEFFERSON INDIAN PEACE MEDAL

Shown Here Actual Size: 102 mm

The largest of three sizes of the Jefferson Indian peace medal, the 102-mm style was made by the fitting together of two silver shells, as there was no press at the Mint with sufficient capacity to strike this diameter. This exceptional specimen has the original loop still attached.

1837 FEUCHTWANGER COINAGE

Rulau HT-268 (cents) • Rulau HT-262 to 266 (three cents) • Cents: 5,000 to 10,000 known • Three-cent pieces: 125 to 200 known

By any reckoning, Lewis Feuchtwanger is one of the most interesting figures in the annals of early American numismatics. Born in Germany in 1805, Feuchtwanger came to America in 1829 and settled in New York City, where in time he opened a pharmacy and imported medicines and other items from his native country. His store must have been interesting to visit, for on display were gems, rare minerals, preserved reptiles, and other curiosities, in addition to items for sale.

In 1829 he introduced Feuchtwanger's Composition, a version of German silver, intended to imitate silver through an alloy of other metals (typically nickel, copper, and tin, sometimes with a trace of silver). The alloy was recommended as an ideal substitute for silver in many uses and for copper in coinage. At the American Institute exhibitions in 1834, 1835, and 1836, silver medals were awarded for his alloy and products made from it.

During the Panic of 1837, when coins in circulation were in short supply, Feuchtwanger created his own "cents," measuring 18.5 mm—much smaller than the copper cents of the day. The *U.S. Gazette*, published in Philadelphia, included this in its issue of September 11, 1837:

> Dr. Lewis Feuchtwanger, of New York, has issued a German silver penny, milled at the edge, on one side a fine bold eagle, and the reverse a wreath, with the words, "one cent," with his name on the circle. It is of the intrinsic value of one cent, and about the size of a dime. They are a first rate substitute for small change.

On the next day this follow-up was printed:

> A friend called on us yesterday, with a sample of Feuchtwanger's coin of "one cent" to which we referred in our morning's paper. It was a beautiful piece of money, if it may be allowed such a title, much more convenient in every way than the copper coin; and should silver and gold ever come again in fashion, we think this kind of "cent" would be a very excellent attendant.[24]

In late summer and autumn 1837, Feuchtwanger spent much time and effort trying to interest Congress in adapting his alloy to make coins, furnishing each member with a sample. However, Mint director Robert M. Patterson rejected the idea.

Likely, a million or more cents were made and used in circulation. As a result, No. 4 among the 100 Greatest is quite affordable today. More than a dozen die varieties are known.

The 1837-dated three-cent pieces were made in limited numbers. Today all are rare. Years later, in 1864, a three-cent piece was made for the numismatic trade; these are also rarities now.

The Feuchtwanger three-cent piece of 1837, HT-262. Featured is an adaptation of the New York state arms. These circulated extensively. Today, most show evidence of wear. Typical grades are Very Fine and Extremely Fine. An estimated 100 to 150 exist.

The Feuchtwanger three-cent piece of 1837, HT-263. The eagle-and-snake motif is similar to that on the cent, but facing to the left. An estimated 30 to 50 are known, mostly in Extremely Fine grade and above.

The Feuchtwanger three-cent piece of 1837, HT-265. Fewer than a dozen are known of this issue, including Proof impressions struck circa 1858.

ESTIMATED MARKET VALUES

One Cent	
MS-63 to 65 (choice to gem):	$500 to $1,000
MS-60 to 62:	$350 to $500
EF-40 to AU-58:	$135 to $350
VF-20 to 35:	$110 to $135

Three Cents With Eagle Reverse	
MS-63 to 65:	$10,000 to $25,000
MS-60 to 62:	$5,000 to $10,000
EF-40 to AU-58:	$2,500 to $5,000

Three Cents With Coat-of-Arms Reverse	
MS-63 to 65:	$3,000 to $5,000
MS-60 to 62:	$2,000 to $3,000
EF-40 to AU-58:	$1,000 to $2,000

COMMENTARY ON VALUE

Commentary: The typically encountered grade range is Extremely Fine to About Uncirculated. Choice and gem Mint State pieces are seldom seen. Scarce die varieties are worth more.

No. 4

COMPOSITION CENTS AND THREE-CENT PIECES
1837 FEUCHTWANGER COINAGE

Shown Here Actual Size: 18.5 mm

The Feuchtwanger cent (HT-268) was widely used in circulation in 1837 and later years. Today, more than a dozen die combinations are known; this is 4-E.

No. 5
AMERICA'S MOST FAMOUS PEACE MEDAL
1792 WASHINGTON PEACE MEDAL FOR RED JACKET
Prucha 25, Baker 174P • Unique

In 1898, the Buffalo and Erie County Historical Society acquired the Red Jacket medal from Minnie Van Rensselaer for $100—a bargain even for the 19th century. The object was the best-known single representative of the Washington peace medal series, a distinguished artifact of a young nation's attempts to commence relations with the largest Native American empire in the New World. The Six Nations of the Iroquois League occupied a territory stretching from Ontario to Virginia and from New Jersey to Michigan, and the U.S. War Department offered peace medals of "the Great White Father" to its representatives throughout that region. One of these was Sagoyewatha, a Seneca chief of the Niagara River valley, who had donned a British red coat during the Revolution, earning himself the nickname *Red Jacket*.

In 1792, Washington himself bestowed the nearly 7-inch-tall silver pendant on Red Jacket in Philadelphia. The exact circumstances of the meeting are unknown, but for the chief, having met the president increased his influence among Indians and white people alike. In his lifetime, Red Jacket made more than 50 speeches on behalf of the Seneca, three to U.S. presidents. He emphasized the need to preserve Seneca lands and traditions against the encroachment of white settlements and ways of life, and with no small diplomacy, managed to sustain the neutrality of his powerful tribe through the War of 1812. After some of his speeches were published, he became a national celebrity. At his passing in 1830, he was interred at an old mission burial ground, and, still later, in Buffalo's elegant Forest Lawn cemetery.

Red Jacket's medal was far too large to have been struck, and was hand engraved on silver sheets placed back to back. Between 1789 and 1795, the government ordered three sizes of this construction, of which 25 to 30 original specimens are known today. Red Jacket's 1792 medal is typical of the largest size, 127 mm × 171 mm. Unlike several later pieces hallmarked by Philadelphia silversmith Joseph Richardson Jr., Red Jacket's piece bears no artist's mark. The medal passed down through the chief's family until 1851, when, before a large assemblage of tribal elders, descendant Ely S. Parker received it at his installation as leading Sachem of the Iroquois Confederacy. In the 1870s, Parker would become the first Native American to head the U.S. Bureau of Indian Affairs. Parker's widow, who later married James Tallmadge Van Rensselaer, relinquished the piece to the Historical Society.

Seneca Chief Red Jacket wearing his Indian peace medal. (Hand-colored, folio-size lithograph by J.T. Bowen, from *History of the Indian Tribes of North America*, by Thomas L. McKenney and James Hall)

Estimated Market Values	Commentary on Value
Typical Oval Washington Peace Medal EF-40 to AU-58: . . . . $250,000 to $400,000 VF-20 to 35: . . . . $125,000 to $250,000	*Commentary:* The Red Jacket medal is unique and in institutional hands, and therefore is priceless. Other engraved oval Washington peace medals occasionally come on the market when fine numismatic collections are sold. Hundreds of false pieces exist, including those that are engraved or cast. To the authors' knowledge, not a single previously unknown authentic piece has been found in the past 20 years, despite many Internet offerings! *Caveat emptor.*

No. 5
AMERICA'S MOST FAMOUS PEACE MEDAL
1792 WASHINGTON PEACE MEDAL FOR RED JACKET

Actual Size: 127 mm wide × 171 mm high

"SEASONS MEDALS"

Baker-170 to 172, Julian IP-51 to 53, Prucha Plate 37 • Silver: 6 to 10 known of each design • Copper: 14 to 18 known of each design

The enduring fame of these British-made Washington peace medals owes much to their designer, American painter John Trumbull, whose artistic talents were invaluable during the Revolutionary War era. He sketched plans of British military installations for use in battle, and immortalized such important scenes as Burgoyne's surrender at Saratoga and the gathering of the founding fathers to draft the Declaration of Independence. Because of these services, and with his many ties to the founding fathers, Trumbull was a natural choice to design the medals.

At Washington's request he composed three agricultural and domestic scenes that might familiarize and attract Indians to the ways of "civilized" people. Previous medals had been designed expressly as peace medals; the domestic, prosperous scenes (oft-misinterpreted as "seasons") on the reverses of these new medals encouraged peace in a subtler way. For die engraver, Trumbull chose that "excellent workman," Conrad Küchler.

Today, these pieces (among them two silver Proof sets, included in the above estimates) are of special interest as America's first *set* of medals. Their three motifs are generally referred to as the Shepherd, the Farmer (or Sower), and the Home (or Spinner); details of each are shown below (all are from copper specimens in the John J. Ford Jr. Collection). Mintages were as follows:

> *The Shepherd*—Silver: 17 without loop, 150 with loop; copper (bronzed finish): 7 without loop, 60 with loop
>
> *The Farmer*—Silver: 17 without loop, 150 with loop; copper (bronzed finish): 7 without loop, 60 with loop
>
> *The Home*—Silver: 17 without loop, 149 with loop; copper (bronzed finish): 9 without loop, 58 with loop

The Seasons medals were the first in the peace series to be struck in round format. These were intended to be distributed during Washington's second term, but production was delayed, and the first 326 silver medals were not shipped until July 1798; unknown quantities of copper strikes were delivered later. Lewis and Clark took 55 silver medals and a supply of copper medals on their 1804–1806 expedition.

Details of "the Shepherd"

Details of "the Farmer"

Details of "the Home"

Estimated Market Values	
Silver Striking, Any Design	
EF-40 to AU-58:	$40,000 to $60,000
VF-20 to 35:	$20,000 to $40,000
F-12:	$10,000 to $20,000
Copper Striking, Any Design	
EF-40 to AU-58:	$15,000 to $22,000
VF-20 to 35:	$6,000 to $15,000
F-12:	$3,000 to $6,000

Commentary on Value

Commentary: Examples are typically marked and nicked. There has been no market-price differential between looped and unlooped pieces, or, in the case of looped pieces, between those with and without the loop remaining.

No. 6

AMERICA'S FIRST SET OF MEDALS
1796–1798 WASHINGTON "SEASONS MEDALS"

"The Shepherd"

Actual Size: 48.3 mm

Silver striking of "the Shepherd," first in the suite of the Seasons medals. Each design was struck in copper and silver using a common reverse. Some have suggested that the standing figures on the Shepherd and the Farmer are Washington himself. (Massachusetts Historical Society)

   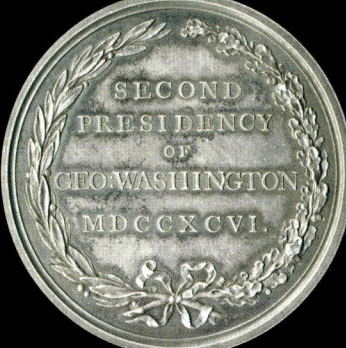

"The Farmer"

Shown Here Actual Size: 48.3 mm

Silver striking of "the Farmer," with a man sowing seeds in the foreground, and in the distance another farmer plowing with two oxen. (Massachusetts Historical Society)

"The Home"

Shown Here Actual Size: 48.3 mm

Silver striking of "the Home." Depicted is an interior scene with a woman operating a spinning wheel, another tending a loom, and at the left foreground, a child near an infant in a cradle. (John J. Ford Jr. Collection)

1737 AND 1739 HIGLEY COPPERS

Crosby pp. 324–326, Breen-238 to 244 • 60 to 80 known of all varieties combined

The copper tokens made by Samuel Higley, of Simsbury, Connecticut, are among the most interesting American colonial issues. A man of multiple talents, Higley held a degree in medicine from Yale, operated a copper mine, and was experienced in making steel from iron (in 1728 he was granted an exclusive 10-year patent to make this alloy in the colony). He cut his own dies and from them struck tokens, each bearing the denomination of threepence. Most had a standing deer on the obverse and either three crowned hammers or a broadax on the reverse.

His threepence coppers were about the same size and weight as ordinary British *halfpence*, then common in circulation. When shopkeepers refused to take in his coins (at a value six times that of the British pieces), Higley changed the inscription from THE VALUE OF THREEPENCE to VALUE ME AS YOU PLEASE. This seems to have solved the matter. As a further touch, certain pieces also bore the inscription I AM GOOD COPPER or I CUT MY WAY THROUGH.

Higley died in May 1737, on a ship en route to England. Some hold that his oldest son, John, and two other men continued the coinage through the year 1739, but there is no evidence to support this.

As all known Higley coppers show wear, and as most are completely smooth in sections of the legends, it is assumed that they circulated widely and for a long time. In his 1875 book, *Early Coins of America*, Sylvester S. Crosby related that a goldsmith who was an apprentice around 1810 told that Higley pieces were hard to find at the time and were in demand to use as an alloy for gold. The goldsmith stated that his master once delayed completing a string of gold beads because he was unable to find a Higley copper with which to alloy the metal.

Higley threepence were early recognized as rarities, and by the mid-19th century, when coin collecting became popular, they were highly prized. Today, several dozen specimens are known to exist. Whenever an example comes on the market—which is not often—it is a focal point for attention.

In 1728 Higley purchased a large tract of land on a slope in the Turkey Hills range, which became the site for his own copper mine and several others, one of which had particularly elaborate underground workings and was later used as the infamous Newgate Prison. Years later the district was divided into the towns of Simsbury, Granby, East Granby, and Canton. As the site of Higley's minting activities later became Granby, and that of his mine, East Granby, some old-time texts call these *Granby coppers*.[25]

Remains of the Newgate Prison in Granby (formerly Simsbury), Connecticut, with the above-ground works as they appeared in the early 20th century. A vast network of tunnels and chambers dug out as a copper mine was later used to confine Tories during the Revolutionary War and criminals at other times.

Estimated Market Values	
Typical Variety With Standing Deer	
VF-20:	$40,000 to $80,000
F-12:	$25,000 to $40,000
VG-8:	$18,000 to $25,000
G-4:	$10,000 to $18,000

Commentary on Value

Commentary: All known examples show wear, usually extensive. Actual size is approximately 27 mm. Typical grades range from Fair (lower than Good) to Very Good or so. All are extremely rare. Certain ultra-rare varieties are worth more.

No. 7
"VALUE ME AS YOU PLEASE"
1737 AND 1739 HIGLEY COPPERS

Actual Size: About 27 mm (varies)

Three varieties of the Higley threepence struck in Simsbury, Connecticut, from 1737 to 1739.

1826 ERIE CANAL MEDAL

HK-1000 (silver), HK-1 (white metal) • Silver: 20 to 30 known • White metal: 150 to 250 known

The Erie Canal completion medal was the first in what is now a distinguished series commemorating such mighty public works as the Atlantic Cable, Transcontinental Railroad, and Panama Canal.

Construction of the first convenient cargo route through the Appalachians from the Atlantic to the West had been slow and difficult. Work on the 363-mile-long canal began at Rome, New York, in 1817, and after two years, only 15 miles had been completed. Strident opponents to the massive state expenditures for the project demanded that the work be abandoned. But supporters persevered, and when the waterway was completed, the City of New York hosted the biggest celebration the nation had ever seen.

On October 26, 1825, the first canal boat left Buffalo. A flotilla of sailing ships and steam barges joined it on the Hudson River at Albany, and escorted it on November 4 to a festive landing at New York's Battery, where Governor Clinton ceremoniously poured a jar of Lake Erie's water into New York Bay. Potentates, organizers, and guests of the city received elegant medals designed by Archibald Robertson and engraved by Edward Thomason of Birmingham, England.

A smaller version was also struck, based on the Thomason piece, but of American materials and by New York artists. According to Robertson's report:

> The medal was engraved by Mr. Charles C. Wright, of the firm of A.B. and C. Durand, Wright and Co. . . . The lettering was by Mr. Richard Trested, engraver and die sinker, upon dies made by Mr. William Williams, Worker in Iron and Steel. The Medals themselves were most elegantly *impressed* by Mr. Maltby Pelletreau of the firm of Pelletreau, Bennett, and Cooke at their Gold and Silver Manufactory, by means of his very powerful and exquisitely adjusted screw press. . . .
>
> Curious woods, such as birdseye, curled maple, red cedar, &c., the produce of the western forests, for making boxes to inclose the medal, were procured and deposited in a canoe made by the aboriginal red men, on the shores of Lake Superior; and embarked on board the first canal boat from the lakes. . . . On the inside of the lid is the crest of the City Arms.

Edward Thomason's elegant 1825 Erie Canal medal (actual size 80 mm), shown here in copper. Charles Cushing Wright copied it in smaller diameter for use on his 1826 medal, our No. 8, shown on the facing page.

Estimated Market Values		Commentary on Value
Silver Strikings		*Commentary:* Occasionally, examples are offered in the small round wooden boxes in which they were distributed, adding $200 to $300 to these estimates. Most have a round paper label.
PF-63 to 65 (choice to gem):	$6,000 to $7,500	
PF-60 to 62:	$4,000 to $6,000	
PF-50 to 58:	$3,000 to $4,000	
White-Metal Strikings		
PF-63 to 65 (choice to gem):	$800 to $1,200	
PF-60 to 62:	$500 to $800	
PF-50 to 58:	$400 to $500	

No. 8
AMERICA'S FIRST PUBLIC-WORKS MEDAL
1826 ERIE CANAL MEDAL

Shown Here Actual Size: 43.9 mm

From dies engraved by Charles Cushing Wright, with lettering added by Richard Trested, the 1826 Erie Canal medal is one of the most historic and beautiful of its era. The motifs are from an 1825 medal struck in England by Edward Thomason.

No. 9

THE FIRST MEDAL STRUCK IN AMERICA
1757 "KITTANNING DESTROYED" MEDAL

Betts-400, Julian MI-33 • 12 to 15 silver originals known

The first medal ever struck within the territory that would become the United States was a combat medal of the French and Indian War (1754–1763). Engraved by Edward Duffield, friend to first U.S. Mint director David Rittenhouse,[26] it was struck by silversmith Joseph Richardson, father to U.S. Mint assayer Joseph Richardson Jr. Some 25 to 50 examples were commissioned by the Corporation of the City of Philadelphia (whose arms appear on the reverse of the medal) to honor Colonel John Armstrong for gallant conduct at a surprise assault on Indian forces at Kittanning, Pennsylvania, in 1756.

Since the fall of 1755, Shawnee chief "Captain Jacobs" and Delaware Chief Shingas had been helping the French try to expel British settlers from the contested Ohio River valley. In April 1756, Governor Robert Morris declared war on the chiefs. Armstrong had ample motivation to march out from newly constructed Fort Shirley with a force of 300 men. He had received intelligence that Jacobs had killed Armstrong's own brother, Edward, during an attack on Fort Granville, and that Jacobs's war party was headquartered in Kittanning, a large Indian settlement about 40 miles north of present-day Pittsburgh.

The phrase "Kittanning destroyed" on the medal is accurate. Armstrong's surprise attack found Jacobs's forces sleeping inside their cabins, many of which were being used to stockpile gunpowder. As the Indians emerged to fight, the soldiers cut them down with musket fire, and those who remained inside were blown to pieces when Armstrong's men set fire to the cabins. Armstrong lost 17 men, and though Shingas and his warriors managed to flee, Jacobs, his wife and son, and many of his men were killed.

In 1821, Philadelphia Athenaeum president and numismatist James Mease announced that Joseph Richardson Jr., who owned the dies, had struck "a few copies" for him in silver (at the U.S. Mint).[27] Mease deposited one strike each of the Armstrong and the Quaker peace medal (No. 13) in the cabinets of the Pennsylvania and New York historical societies. The Mint later used the original dies for restrikes in bronze, until they cracked and eventually broke; copper strikes of the 1860s show the die cracks. In 1874, the Mint made copy dies and resumed restriking. To mark the 250th anniversary of the French and Indian War, the Armstrong County Tourist Bureau sold brass and silver copies of the medal as souvenirs of an elaborate battle reenactment. These differ slightly from the original design and are edge-stamped "1756–2006."

The September 10, 2006, reenactment of the battle of Kittanning likely took more planning than the original attack. A historically authentic village of cabins was constructed for the 250th-anniversary battle, and more than 90 reenactors fired off over 200 pounds of black powder. Mike Slease, who played General Armstrong, reports that fire can blow as far as 12 feet from the touchhole of a musket.

ESTIMATED MARKET VALUES	COMMENTARY ON VALUE
SILVER	
EF-40 to AU-58: .... $50,000 to $100,000 + VF-20 to 35: .... $20,000 to $50,000	*Commentary:* Actual market prices can vary widely, depending upon the condition of the medal, the expertise (or lack thereof) accompanying an auction offering, and the medal's pedigree. Market appearances of originals are infrequent. The Ford Collection example illustrated here, believed to be the finest known, sold for $103,500 in May 2006, with a detailed historical and numismatic description (by Michael Hodder for Stack's).

No. 9
THE FIRST MEDAL STRUCK IN AMERICA
1757 "KITTANNING DESTROYED" MEDAL

Shown Here Actual Size: 46 mm

The Kittanning medal, original striking in silver. A superb impression from the John J. Ford Jr. Collection, the largest cabinet of Betts medals ever formed.

ABOLITIONIST MEDALS
1838 "AM I NOT A WOMAN & A SISTER" AND "AM I NOT A MAN & A BROTHER" TOKENS

Low-54 and 54A, Rulau HT-81 and 82 • Am I Not a Woman: 500 to 1,000 known • Am I Not a Man: 3 known

In 1787, London's Society for Effecting the Abolition of the Slave Trade needed propaganda for their cause. They commissioned Staffordshire potter Josiah Wedgwood to create colorful jasperware cameos of their official seal, which showed a kneeling slave bound in chains, under the legend AM I NOT A MAN AND A BROTHER? Wedgwood adapted these for snuffboxes, hatpins, and brooches, and in 1788 shipped a case to Benjamin Franklin, who replied:

> I am distributing your valuable present of cameos among my friends in whose countenances I have seen such marks of being affected by contemplating the figure of the Suppliant (which is admirably executed) that I am persuaded it may have an effect equal to that of the best written pamphlet in procuring honour to those oppressed people.[28]

By the 1830s, "Am I not a man and a brother?" had become the rallying cry of the abolitionist movement in America as well as England. The enchained-slave image could be seen on British trade tokens of the 1790s, American handbills, shaving mugs, sugar bowls, and needlepoint samplers. In April 1837, Bostonian William Lloyd Garrison's abolitionist journal *The Liberator* began printing, beside features in its "Ladies Department," the image of a bound female slave under the slogan AM I NOT A WOMAN AND A SISTER? In December, Charles Denison's New York paper *The Emancipator* advertised new tokens for sale at the Anti-Slavery Office on Nassau Street. They were "similar in appearance to new cents—nearly as heavy and made of pure copper," and they bore the woman/sister device and the date 1838. Modern researchers have determined they were made by Gibbs, Gardner & Company of Belleville, New Jersey, producer of many other tokens in the Hard Times series.[29] Only three pieces of the man/brother token by the same firm, also dated 1838, are known.

An overseer with whip in hand watches slaves in a cotton field. Planters Bank of Fairfield, Winnsboro, South Carolina, $5 note, December 1, 1855. Printed by Toppan, Carpenter, Casilear & Co., Philadelphia and New York.

Cotton, an element of the "wealth of the South" (see No. 64), was typically picked by slaves. Bank of Lexington, payable at Graham, North Carolina; $5 note dated April 6, 1861, printed by the American Bank Note Co., New York.

A young slave cranks a grinding wheel while a mechanic sharpens a scythe blade. Two other slaves are at work in the field to the right. Bank of Hamburg, South Carolina, $5 note dated January 4, 1860, printed by the American Bank Note Co., New York.

Men and women slaves harvesting sugar cane (another element of the wealth of the South). Central Bank of Tennessee, Nashville, $1 note dated June 25, 1855. Printed by Danforth, Wright & Co., New York and Philadelphia. Three known.

Estimated Market Values	Commentary on Value
Am I Not A Woman & A Sister	
MS-63 to 65 (choice to gem): $600 to $1,000	*Commentary:* These are usually found well struck and on excellent planchets. Uncirculated examples are rare, and when seen have natural toning.
MS-60 to 62: $350 to $600	
EF-40 to AU-58: $225 to $350	
VF-20 to 35: $150 to $250	
Am I Not A Man & A Brother	
VF-20 to 35: $50,000 to $80,000	

No. 10
ABOLITIONIST MEDALS
1838 "AM I NOT A WOMAN & A SISTER" AND "AM I NOT A MAN & A BROTHER" TOKENS

Actual Size: 28 mm

No. 11
"HE IS IN GLORY, THE WORLD IN TEARS"
1800 WASHINGTON FUNERAL MEDAL BY PERKINS

Baker-165 and 166 • Skull and Crossbones (B-165): 2 known in gold, 2 to 4 in pewter, 1 in copper, 15 to 20 in silver
• **Funeral Urn (B-166):** 18 to 22 in gold, 150 to 250 in silver, 200 to 300 in pewter, 2 or 3 in copper

Actual Size: 48.3 mm

Following George Washington's death on December 14, 1799, the nation went into mourning. Many mementoes were made, including ribbons, booklets of eulogies, and medals. Most famous of these is the series of so-called Washington funeral medals, round and of the diameter of a then-current copper cent, by Jacob Perkins, of Newburyport, Massachusetts. These occur in several different die combinations, most showing a portrait of Washington on one side and a funeral urn on the other (Baker-166). The obverse inscription is HE IS IN GLORY, THE WORLD IN TEARS. Medals were holed at the top for suspension on a cord or ribbon. The *Massachusetts Mercury*, January 3, 1800, noted:

> Mr. Jacob Perkins, of Newburyport, has designed and executed a very beautiful medal of Gen. Washington. On one side is a likeness of that illustrious personage; and on the reverse, a memoranda [sic] of the most remarkable periods of his life. They are struck off in gold, silver, or white metal and may be purchased of Mr. Perkins, or at the book stores in Newburyport, and of Mr. Eben Moulton, goldsmith, in this town.[30]

Many of these were worn in parades held on Washington's birthday, February 22. Other varieties included the style with a skull-and-crossbones motif on the reverse (Baker-165) and examples of elliptical format. A few are said to have been restruck in gold in the mid-19th century by Dr. Francis Smith Edwards, who had the original dies (later destroyed).[31]

The *Essex Journal*, January 10, 1800, printed this item, datelined January 7:

> Jacob Perkins takes leave to inform the public that he will now be able to answer orders for the Medals in memory of the late illustrious Gen. WASHINGTON, from any part of the continent, and to any amount, executed on Gold, Silver, or White Metal, with punctuality and dispatch—from 3 to 5 thousand can be made daily. A liberal discount will be made to those who purchase quantities to sell again. Jan 7.

Perkins operated in a three-story wooden building on Market Square.[32] Later, he and his associates produced bank notes in a small Fruit Street building that still stands today.

The funeral medals attracted attention when numismatics became a popular hobby. *Historical Magazine*, July 1858, included a history of them, in response to an inquiry from a reader. They remain in demand to this day. Most often seen are examples with the urn reverse, in silver; occasionally one finds offerings of pewter strikings and, at widely spaced intervals, impressions in gold.

The commercial district of Newburyport in the early 19th century. (Vignette from a $1 note of the Newburyport Bank; American Antiquarian Society)

ESTIMATED MARKET VALUES

Silver with Funeral-Urn Reverse, Holed for Suspension		Gold Strikings		White-Metal Strikings	
EF-40 to AU-58:	$2,000 to $4,000	EF-40 to AU-58:	$20,000 to $30,000	EF-40 to AU-58:	$2,500 to $4,000
VF-20 to 35:	$1,500 to $2,000	VF-20 to 35:	$15,000 to $20,000	VF-20 to 35:	$1,500 to $2500
F-12:	$1,000 to $1,500	F-12:	$10,000 to $15,000	F-12:	$750 to $1,500

No. 12

POST TRADER CURRENCY
1820 NORTH WEST COMPANY BEAVER TOKEN

Rulau Ore-1 to 3 • 100 to 150 known

Actual Size: 29.3 mm

When Captain James Cook published the account of his 1778 voyage to the Pacific Northwest, detailing the vast populations of fur-bearing sea otter as well as coastal topography favorable for shipping and settlement, he precipitated a rush to take advantage of the region's wealth. Expeditions set out from Boston (see No. 31), Canton, Macao, Calcutta, Bombay, London, and Ostend.[33] By the end of the century, trading ships regularly visited coastal settlements extending from the Columbia River to Cook's Inlet in Alaska.

Traders bringing furs and goods westward from the interior represented dozens of French, British, and American firms, with the British-Crown-supported Hudson's Bay Company dominating the Canadian portion of the trade. After 1807, John Jacob Astor's American Fur Company competed in the area west of the southern Great Lakes, all the way to the Oregon coast. His settlement at Astoria on the Columbia River was a major outlet to the markets of Asia, and a great prize for the British, who seized it in the War of 1812. The North West Company, a large French Canadian firm that had sided with Britain during the war, moved into Astor's Pacific territory after the takeover. By 1820, the company had issued brass and copper tokens, specimens of which have been found at trading post sites in the lower Columbia and Umpqua River valleys of "Oregon Country."

Sea-otter populations were depleted by 1821, when the Hudson's Bay and North West Companies merged under the Hudson's Bay name and focused on harvesting beaver. At many of its remote trading posts, the company used tokens as a medium of exchange. Prices were expressed in units of "made beaver," or dressed adult beaver pelts, since the predominantly Native American trappers had no access to, or understanding of, government coinage. The North West Company tokens were valued at one made beaver, although later Hudson's Bay issues added denominations of 1/8, 1/4, and 1/2 made beaver. The majority of North West Company issues are holed, since trappers strung them on leather cords suspended from their belts. Nonholed specimens are exceedingly rare; in 2004 a specimen from the collection of John J. Ford Jr. sold for $48,300. Of the usually encountered pierced examples, perhaps 100 to 150 are known, most of which are well worn, porous, or both.

1925 Fort Vancouver Centennial commemorative half dollar (actual size 30.6 mm) celebrating the 100th anniversary of the fort, which was set up by the Hudson's Bay Company. No doubt North West Company tokens were often seen there.

ESTIMATED MARKET VALUES	COMMENTARY ON VALUE
BRASS OR COPPER, HOLED FOR SUSPENSION	*Commentary:* These have a small hole at the top for suspension. Most tokens show oxidation or other roughness from burial as well as hard use. Some are lightly struck at the centers.
VF-20 to 35: $5,000 to $7,000	
F-12: $2,500 to $5,000	
VG-8: $1,200 to $2,500	
G-4: $600 to $1,200	

No. 13

EMBLEM OF QUAKER GOODWILL
GEORGE II INDIAN PEACE MEDAL

Betts-401 • 15 to 20 silver originals known

Shortly after Colonel John Armstrong's forces handed the Indians their 1756 drubbing at Kittanning (see No. 9), a powerful segment of Philadelphia society that did not see the bloodshed as cause for celebration issued a silver medal of its own. Edward Duffield and Joseph Richardson, the artisans of the "Kittanning Destroyed" medal, now created pieces having an entirely different intent. Richardson was a founder and trustee of the Friendly Association for Regaining and Preserving Peace with the Indians by Pacific Measures, a Quaker group deeply concerned about Pennsylvania's aggressive new policies toward its native inhabitants. While the Quakers agreed that *something* must be done about the vicious attacks being suffered by western settlers, they believed military action and bounties on Indian scalps would only provoke more tribes to join with the French, and could lead to an all-out war with a populous and formidable enemy.

Actual Size: 43.7 mm

The legend on their medal, LET US LOOK TO THE MOST HIGH WHO BLESSED OUR FATHERS WITH PEACE, was as much a political statement to the government of Pennsylvania as it was a plea to the Indians.

The group's charter declared the intention to uphold the precedents for fair dealing with Indians established by colony founder William Penn. At their first meeting in April 1756, they backed their plans with serious money, raising £2,000 in subscriptions, with £18,000 more added over the seven-year life of the organization.[34] The funds were to be spent on sending emissaries to deliver peace offerings to tribes across the colony, in the form of medals, looking glasses, sewing needles, fabric, finished clothing, and other useful articles.

Critics of the Quaker plan, including colonial governor Robert Morris and the official superintendent of Indian affairs, Sir William Johnson, viewed the offerings as "conscience money" for the infamous Walking Purchase of 1737, wherein the sons of William Penn defrauded the Delawares out of huge tracts of land, making them all too willing to join with the French in 1756.

In 1827, Philadelphia historian Roberts Vaux stated that Joseph Richardson Jr. personally explained to him the process used by his father for both this and the Armstrong medal: "The coining press being unknown in this country, the dies were cut on branches fixed in a socket, and the impressions made by the stroke of a sledge hammer."[35]

Another Indian peace medal (actual size 40 mm) issued by the Quakers, this one in 1775, is listed as Betts-531. The Indian on the reverse was obviously copied by Thomas Webb, engraver of the Washington medal published by Eccleston (No. 24)—or perhaps both images are from an earlier common source. The dies were engraved by Lewis Pingo, who in 1776 was appointed as an assistant engraver at the Royal Mint in London. From 1779 to 1815 he served as chief engraver.

ESTIMATED MARKET VALUES	COMMENTARY ON VALUE
ORIGINAL STRIKING IN SILVER	
MS-60 to 62: .... $75,000 to $100,000	*Commentary:* Proof restrikes are seen with some frequency. A typical choice Proof restrike has a market value of about $1,000 to $1,500.
EF-40 to AU-58: .... $50,000 to $75,000	
VF-20 to 35: .... $25,000 to $50,000	

No. 14
COLORFUL MONEY FOR AN EMERGENCY
1862 ENCASED POSTAGE STAMPS

EP, HB, and Reed catalog listings • Rarity varies widely depending on variety

The United States of America declared war against the Confederate States of America on April 15, 1861. The Union anticipated an easy victory, as most of the nation's manufacturing resources were in the North. It did not work out that way, however, and after a decisive Union loss at Bull Run on July 17, both sides planned for an extended conflict. By late 1861 there was still no clear victor. Citizens, fearful that paper money would become worthless, began hoarding coins. By the second week of July 1862, even one-cent pieces had disappeared from circulation. It was impossible to find a coin to buy a newspaper or get a haircut.

Filling the gap, many merchants, towns, and other entities issued tickets and scrip notes. In time, many merchants issued bronze tokens the size of cents, which served for that value. On July 17 the U.S. government decreed that ordinary postage stamps could be used as money. Some were housed in paper envelopes, others pasted to cards. Among the entrepreneurs with an eye toward profit was John Gault, a Boston inventor and entrepreneur who had moved to New York City earlier in the year. Recognizing that stamps would soon become discolored or damaged, and that those in envelopes would be clumsy to inspect, he felt that "encased postage stamps" would serve a need.

Basically, the unit consisted of multiple parts displayed in a circular frame made of brass. On the face, under clear mica, a postage stamp was displayed. The back was embossed with advertising. After patent number 1627 was granted for this device (August 2, 1862), production commenced at the Scovill Manufacturing Co.; it lasted through spring 1863, at which time Postage Currency notes issued by the Treasury Department flooded circulation.

During this time, 31 different merchants signed up to advertise, including Lord & Taylor, the Tremont House, and Mendum's Family Wine Emporium. Products included patent medicines, hotels, food, wine, dry goods, Brown's Bronchial Troches, Aerated Bread, and Drake's Plantation Bitters. Most stamps were of low denominations, such as 1¢, 3¢, and 5¢, but higher values included 10¢, 12¢, 24¢, and 90¢.

Actual Size: About 25 mm (varies)

Today, encased postage stamps are enthusiastically collected. A popular objective is to acquire one from each merchant, the three rarest being B.F. Miles (a druggist in Peoria, Illinois), Arthur M. Claflin (a clothier in Hopkinton, Rhode Island), and Sands Ale.[36]

Ayer's Sarsaparilla was advertised on encased postage stamps and in other media, such as this trade card.

ESTIMATED MARKET VALUES	COMMENTARY ON VALUE
COMMON VARIETIES	*Commentary:* Prices are for the more plentiful issues (consult specialized texts for listings) of lower denominations such as 1¢, 3¢, and 5¢. At the Very Fine level there may be some laminations or flakes in the mica, but the overall appearance must be attractive. Some higher-grade examples have full or (usually) partial silvering on the back of the case.
Basic Unc., choice mica, bright stamp: $500 to $1,000	
EF to AU, choice mica, bright stamp: $250 to $500	
VF, average mica and stamp: $175 to $250	

No. 15
1863 MESSAGES OF PATRIOTISM
PATRIOTIC CIVIL WAR TOKENS

Fuld-1 through 500 series • Estimated 1,000,000+ known

Actual Size: About 19 mm (varies)

Patriotic Civil War cents (or simply *patriotics* to collectors) are mostly dated 1863, although they were made earlier in the war, continuing through 1864. The size of a contemporary Indian Head cent, but usually bronze, these served in commerce at the value of a cent. Beginning in August 1862, one-cent pieces were hoarded by the public: with the outcome of the Civil War uncertain, citizens preferred hard money or coins to Legal Tender paper notes with no intrinsic value. Earlier in the year, silver and gold coins had disappeared from circulation.

Serving as substitutes were several other forms of money, including Postage Currency, encased postage stamps, privately issued scrip notes, and Civil War tokens, the last being of patriotic (as here) and store card (No. 16) types.

Inscriptions on patriotics—usually found on the reverse—are varied, but most relate to the war or money. They include NOT ONE CENT (many variations), THE FLAG OF OUR UNION, ARMY & NAVY, THE UNION MUST AND SHALL BE PRESERVED, UNION FOREVER, KNICKERBOCKER CURRENCY, and more.

On the obverse, portraits were widely used, including the French Liberty Head (a turbaned head created by Robert Lovett Jr. of Philadelphia after a French coin, and widely copied), many Indian heads, princesses with plumed headdresses, Benjamin Franklin, George B. McClellan, Abraham Lincoln, and George Washington—the latter in various poses. Guns, flags, and military regalia are seen on many tokens, as are buildings, statues, and ships.

Most patriotics were made in New York City by diesinkers such as Emil Sigel, Charles D. Horter, George H. Lovett, William H. Bridgens, John D. Lovett, and Frederick B. Smith. Scovill Manufacturing Co. (Connecticut) and several shops in Philadelphia and Cincinnati were also important producers.

About 2,000 varieties of patriotics are known today, counting variations in metal composition. The bible of the series is *Patriotic Civil War Tokens*, by Melvin and George Fuld, now in its fifth edition from the Civil War Token Society. Each die is given a reference number; for example, a token described as Fuld-254/255a combines die 254 with die 255. These tokens are popular and plentiful. A fine representative collection can be obtained at a modest cost and is fascinating to gather.

A selection of interesting Civil War patriotic tokens.

ESTIMATED MARKET VALUES
COMMON VARIETIES IN COPPER
MS-63 to 65 (choice to gem): .... $60 to $100
MS-60 to 62: .... $35 to $60
EF-40 to AU-58: .... $20 to $35
VF-20 to 35: .... $15 to $20
F-12: .... $10 to $15

COMMENTARY ON VALUE

Commentary: Interesting designs and varieties will bring higher prices, as will rare dies and combinations, which may bring thousands of dollars. Striking will vary from issue to issue. The quality and appearance of white-metal strikings varies; prices are usually higher than for copper. Overstrikes on copper-nickel cents sell for several hundred dollars and up, and overstrikes on dimes are well into the four-figure range.

No. 16
MANY GOODS AND SERVICES FEATURED
CIVIL WAR STORE CARDS

Fuld Alabama to West Virginia Listings • Estimated 1,000,000+ known

Actual Size: About 19.1 mm (varies)

The history of Civil War store cards (metal tokens bearing advertisements) goes hand in glove with that of the patriotic issues (No. 15). Many of the same engravers and shops made both types, although for store cards Cincinnati was most prominent. In that city John Stanton and William K. Lanphear produced countless millions. Most of Stanton's featured an Indian Head on the obverse and an advertisement on the reverse. Lanphear's shop was more imaginative, and his staff turned out many different motifs, ranging from Liberty Heads to a hippocampus. In New York City, William H. Bridgens produced various pictorial tokens, including one showing the American eagle smoking a cigar! Chicago's Shubael Childs was another prolific maker of store cards, most of which had a distinctive Liberty Head on the obverse.

Store cards bear the name, initials, or other identification of a merchant, business, steamship, toll-bridge crossing, professional person, or other commercial entity. Most identify the town of issue, and many also give the state. In instances in which locations are not given, many merchants have been identified from old advertisements, directories, and other listings.

Tokens are known from more than 1,500 advertisers. Often tokens would catch on in a particular town, city, or district, and many different merchants would issue them. Over two dozen merchants in Indianapolis issued more than 125 die combinations and varieties. All told, 69 different Indiana municipalities were home to token distributors. In contrast, in the state of Maine just two merchants advertised on tokens, in New Hampshire just one, and in Vermont none at all.

Today, more than 8,600 varieties of store cards are known, including die combinations and different metals. These tokens can be collected in many different ways: One can specialize in trades and professions, collecting, say, a token from each of the different watchmakers and jewelers, medical doctors, hotels, restaurants, stages and railroads, or dry-goods stores. Or one may seek a token from each issuer in a given state (noting that certain states, including Alabama, Iowa, and Missouri, are "rare").

The standard reference is *A Guide to Civil War Store Card Tokens*, by Melvin and George Fuld, published by the Civil War Token Society. Such tokens are interesting to study and own, and plentiful enough that there will always be the opportunity to add new pieces to even an advanced collection.

A selection of interesting Civil War store cards.

ESTIMATED MARKET VALUES	
COPPER STRIKINGS FROM COMMON TOWNS	
MS-63 to 65 (choice to gem):	$50 to $100
MS-60 to 62:	$30 to $50
EF-40 to AU-58:	$20 to $30
VF-20 to 35:	$16 to $20
F-12:	$12 to $16

COMMENTARY ON VALUE

Commentary: Pricing depends on rarity. The above prices are for tokens from merchants in populous states who issued many tokens. Tokens from scarcer states—such as Iowa, Kansas (just one issuer), Alabama, and Missouri—or from merchants for which only one or a few examples are known, may bring up to several thousand dollars, even if well worn. Scarce die varieties are always worth more, but if common varieties are known for the same merchant, the premium for rare die combinations for the same merchant can be modest. Silver impressions are rare and expensive.

No. 17
FIRST AUTHENTIC WASHINGTON PORTRAIT ON A STRUCK MEDAL
1790 WASHINGTON MANLY MEDAL

Baker-61 • Gold: 2 or 3 known • Silver: 5 to 7 known • White metal: 15 to 20 known • Brass: 150 to 250 known

In October 1789, George Washington visited Harvard College in Cambridge, Massachusetts. While he was there, Edward Savage painted a full-length portrait of him and presented it to the college. During this visit the president was probably sketched by Samuel Brooks, a well-known Boston maker of portrait profiles (silhouettes) and painter of miniatures. In 1790 Brooks advertised "correct likenesses in two minutes' sitting." The Brooks and the Savage likenesses are very similar. Soon Brooks produced dies for what would become the first medal depicting Washington as he appeared in life. (Up to this time, the only struck "Washington medal" was that published in Paris by Voltaire in 1778—No. 59 in the 100 Greatest—with a *fictitious* portrait. Although Americans knew of his exploits during the Revolutionary War and as president, his portrait was less familiar.)

In 1790 the *Freeman's Journal* and the *Gazette of the United States* carried notices that "an artist" proposed "a subscription for a medal of George Washington." Inquiries were received in Wilmington, Delaware by Peter Rynberg and in Philadelphia by J. Manly "in the care of Robert Patton, postmaster." On March 7, 1790, the *Pennsylvania Packet and Daily Advertiser* offered these for sale, accompanied by a certificate dated February 22, 1790 (Washington's birthday), and bearing the names of Thomas Mifflin, governor of Pennsylvania; Richard Peters, speaker of the House of Assembly; Christian Febiger, treasurer; and Colonel Francis Johnston of the army, attesting that the image on the medal was a "strong and expressive likeness and worthy of the attention of the citizens of the United States of America." Prices were one dollar for a medal in "fine white metal, to resemble silver," two dollars for one in gold-colored metal (brass), and gold at a price "in proportion to weight."

The Manly medal (Baker-61), named for the seller, J. Manly & Co., is signed BROOKS F. on the neck truncation. The medals were produced quickly, with the first examples ready by February 20, 1790, just in time to go on sale. The reverse gives Washington's birth date, February 11, 1732 (old calendar), in abbreviated form, with other events in his life, as illustrated. To minimize metal movement during striking and to facilitate production, the Manly medals were cast in their approximate form and then were struck with dies to sharpen the details.

These were popular in their own time. In 1801, when the east pier of the Market Street bridge was being constructed in Philadelphia, among the other mementoes placed inside were a Manly medal and a Westwood medal, each depicting Washington.[37] Circa the 1850s another Brooks obverse die, not known to have been used in 1790, was resurrected, and additional medals (Baker-62) were struck.

Actual Size: 48.5 mm

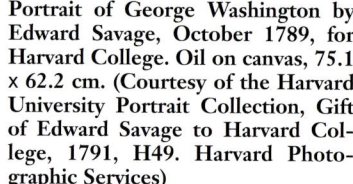

Portrait of George Washington by Edward Savage, October 1789, for Harvard College. Oil on canvas, 75.1 x 62.2 cm. (Courtesy of the Harvard University Portrait Collection, Gift of Edward Savage to Harvard College, 1791, H49. Harvard Photographic Services)

First obverse die (Baker-62) with different inscription, in Latin. This die may have been cut earlier than Baker-61. Signed S.B.F. on the neck truncation. The literature suggests that these were first made in the 1850s from original dies, and struck on a powerful medal press.

ESTIMATED MARKET VALUES

BRONZE STRIKINGS		SILVER STRIKINGS		WHITE-METAL STRIKINGS	
MS-60 to 62:	$2,500 to $5,000	MS-60 to 62:	$20,000 to $30,000	MS-60 to 62:	$3,500 to $6,000
EF-40 to AU-58:	$1,000 to $2,500	EF-40 to 58:	$10,000 to $20,000	EF-40 to 58:	$2,000 to $3,500

No. 18

"PIKES PEAK SILVER MINE"
1900–1901 LESHER "DOLLARS"

HK-787 to 797 • Varieties range from extremely rare to several hundred known

Actual Size: 35 mm

Issued in 1900 and 1901, Lesher Referendum Souvenirs (as the seller called them) were denominated $1.25, but they have long been called Lesher *dollars*. These were the brainchild of Joseph Lesher, who lived high on a slope of Pikes Peak in the mining town of Victor, a few miles from the world-famous Cripple Creek. His house on the main street was two doors left of the Town Hall. Lesher came to Colorado from Fremont, Ohio, to make his stake in the silver-mining business, which created boom times beginning in the 1860s. After 1873, however, the price of silver declined sharply on world markets, primarily due to European countries' abandoning the metal as a monetary standard. Meanwhile, new discoveries in Colorado and elsewhere in the West resulted in an oversupply of silver, causing prices to drop even further. Lesher went back to Ohio to engage in livery and farming.

In the early 1890s, gold was discovered on the west side of Pikes Peak. This developed into a bonanza, and by 1900 mines were scattered all over the area, which had come to be called "the richest gold district on earth." Lesher relocated to the scene of activity and became a successful real estate investor. He maintained his love for silver, however, and in 1900 he created a design of an octagonal dollar or medal depicting the nearby mountain, with the inscription PIKES PEAK SILVER MINE. Frank Hurd struck the pieces with dies cut by Herman Otto, using 412 grains of silver alloy—the same as in a silver dollar. The first issues, dated 1900, were denominated $1.25; those of 1901 were valued at $1 in exchange.

Lesher issued many of his dollars for his own account, passing them out and redeeming them from his Victor home and through local businesses and banks. Many were distributed by local and regional merchants (plus one in distant Holdrege, Nebraska), and had their imprint stamped on them. Distribution continued through 1903. The dollars were serially numbered, an unusual practice for a monetary token, but one that permits easy numismatic attribution today as to their recorded appearances.

The Lesher dollars soon attracted the interest of numismatists, and accounts of them were printed in *The Numismatist* (first noticed in February 1901), the *Numismatic Scrapbook*, and elsewhere. Adna Wilde's February 1978 study in *The Numismatist*, "Lesher Referendum Dollars: Where Are They Today?" brought together past knowledge and new research to create what is now the standard authority on these pieces, delineating six types and 11 varieties.[38] It is likely that slightly more than 3,000 Lesher dollars were distributed, of which only a few hundred survive today.

A typical 1901 Lesher "dollar" with a panoramic view of Pikes Peak and mention of the "Pikes Peak Silver Mine." Never mind that the mines on the slope of that mountain all produced *gold*.

ESTIMATED MARKET VALUES	
TYPICALLY AVAILABLE VARIETIES	
MS-60 to 62:	$2,500 to $4,000
EF-40 to AU-58:	$1,200 to $2,500
VF-20 to 35:	$1,000 to $1,200

COMMENTARY ON VALUE

Commentary: Prices are for generally available imprints such as A.B. Bumstead. Scarce and rare varieties can sell for much more.

No. 19
Triumphs of Medallic Sculpture
1930–1995 Society of Medalists Issues

SOM-1 to 129 • Several hundred each known of most varieties

It was obvious to our voters that any book whose theme is greatness in medals must give prominence to that remarkable 20th-century phenomenon, the Society of Medalists series.[39] Electing just one of the 129 art-medals issues created between 1930 and 1995 proved too difficult, so the entire series took our 19th spot.

Conceived by America's leading sculptors under the aegis of the American Federation of Arts, the society was intended as a forum for experimentation with medallic sculpture. Medallic Art Company was the ideal choice for a mint, as its Janvier pantographic equipment allowed artists to model their designs in a 9-inch to 12-inch format, to be mechanically reduced onto medal dies. Almost every important sculptor submitted designs to the society's review committees, who invited just two artists per year to create a medal. Each medal struck in silver and bronze was edge-marked with the issue number and year, and the number of medals issued was governed by, but not limited to, the number of subscribers in a given year.

The first five participants, Laura Gardin Fraser, Paul Manship, Hermon MacNeil, Frederic MacMonnies, and Lee Lawrie, were thrilled to have total control over subject matter, design, shape, metallic content, and finish—something not available to them as commissioned makers of commemorative and award medals. They were joined by a stellar lineup of successors: John Flanagan, Herbert Adams, Carl Jennewein, Chester Beach, Walker Hancock, Adam Belskie, Marcel Jovine, Karen Worth, Alex Shagin, and many more. The result of all that talent and imagination was a 65-year-long emission, representing 129 different artistic approaches and as many creative visions. (One of those approaches, the 128th, was actually a cased set of six medals, featuring dinosaurs by Don Everhart.) From time to time the medalists provoked controversy with their subject matter (as artists often do). At the height of Prohibition in 1930, Paul Manship saluted Dionysus, the god of wine. In his 1971 cautionary statement PANDORA ONE, PANDORA TWO, Elbert Weinberg associated the atomic bomb with Pandora's box, the mythical locus of evil. The impact of modern design, photography, and other stylistic innovations is also apparent throughout the series.[40]

Actual Size: 72 mm

With the retirement of Joseph Veach Noble, the society's administrative guiding light in the final 30 years, the series came to an end in 1995. The dies survive in the possession of the Medallic Art Company, which has no immediate plans for making restrikes.[41]

Elbert Weinberg's 1971 Society of Medalists issue (actual size: 71 mm) juxtaposes the mythical Pandora's box with the atomic bomb.

Estimated Market Values	Commentary on Value
Examples from Popular Artists or With Popular Themes MS-63 to 65: .... $150 to $400 **Examples from Less-Popular Artists With Less-Popular Themes** MS-63 to 65: .... $30 to $50	*Commentary:* Prices vary depending upon design and rarity. Most medals survive in the condition as issued, typically with a matte or antiqued finish. It is desirable to have the original leaflets and containers. Except among medal specialists, this fascinating series is not well known. If it were to become so, prices would likely escalate sharply.

No. 20
"UNSURPASSED IN BEAUTY AND DESIGN"
1796 P.P.P. MYDDELTON TOKEN

Breen-1073 and 1074 • Silver: 20 to 30 known • Copper: 18 to 25 known

When Sylvester S. Crosby wrote his 1875 magnum opus, *The Early Coins of America*, he paid our No. 20 the ultimate compliment: "In beauty of design and execution, the tokens are unsurpassed by any piece issued for American circulation."

In 1796 in England, Philip Parry Price, either surnamed Myddelton or from Myddelton, planned a real estate promotion whereby British citizens were to purchase tracts of land in Kentucky. To further this ambition, he commissioned the Soho Mint, a private enterprise in Birmingham operated by Matthew Boulton and James Watt, to create an appropriate token or medalet. Most likely, these pieces were produced primarily for the numismatic trade in England, rather than prospective customers for land. Today, several dozen examples exist in silver (primarily) and copper, all with Proof finish.

The obverse is inscribed BRITISH SETTLEMENT KENTUCKY and illustrates Hope (representing Britain) presenting two of her children to the goddess Liberty, who welcomes them with an outstretched arm; behind her, a cornucopia represents the bounty of America.

The reverse shows the goddess Britannia, dejected and defeated, possibly an allegory for the loss of her citizens or, reaching further back in history, the British defeat in the Revolutionary War. Related in concept is the reverse of the Libertas Americana medal (No. 1).

The dies were cut by Konrad Heinrich Küchler (usually given as Conrad H. Küchler), a gifted German artist who also prepared the three different Washington Seasons medals (see No. 6) at about the same time. Begun in 1759, the Soho Manufactory, as it was called, was well known by the time of Küchler's arrival. The facility was situated on Hockley Brook, a convenient power source until it dried up. James Watt, maker of steam engines, came to the rescue and set up a steam plant, which drove dozens of machines. The three-story structure and outbuildings at one time employed about 600 people. The "Soho Mint" part of the complex made circulating coins for the British government as well as for other countries.

Eagerly collected by British numismatists in an era in which there was little such interest in the United States, the remaining

Actual Size: 28.9 mm

P.P.P. Myddelton tokens found ready buyers on this side of the Atlantic when the hobby began to develop in the 1850s. Today they are classics.

The obverse of the Copper Company of Upper Canada token, shown here, is the same as that of the Myddelton token. Actual size: 28.9 mm.

ESTIMATED MARKET VALUES		COMMENTARY ON VALUE
SILVER STRIKINGS		*Commentary:* The above prices are for silver strikings. Copper impressions are rarer, but sometimes sell for 10% to 20% less. The eye appeal of most surviving examples is very good.
P-63 to 65 (choice to gem):	$18,000 to $25,000	
P-60 to 62:	$15,000 to $18,000	
P-50 to 58:	$9,000 to $12,000	

No. 21

EARLIEST AMERICAN-MADE BRITISH PEACE MEDAL

1764 "HAPPY WHILE UNITED" INDIAN PEACE MEDAL

Betts-510, Fuld/Tayman HWU-1 through 16 • 20 estimated to exist today (some of each size)

Actual Size: 73 mm

After British forces took Montreal in 1760, the competition between the British and the French for influence with the Indians was ended. The British now had a clear field and, rather than attempt to win over the Indians who had supported the French, they elected to weaken their position across the board. The Indians—even Britain's close allies—were denied access to trade at the forts. Sale of ammunition was strictly forbidden. The annual present, normally a substantial one, was eliminated.

These draconian new policies, authored by commander-in-chief Lord Jeffrey Amherst, created seething discontent. In the spring of 1763 a charismatic Ottawa chief named Pontiac organized a widespread revolt. Although Amherst opined that no fort commanded by a British officer was vulnerable to an attack by "savages," fully eight of the 10 forts west of the Alleghenies fell to the Indians, with only Detroit and Pittsburgh holding out. Panic spread throughout the frontier and, not surprisingly, Amherst was recalled.

Sir William Johnson, the longtime superintendent of Indian affairs, who had advised Amherst against the new policies, assumed responsibility for restoring the status quo. He invited Pontiac and other influential chiefs to a peace council at Fort Niagara in the summer of 1764. Pontiac could not attend the first council, so Johnson invited him to a second at Fort Oswego in the summer of 1766.

As an expert in Indian diplomacy, Sir William provided peace medals for the two councils. He knew the high value placed on these symbols so, in the interest of time, he purchased a relatively crude product from a domestic source rather than wait for a higher-quality design to be executed in England. He ordered 60 medals for each of the two councils, split between large (73 mm) and medium (56 mm) sizes. The artist who provided the silver-chased castings was Daniel Christian Fueter, a New York City silversmith. Roughly 20 of the original 120 medals are known today, an amazingly high survival rate.

Unlike Indian peace medals of the federal period, Happy While United medals were awarded to chiefs who represented a potent fighting force. In the 1760s, they had very nearly pushed the white man back across the Allegheny Mountains. These medals are eloquent reminders of turbulent times and the diplomacy that was brought to bear to restore the situation.

Cast copy or study piece, Ford Collection, of the Happy While United medal, smaller size (56 mm). The theme is the same as the larger version, but with differences in the lettering and arrangement.

ESTIMATED MARKET VALUES	COMMENTARY ON VALUE
CAST COPPER AS ISSUED VF-20 to 35: .... $200,000 to $300,000	*Commentary:* Values are highly speculative, because most pieces exist in museums, and there are no modern sales records on which to base them. Not even the John J. Ford Jr. Collection had an example. A leading specialist advised the authors that he would pay $200,000 for a nice example.

No. 22
"SILVER-TONGUED ORATOR OF THE PLATTE"
1896 BRYAN "CARTWHEEL" DOLLAR

HK-780 to 782 • 500 to 1,000 known

In the limelight in 1896 were Republican presidential contender William McKinley, a conservative of the old school, and Democrat William Jennings Bryan, "the silver-tongued orator of the Platte." *Silver* was the burning question of the day, debated with fiery enthusiasm. In the American West, the metal had been mined in large quantities ever since the Comstock Lode in Nevada was exploited in the 1860s. By 1896 many other strikes had been made, including vast deposits in Colorado and Utah. Unfortunately for the mining interests, in the 1870s European nations went off the silver standard, switching to gold exclusively. The price of silver dropped sharply, and by 1896 a silver dollar contained just 48 cents' worth of metal.

In the plains states and the West, "Silverites" or "Free Silver" adherents proposed that the economy would revive if the U.S. government made silver coins worth full silver content, as was the current case with gold coins.

At the Democratic convention held on July 8, 1906, Bryan gave his famous "Cross of Gold" speech, concluding with the ringing statement "You shall not press down upon the brow of labor this crown of thorns, you shall not crucify mankind upon a cross of gold." Bryan was swept into the nomination.

Almost immediately, Republicans and other Bryan detractors turned loose a flood of satirical medals, some showing how large the diameter would be if a silver dollar contained full value of the metal, as illustrated here. In *The Numismatist* in July 1896, editor George F. Heath mused: "The medal fiend is abroad in the land.... The presidential campaign is creating... ingenious chaff, whole volumes of abnormal art and stacks upon stacks of outrageously distorted lines."

The same magazine in July 1926 was devoted to a book-length study of Bryan money by Farran Zerbe, which set the stage for increased collecting interest. As to Bryan, he lost the Electoral College vote 292 to 155 in 1896. He ran again in 1900 and 1908, but lost both times. His last appearance in the public spotlight was in 1925, when he served as attorney in opposition to Clarence Darrow in the Scopes "Monkey Trial" in Dayton, Tennessee. Bryan died five days after the trial ended.

Actual Size: 51.2 mm

William Jennings Bryan, Democratic Party presidential candidate in 1896, 1900, and 1908. (*Harper's Weekly*, July 18, 1896)

ESTIMATED MARKET VALUES	COMMENTARY ON VALUE
MS-60 to 62: .... $300 to $500 **EF-40 to AU-58:** .... $150 to $300	*Commentary:* Prices are for varieties with a spoked wheel as part of the design. Others can bring more or less.

No. 23

SOUVENIR OF AMERICA'S FIRST CIRCUS
1793–1795 RICKETTS'S CIRCUS TOKEN

Julian UN-23, Rulau Pa-428 and 430 • Silver, reeded edge (thin-planchet originals): 2 to 4 known • Copper, plain edge (thick-planchet restrikes): 8 to 10 known • Copper, reeded edge (thin-planchet originals): 4 to 6 known

Actual Size: 28.2 mm

It is not clear whether the tokens of Ricketts's equestrian circus were intended as admission passes or souvenir pieces, but they may well have been the first token issue struck at the U.S. Mint. Robert Julian and Russell Rulau assign them to the early 1790s; perhaps they were issued in time for America's first circus performance, in Philadelphia in April 1793. In 1912, *The Numismatist* reported original strikes in copper and silver "on thin and thick planchets, with plain and reeded edges." Rulau pictures two Ricketts tokens, calling the thick-planchet plain-edge specimen (170.9 grains) a restrike and the thin-planchet reeded-edge example (84.3 grains) an original. The latter variety is also found struck in silver.

Scotsman John Bill Ricketts arrived in Philadelphia "with all his horses, & dancing devils, & little devils"[42] in October 1792, having learned his trade from Charles Hughes of London's Royal Circus. For some years, Ricketts rotated performances between Philadelphia and New York in summer and Charleston in winter, in each location performing in a wooden amphitheater complete with box seats. By 1799, Ricketts had carried his show to Albany, Boston, and Canada.

His entertainments varied over time and included acrobatics on horseback, performances by trained horses, the antics of Matthew Sully the English Clown (father of painter Thomas Sully), tightrope dancing by a Seignior Spinacuta, and "Italian fireworks," among other attractions. George Washington's attendance at the circus was reported in the newspapers as well as his own correspondence. The president admired Ricketts's feats of horsemanship, such as standing erect on a galloping horse, with two raw eggs fastened to the bottoms of his feet, and his mounted broadsword exhibition, "going through the offensive and defensive guards of different nations, in real action, upon the celebrated horse, Cornplanter." In 1797, Washington sold Ricketts his horse "White Jack" for $150; the animal became a most capable performer.

On the night of December 17, 1799, a fire destroyed Ricketts's main amphitheater in Philadelphia, and after a final U.S. performance in April 1800, he relocated his company to the West Indies. Only three years later, on a voyage to England in 1803, the ship carrying his troupe never arrived at its destination, and was presumed lost.

This portrait of John Bill Ricketts, by none other than master portraitist Gilbert Stuart, was terminated halfway through, when the artist became frustrated with the performer's recurrent tardiness. It is reported that Stuart flung his paintbrush into the face of the portrait and declared he would have nothing more to do with its subject.

Estimated Market Values	Commentary on Value
Copper Originals EF-40 to AU-58: . . . . $5,000 to $10,000 **Copper Restrikes, Plain Edge, Thick Planchet** MS-60 to 62: . . . . $4,000 to $7,000	*Commentary:* Original strikings in copper and silver with reeded edge (1790s) and restrikes with plain edge (circa 1840) from dies held at the Mint have not been clearly delineated in the literature. Thin-planchet reeded-edge copper pieces include the Roy Van Ormer Collection specimen, 1985, at $3,300, and the Betts-Wright-Zeddies example for $3,520 in 1990, which would bring much more today.

No. 24

"THE LAND WAS OURS"
1805 WASHINGTON MEDAL BY ECCLESTON

Baker-85 • Copper: 250 to 400 known

Among the numismatically popular early medals associated with the life of George Washington, the 1805 Eccleston medal, from dies cut by Thomas Webb, is certainly the largest (76 mm)—and it is among the most interesting, as well.

At first glance, this seems to be a satirical medal. Washington, on the obverse, is encased in a heavy suit of armor: "a singular conceit," noted W.S. Baker in his 1875 book on Washingtoniana. At the center of the reverse is a Native American leaning on a bow, with the surrounding inscription THE LAND WAS OURS. According to Rulau and Fuld, Eccleston had a lifelong interest in aboriginal rights. His juxtaposition of a downcast-looking brave with a warrior-styled Washington might be taken to imply a view of Washington as an invader. However, it seems that Eccleston, a highly eccentric Englishman, did mean the medal as a straightforward tribute to Washington.

According to his own account, Eccleston spent time in America in the late 18th century and was Washington's guest at Mount Vernon. However, no confirmation of this has been found by the authors.

Eccleston wrote to Thomas Jefferson in May 1807, enclosing a specimen of the medal, which is in the collection of the Thomas Jefferson Foundation and is on display at Monticello:

Actual Size: 76 mm

> Sir,
>
> I beg your acceptance of a Medallion of your Great Predecessor in the high station which you at present so worthily fill, which I have lately had struck off to his memory, and request the favours of your forwarding a couple to the honourable Bushrod Washington [Washington's nephew, a Supreme Court justice at the time], for himself, and Judge Marshall.
>
> Notwithstanding the Date on the Medallion, these are some of the first I have issued. I believe it is the largest medal, and in the highest relief that has been struck off in this country for some time.
>
> If it would not be occupying too much of your time, I should be glad just to be informed of the safe arrival of this small parcel and I am,
>
> Sir, Your assured friend, Daniel Belteshazzar Plantagenet Eccleston[43]

On December 21, 1816, the weekly *Lancaster Gazette* published a premature notice of Eccleston's death and described his life and accomplishments. The memorial noted his many eccentricities and his diverse projects and business ventures in Lancaster, including brokering insurance and selling liquor. Among his inventions was a cast-iron loom for weaving sailcloth, a device that was widely used and brought him much profit. He was also a member of the Religious Society of Friends (Quakers)—and a numismatist.

It is not often than someone can read his own obituary, but Eccleston seems to have done so—or perhaps the entire affair was a stunt. In the next issue of the *Gazette* he announced that he was alive and well, signing himself as Daniel Belteshazzar Fitz William Caractacus Cadwallador Llewellyn Ap-Tudor Plantagenet Eccleston.

A British tradesman's token bearing a portrait of Eccleston is a well-known member of the Conder series (see the introduction). Apparently Eccleston issued it himself. Today, his medal to Washington stands as an elegant specimen of art, and one of the most intricate in the Washington series.

ESTIMATED MARKET VALUES	COMMENTARY ON VALUE
COPPER STRIKINGS	*Commentary:* These are always well struck and are usually found in higher grades. These prices reflect typical rough planchets; pieces with smooth planchets are worth more.
P-60 to 62: .... $800 to $1,600	
P-50 to 58: .... $400 to $800	

No. 25

ENIGMATIC EARLY ISSUE
NEW YORKE IN AMERICA TOKEN

Rulau NY-621, Breen-245 to 247 • Brass: 20 known • Lead or pewter: 4 known • Copper: 1 reported

The brass and lead trade tokens struck on behalf of New York's second colonial governor, Francis Lovelace, never reached circulation in America due to the conquest of New York by Dutch forces July 30 to August 9, 1673. Lovelace, who had managed the colony for Britain since 1668, was charged with its loss, stripped of his property, and imprisoned in the Tower of London, where he died in 1675. Although the Dutch held New York for a mere 15 months, it was long enough to eliminate any need for Lovelace's tokens. According to research by John Kleeberg, the tokens were likely produced in England, and all surviving strikes were undoubtedly patterns. The circulation wear apparent on all examples is consistent with that seen on certain other British patterns of the period, since it was often the practice to place them in circulation after they had been reviewed, as such pieces readily traded along with official issues, tokens, and other coins of similar metal and diameter.

Actual Size: 22 mm

As a governor, Lovelace perhaps did not merit all of the shame and blame his countrymen heaped upon him. He was well aware of the threat posed by the Dutch, whose resentment had festered ever since the English wrested New Amsterdam from Peter Stuyvesant and renamed it New Yorke in 1664. From the start, Lovelace advised his executive council, "We cannot expect they love us," and issued strict orders to watch for breaches of the peace throughout the scattered Dutch, Swedish, English, and Finnish settlements that made up his colony. From his seat of government at Fort James on Manhattan's Battery, Lovelace administered a variety of activities, including judicial services, census taking, ship-building, and ferry services. He acquired the colony's first printing press and instituted the first merchants' exchange and horse-breeding program. He perceived the strategic importance of Staten Island, which overlooked the entrance to Upper New York Bay, and bought it from the Indians in 1670. At the time of the Dutch invasion, he had been visiting the governor of Connecticut to enlist his help in opening America's first post road.

His single error as a governor was catastrophic. Though he had put his administration on a state of high alert at King Charles II's declaration of war with Holland in 1672, he chose to ignore the intelligence that a squadron of Dutch naval vessels was on its way from the West Indies, and left the garrison at Fort James manned by only 80 soldiers. These men offered valiant resistance to the Dutch broadsides, until they ran out of powder and surrendered.

Fort Amsterdam was built by the Dutch in 1626. The English renamed it Fort James, and later Fort George. The 1907 U.S. Custom house now stands on the site at the foot of Broadway in lower Manhattan.

ESTIMATED MARKET VALUES		COMMENTARY ON VALUE
BRASS STRIKINGS		
EF-40 to AU-58:	$35,000 to $50,000	*Commentary:* Market offerings are infrequent, and years may pass between them. Pewter strikings are worth 30% to 40% more than the above estimates.
VF-20 to 35:	$20,000 to $35,000	
F-12:	$10,000 to $20,000	

No. 26
FIRST STRUCK MEDAL IN THIS SERIES
1801 THOMAS JEFFERSON INAUGURAL MEDAL

Julian PR-2 • Silver: 6 to 8 known (estimates vary) • White metal: 3 or 4 known

Throughout the 1790s, the Philadelphia newspaper *Aurora General Advertiser* stridently opposed the Federalist policies of presidents Washington and Adams. In 1800, it became the standard-bearer for the Democratic Republican candidacy of Thomas Jefferson. In the months leading up to the election, attacks on Adams and praise of Jefferson were the paper's daily fare, so it was only natural that the *Aurora* should support the sale of Jefferson's inaugural medals when he won the presidency. A notice appearing in the February 17, 1802, issue described them:

Actual Size: 45.8 mm

> A STRIKING LIKENESS OF THOMAS JEFFERSON, PRESIDENT OF THE UNITED STATES; ON a Medallion, executed by Mr. Reish [sic] the celebrated German Artist, to commemorate, at once, the Era of American Independence, and the auspicious day, which raised Mr. JEFFERSON to the dignity of President over a free people. On the reverse of this elegant medallion, are represented emblematical figures, in a style of workmanship never equalled before in this country, and excelled in none.
>
> It will depend on upon the encouragement Mr. Reish meets with, in this first exhibition of his talents in this country, whether he will reside in America, or return to Europe. Patriots . . . may be supplied with medallions in Silver or White Metal, at the Aurora Book-Store, and no where else in Philadelphia.

The famous obverse portrait is very similar to that on Reich's Indian peace medal (No. 3). On the reverse, wisdom goddess Athena lays the Declaration of Independence atop the Constitution, a reminder of Jefferson's contributions to these documents; the legend UNDER HIS WING IS PROTECTION conveys that the new president will defend the principles of both. His success is symbolized by an eagle carrying a laurel wreath of the type laid upon a victor's brow. Although Reich made the dies, the U.S. Mint performed the striking work, possibly with Mint director Elias Boudinot himself assuming the production cost. If this was so, it would account for the dies' being recorded as "lost" in Franklin Peale's 1841 register of Mint medal dies, because Boudinot resigned in the summer of 1805, and under this scenario he may have taken the dies away with him.

It is believed that the medals proved quite popular with the public, but no records survive as to precisely how many were struck. Copper strikings, though not advertised in the *Aurora*, were certainly made.

Monticello, Jefferson's home, as it appears today.

ESTIMATED MARKET VALUES

Striking in Silver, Unholed	Striking in Copper	Striking in White Metal
VF 20 to 30: . . . . $10,000 to 20,000	PF-40 to 58: . . . . $20,000 to $30,000	PF-40 to 58: . . . . $12,000 to $20,000
	VF to EF, holed: . . . . $5,000 to $8,000	VF to EF, holed: . . . . . . $6,000 to $10,000

No. 27
DESIGNED BY SAINT-GAUDENS, SCULPTED BY WEINMAN
1905 THEODORE ROOSEVELT INAUGURAL MEDAL
Baxter-78 • Gold: 3 cast • Bronze: 125 cast

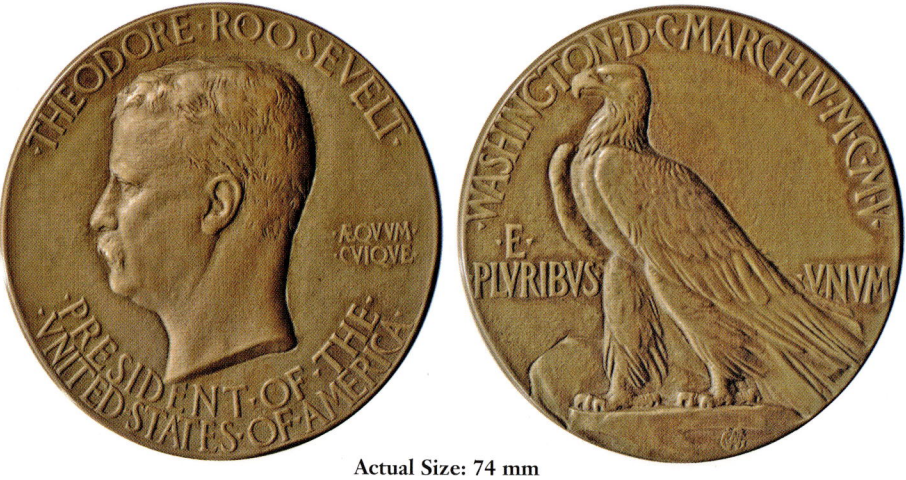

Actual Size: 74 mm

At the turn of the 20th century, sculptor Augustus Saint-Gaudens had many admirers who mattered in America: members of high society, politicians, literati, and the majority of his fellow artists, who acknowledged him as the nation's preeminent sculptor. The ultracynical Henry Adams felt he "counted as a force even in the mental inertia of sixty or eighty million people," and that "the one step essential to immortality" was to have Saint-Gaudens model one's head.[44] The president himself professed a strong attraction to the artist's work, corresponded with him, and met him socially. At Roosevelt's request, in 1904 the Inaugural Committee invited him to create a medal for the president's second term.

Busy though he was with other commitments, no project could be more important than a president's medal, so the sculptor agreed to design the piece if the committee would approve his former student, Adolph Weinman, to do the modeling work. He relished the idea that his portrait would replace the one by Mint engraver Charles E. Barber that had been previously accepted by the committee but rejected by Roosevelt. Eleven years earlier, it had been Barber's reverse that supplanted the Saint-Gaudens design on the official Columbian Exposition medal (see our No. 53), and Saint-Gaudens still harbored some resentment.

The superb result of the two artists' collaboration was a Saint-Gaudens product all the way: the master checked frequently on its progress and oversaw every step of its production. In homage to the Renaissance style of Pisanello, he specified that it would be cast, rather than struck, by Tiffany Studios in New York. On seeing the outcome, the president wrote him to say, "I like the medals immensely; but that goes without saying; for the work is eminently characteristic of you. . . . Thank Heaven we have at last some artistic work of permanent worth done for the government."[45]

Faced with the problem of how to fulfill its contract with Joseph Davison's Sons, the Inaugural Committee ordered 3,000 bronze medals of the Barber design, struck in 44 mm size, for customary distribution to members of the subsidiary inaugural committees.

Joseph K. Davison's Sons struck 3,000 official medals with Charles Barber's 1901 presidential portrait and a new reverse by George T. Morgan.

The 1907 $10 gold coin (actual size 27 mm) designed by Saint-Gaudens features the same type of eagle employed on his 1905 inaugural medal for Roosevelt.

Estimated Market Values	
MS-60 to 62:	$20,000–$30,000
AU-50 to 58:	$15,000 to $20,000

Commentary on Value

Commentary: Today this medal is perhaps the most desired of all 20th-century medals relating to an American president, mainly due to the fame of Saint-Gaudens. Only a few dozen of the 125 bronze examples have been traced on the numismatic market, and each attracts attention when it appears.

No. 28
Testing the Nation's Coinage
ASSAY COMMISSION MEDALS

Julian AC-1 onward • 10 to 30 known for most years 1860 to 1976; 1977 is common

The late 18th century saw the start of an annual custom, in which an Assay Commission (a group of government officials and presidentially invited citizens) met at the Philadelphia Mint to review the quality of the gold and silver coins struck in the year just concluded. During that year, numerous examples of the precious-metal issues had been extracted at random and set aside for the Assay Commission's review. From those examples, the commission members would select certain pieces for elemental analysis. The object was to verify that the coins were of full weight and metal value to conform with U.S. coinage laws. (In England, a related ceremony, called the trial of the pyx, had been conducted for a long time.)

The first Assay Commission met on March 20, 1797. Beginning with the 1860 gathering, special Assay Commission medals were struck for presentation to those attending. The first such medal was from dies by Chief Engraver James B. Longacre and featured the French Liberty Head design used in 1859 to strike pattern half dollars. Certain other medals also began to be minted at that time for private sale to the collectors' market; Mint officials kept no records of their production. Composed of silver, copper, or aluminum, these rarities occasionally combined the Assay Commission–medal dies with "rare" dies or dies from earlier years.

By the early 20th century, the making of these fancy pieces had essentially ended, and for any given year just one variety was made. By the 1920s it had become standard to make these medals in brass. On February 11, 1976, the last public meeting of the Assay Commission was held; the commission continued for four years after that, but only government officials were present. The last such meeting was on February 13, 1980. The next day, President Jimmy Carter abolished the commissions, on the grounds that gold coins had not been struck since 1933, and silver-content pieces since 1970.

Beginning in 1982, however, the Mint began to produce new *commemorative* coins with silver content, and in subsequent years, in gold as well; and in 1986 bullion coins began to be made in the same metals. Accordingly, it would seem that today the oversight of the Assay Commission would be a safeguard.

Actual Size: 34 mm

Today, with the exception of the 1977 medal struck in *pewter* and placed on open sale to collectors, all Assay Commission medals are rare, and some special pieces are exceedingly rare or even unique.

Assay Commission room at the new Philadelphia Mint in 1902.

Estimated Market Values	
Typical 19th-Century Issues in Copper	
PF-63 to 65 (choice to gem):	$400 to $600
PF-60 to 62:	$200 to $400
AU-50 to 58:	$150 to $200

Commentary on Value

Commentary: Although all are scarce, most often seen are 19th-century issues in copper. Those in silver or aluminum are rarer and more valuable, as are rare die varieties and combinations in all medals. Many 20th-century strikings are in brass, typically selling for the same rate of $150 to $600. Rare varieties can sell for much more, and the 1977 pewter issue is valued at about $25 to $35.

No. 29
TRIBUTE TO A BELOVED STATESMAN
1777 FRANKLIN AMERICAIN MEDAL

Fuld FR.ME.L.3 (terra-cotta), Betts-548 (bronze) • Silver: 2 known • Bronze: 15 to 20 known
• Terra-cotta (uniface original format): 100 to 200 known

Medal collectors usually seek objects struck in metal, but the piece our voters ranked 29th is a medallic masterpiece in terra-cotta. A particularly fine blend of the clay was discovered in 1772 along the Loire river, on the grounds of the Château de Chaumont. The château and its famous glassworks were owned by Jacques Donatien Le Ray de Chaumont, a French courtier, who immediately constructed a ceramics plant and invited Italian master engraver Giovanni Battista Nini to serve as its superintendent.

In his capacity as American commissioner to the court of Louis XVI, the 70-year-old Benjamin Franklin arrived in Paris in December 1776. He accepted de Chaumont's offer of the use of his vacant home in Passy, a Parisian suburb, and lived there for nine years. In this house Franklin conducted his work on behalf of the United States and wrote most of his autobiography, and on its roof he erected Europe's first lightning rods. Thomas Walpole, the son of an English banker, visited there to make sketches of the diplomat. In 1777, in honor of his guest, de Chaumont arranged to have five of these sketches sent to Nini to be made into medallions. In one of them, Franklin wore spectacles; in another, Rousseau's cap; in a third, a liberty cap; and in the fourth, no cap at all.[46] Nini created wax molds for uniface casts of all of these, but it was Walpole's fifth drawing, of Franklin in a fur cap, that he chose for the production version. Under the truncation of Franklin's shoulder, he included a tiny design of a shield with a lightning rod and lightning bolt beneath a crown, a reference to a statement heard throughout Europe at the height of Franklin's popularity: "He snatched lightning from the sky and the scepter from tyrants."

When sending a copy of the medallion to his daughter in Philadelphia, Franklin wrote, "A variety of others have been made since of different sizes; some to be set in the lids of snuffboxes, and some so small as to be worn in rings; and the numbers sold are incredible." Bronze versions were cast as well, and England's Josiah Wedgwood produced colorful versions in porcelain. Franklin's fur cap became so fashionable that women at the French court altered their hairstyles to resemble it. In the United States, fur-capped Franklin busts can be found on the Wright & Bale store cards of 1829, the Franklin Institute medals (No. 65), and several Civil War tokens.

Actual Size: 112.6 mm

Estimated Market Values	
Terra-Cotta Impression (Uniface)	
MS-60 to 62:	$2,000 to $3,000
EF-40 to AU-58:	$1,000 to $2,000

No. 30
"GOD PRESERVE" ISSUES
CAROLINA AND NEW ENGLAND ELEPHANT COPPERS

Rulau YG-10 and 11 (New England) and CG-1 and 2 (Carolina) • New England: 2 known • Carolina PROPRIETERS: 8 to 11 known
• Carolina PROPRIETORS: 25 to 40 known

For a long time, much more was known about the "what" of the Carolina and New England Elephant coppers than the "why." These pieces, a few of which may have been brought to the colonies in the pockets of English emigrants, shared their obverse design of a nicely engraved bull elephant with some British halfpenny tokens, which bore the reverse legend GOD PRESERVE LONDON. Reverse legends on the American-linked tokens read GOD PRESERVE CAROLINA AND THE LORDS PROPRIETERS 1694 and GOD PRESERVE NEW ENGLAND 1694. Some of the later Carolina examples from the same die have the correct PROPRIETORS, made by punching an O over the erroneous E.

R. Neil Fulghum, curator of the University of North Carolina's North Carolina Collection, has proposed a reason for their existence.[47] The token may have been issued by the eight-member ruling body of the Province of Carolina, the Lords Proprietors, in hopes of drumming up investments in their colony. The Lords Proprietors held regular meetings in London in 1694, and they may have issued the token to be spent at the Carolina Coffee-House located near the Royal Exchange, the seat of England's wealthiest investors. There were several other coffee-houses around London where one could get American news, discuss the colonies, and perhaps decide to invest in them: on Birchin Lane was the Pennsylvania Coffee-House, on St. Michael's Alley was the Virginia Coffee-House, and—most notably for our tokens—on Threadneedle Street, just behind the Royal Exchange, were both the New England Coffee-House and the London Coffee-House!

It has long been assumed that the elephant engraving was done at the Royal Mint. Fulghum found mention of an "old elephant die" in the mint's huge inventory of hardware for the year 1769, and this die remained in the inventory until 1910, which seems to confirm this theory. The meaning of the elephant on the tokens remains a mystery, other than it may have been an attraction as an exotic animal.

Actual Size: About 29 mm (varies)

The London Elephant token is the most familiar in this series, with multiple die varieties known, including the one pictured here. The same obverse motif was used on dies for the far rarer Carolina and New England tokens.

ESTIMATED MARKET VALUES	
CAROLINA PROPRIETORS (SECOND O OVER E)	
MS-60 to 62:	$30,000 to $50,000
EF-40 to AU-58:	$18,000 to $25,000
VF-20 to 35:	$10,000 to $18,000

COMMENTARY ON VALUE

Commentary: In 1860, Joseph Merriam made copy dies of the New England tokens for Alfred S. Robinson and struck three in silver and 15 each in copper, brass, and nickel.[48] In 1863, John Bolen struck 40 copies of the Carolina tokens in copper, two in silver, and five in brass, after which the dies were canceled.[49]

No. 31

AN EARLY AMERICAN CLASSIC
1787 COLUMBIA AND WASHINGTON MEDAL

Rulau Ore-4 • Silver: 6 known (3 in private hands) • Copper: 4 to 6 known • White metal: 2 or 3 known

Actual Size: 40.2 mm

By any account the Columbia and Washington medal is one of America's most historical and important. In 2005 Anne Bentley, curator of the Massachusetts Historical Society, stated that this medal was the most important item in their collections! This piece is shown above.[50]

Depicted on the obverse of this 40 mm medal are two ships, with the inscription, "COLUMBIA and WASHINGTON, commanded by J. KENDRICK." The *Columbia Rediviva*, usually called the *Columbia*, was a full-rigged ship, 83 feet long, which displaced 212 tons. Providing a consort for her was the *Lady Washington*, a sloop of 90 tons under Captain Robert Gray, usually cited simply as the *Washington*. Interestingly, the dropping of the *Lady* in popular usage has resulted in some demand for this medal by collectors of *George* Washington numismatica.[51]

The reverse bears this inscription: "Fitted at Boston, N. America, for the Pacific Ocean, by J. Barrell, C. Brown, C. Bulfinch, J. Darby, C. Hatch, J.M. Pintard, 1787." Charles Bulfinch was one of America's best-known architects. The dies are attributed to Joseph Callender, who also cut dies for 1787 and 1788 Massachusetts copper coins. There were two reverses made, with slight differences in the arrangement of the lettering and ornaments.

The ships were set to sail from Boston to explore the distant coast of the Pacific Northwest, in the area now known as Oregon and Washington. Medals were struck, some say by Paul Revere. A few silver impressions seem to have been for presentation or the ship's owners, and some white-metal pieces were made. Comprising most of the production were several hundred copper examples to be taken for distribution in the lands of destination, including to Native Americans. Also taken were newly minted 1787 Massachusetts half cents and cents.

The ships set sail on September 30 of that year, with Captain John Kendrick in charge of the expedition. They traveled together as far as Cape Horn at the tip of South America, where they separated, not to see each other again until they arrived at Nootka Sound on the Northwest Pacific coast.

Today the larger ship is remembered in the name of the Columbia River, first seen by Captain Gray. The voyage was the first in which the American flag was carried to this district of the Pacific Northwest. The *Columbia* returned to Boston on August 9, 1790, the first American vessel to have circumnavigated the globe.

The first reverse, as illustrated by this somewhat oxidized white-metal example in the Massachusetts Historical Society collection. Note the rosette at the top center border, in comparison to the spidery "star" on the second reverse.

ESTIMATED MARKET VALUES	
SILVER STRIKINGS	
MS-60 to 62:	$100,000 upward
EF-40 to AU-58:	$40,000 to $70,000
VF-20 to 35:	$25,000 to $40,000
COPPER AND WHITE-METAL STRIKINGS	
MS-60 to 62:	$20,000 to $25,000
EF-40 to AU-58:	$10,000 to $20,000
VF-20 to 35:	$5,000 to $10,000

COMMENTARY ON VALUE

Commentary: Values are highly conjectural due to the extreme rarity of these medals. A superb high-grade copper medal in the Massachusetts Historical Society, presented by one of the voyage's planners, is the key item in that museum and is priceless.

No. 32

Repealing the Stamp Act
1766 William Pitt Token

Betts-519 and 520, Rulau E NY-176 and 177 • 23 mm "farthing": 10 to 15 known • 28.5 mm "halfpenny": 300 to 500 known

At the Peace of Paris in 1763, Britain won new North American territory and new status as a world power, but at the same time gained the expense of administering an expanded empire. The war had nearly emptied the exchequer, and citizens at home vigorously resisted any additional taxation. Parliament saw a solution: increase the revenues coming from the colonies. Their Stamp Act of 1765 placed a tax on every piece of paper printed in the colonies, which included newspapers, legal documents, and even playing cards. Although the actual amounts levied were small, the colonists found the precedent ominous, and their resistance was fierce.

In Virginia, Patrick Henry denounced the Act in the House of Burgesses. In New York, two groups formed to make their displeasure known. The Sons of Liberty, composed of workingmen from the poorer classes, advocated a punishing boycott of all British imports. They tore down posted tax notices, organized street rallies—which often turned into brawls—and physically menaced the tax agents. (The Massachusetts branch held its famous "Tea Party" in Boston in 1774.) The second group, called the Friends of Liberty and Trade, was made up of prosperous merchants, landowners, and importers who opposed the tax but stood to lose much from a comprehensive boycott of English goods. They enlisted the aid of some potent allies: member of Parliament William Pitt and a number of British manufacturers and export merchants with whom they did business. In heated speeches before the House of Lords, Pitt openly supported the colonists' disobedience, and argued that taxing the colonies was a violation of English law that would harm English trade.

In May 1766, Parliament succumbed to the combined political and civil pressure and repealed the Stamp Act. The relieved Friends of Liberty and Trade issued our subject token in celebration. Numismatic tradition indicates that they commissioned gunsmith James Smither of Philadelphia to strike the copper tokens bearing the bust of their hero,[52] and credited their own organization on the reverse with the legend NO STAMPS: THANKS TO THE FRIENDS OF LIBERTY AND TRADE. In 1783, William Pitt became Prime Minister of England.

Actual Size: 32 mm

The 28.5 mm version is sometimes called the Pitt halfpenny, while the much rarer 23 mm size is called the farthing. In actuality, neither had any monetary value.

New Hampshire's Stamp Act Island, on Lake Wentworth, was named for the detested legislation that residents were determined never to forget. (1920s view by Tichnor Brothers)

Estimated Market Values

"Halfpenny" Size

MS-63 to 65 (choice to gem):	$9,000 to $15,000
MS-60 to 62:	$5,000 to $9,000
EF-40 to AU-58:	$3,000 to $5,000

No. 33

A MOST CURIOUS RARITY
1714 GLOUCESTER COURT HOUSE TOKEN

Crosby p. 323, Breen-237 • 2 known

Actual Size: 24 mm

A prime fascination of medals and tokens is that for many issues very little is known about their origin. Thus arises the opportunity for research and discovery, a stimulating aspect not generally available to, say, collectors of modern coins. The 1714 Gloucester token is one such piece—to paraphrase Churchill, a mystery wrapped in an enigma.

An early notice of this piece appeared in Edward Cogan's sale of the E.J. Farmer Collection on April 13–14, 1869, where most attention was paid to the stunning price ($100) paid for a choice 1796 half dollar. Attending the sale was E.L. Mason Jr., who commented on the Virginia token:

> There were other attractions in the sale [including] a *unique* "Virginia shilling," or as Brother Cogan terms this peculiar little brass piece "store card." Let it be what it may,—and our word for it, there is a young mint for the happy possessor of this piece, not far in the future,—it is of absorbing interest, and some close student of Virginia's romantic history may some day unravel the mystery which befogs the proper understanding of this *rara avis*. Who was this "Richard Dawson," whose name is inscribed upon the card or coin, or medal, etc. . . .

In *Early Coins of America*, 1875, S.S. Crosby noted:

> Of the history . . . of the Gloucester token, nothing is known. It appears to have been intended as a pattern for a shilling of a private coinage, by Richard Dawson of Gloucester (county?) Virginia. . . . But two specimens of this are known, both struck in brass.[53] A full description cannot be given of it, as both impressions are very imperfect, and together they do not supply the entire legends with certainty. . . .

> The house upon this token may have been designed to represent a warehouse, but is of a style corresponding more closely to that of some of the public buildings of olden times. Possibly it may have represented the court house of Gloucester County, and the legend, should any specimen fortunately be discovered to supply the missing portions, may prove to be GLOVCESTER CO HOUSE VIRGINIA. . . .

Today, the reverse inscription is thought to read RIGHAVLT DAWSON ANNO DOM 1714. The Righault and Dawson families owned land in Gloucester County. The XII denomination in combination with the use of brass (instead of silver) may indicate that this piece was intended not as a coin but as a check for tobacco, which was legal tender in the colony at the time.[54] Or it may have been a store card issued by a Righault-Dawson partnership. The depiction of a courthouse may refer to the nearest business and judicial center.

It is evident that, other than identifying the name Righault, we know little more today than Crosby did in 1875!

Estimated Market Values	Commentary on Value
Fine: $80,000 to $150,000 **Good:** $30,000 to $50,000	*Commentary:* The Garrett coin sold for $36,000 and the lesser-grade Roper coin for $20,900 more than two decades ago. Kenneth E. Bressett graded the first as Fine and the second as Good. Both have incomplete legends as struck. The estimated values given here are highly conjectural.

No. 34

POLITICAL AMERICANA
SATIRICAL HARD TIMES TOKENS

Low-17, 51, and 55, Rulau HT-31, 63, and 70 • Several hundred to several thousand of each

During the contentious elections of the 1830s, many political-campaign tokens took aim at candidates and causes. Three of these satirical pieces have been elevated to the top 100 by our voters. The "I Take the Responsibility" token of 1833 (HT-70) made the list as the probable earliest issue in a cascade of cent-sized satirical tokens. The "Illustrious Predecessor" token of 1837 (HT-31), as well as the curious "Loco Foco / Benton Mint Drop Experiment," a Whig token of 1838 (HT-63), poked fun at the opposition. Many circulated in place of U.S. cents during and after the Panic of 1837, when the suspension of specie payments by American banks precipitated a nationwide economic depression that continued through 1843. The hoarding of U.S. coins, coupled with a high profit margin for token producers, increased the issuance of both political and merchant-advertising pieces.

Actual Size: About 29 mm (varies)

The HT-70 token was a Whig issue portraying incumbent Andrew Jackson as a greedy tyrant, a thief coming out of a bank safe with a moneybag and a sword in his hands, turning his slogan "I take the responsibility" into a sneer at his motives. Its reverse, depicting a jackass, equated Jackson's espoused "Roman firmness" with mulish stubbornness, and implied that his love of "veto" made him an enemy of the constitution "as I understand it." More tokens of this design were issued in 1837.

When Jackson's hand-picked protégé, Martin Van Buren, won the election of 1836, Whigs showed their displeasure with tokens that mocked Van Buren's inaugural statement. Van Buren had sworn to follow the course of his "illustrious predecessor," so the tokens depicted a running jackass. The "executive experiment" symbolized by a tortoise on the obverse carrying a safe seems to refer to the slow movement of federal funds to Jackson's so-called pet banks. Alternatively, it could refer to Van Buren's Independent Treasury Bill, which—though ultimately successful—was all too slow in bringing recovery from the bank failures of 1837.

Several versions of a "Mint Drop" token were produced to jab at Thomas Hart Benton and the Democrats, who believed a system of gold and silver specie–backed banking was the way to national economic stability. Benton composed legislation to lower the fineness of the $5 gold piece, and the BENTON MINT DROP EXPERIMENT legend on these tokens derided the devaluation. LOCO FOCO (on the headband of a very ugly Miss Liberty) was a New York newspaper's nickname for the Democratic Party.

The "Executive Experiment" and "LocoFoco" varieties of the Hard Times tokens.

ESTIMATED MARKET VALUES

COMMON VARIETY WITH JACKSON AND MULE, COPPER

MS-63 to 65 (choice to gem):	$300 to $50 +
MS-60 to 62:	$150 to $300
EF-40 to AU-58:	$30 to $150
VF-20 to 35:	$20 to $30

No. 35

FIERCE NAVAL BATTLE DEPICTED
1779 JOHN PAUL JONES MEDAL

Julian NA-1, Loubat-17, Betts-568 • 5 to 7 silver originals known

As a young lieutenant of the American navy in December 1775, John Paul Jones was the first sailor to hoist the Grand Union flag on a Continental warship. After receiving his captain's commission in 1776, he took part in several successful engagements off the American coast and in 1777 took command of the *Ranger*, a brand-new sloop of war built in Portsmouth, New Hampshire. Carrying the news of Burgoyne's surrender in 1779 (see No. 56), he sailed for Europe and commenced a series of raids on British shipping. Congress voted Jones our No. 35 medal to recognize his remarkable September 1779 victory off the Yorkshire coast. Sailing the *Bonhomme Richard*, lent him by the French king, he engaged and bested the British *Serapis* despite his vessel's inferior maneuverability and cannon power. Every schoolchild knows that most of the battle went against Jones, but when the British commander invited him to surrender he replied, "I have not yet begun to fight," galvanizing his men and reversing the course of the conflict. The badly damaged *Bonhomme Richard* sank, not beneath Jones as he claimed victory (as told in some schoolbooks), but a month later. Louis XVI presented Jones a sword and the command of *Serapis*, and the U.S. Congress awarded him a gold medal.

The medal authorized in 1787 was the only such honor accorded to a naval officer of the Revolutionary War. Engraver Augustin Dupré executed the dies in 1789. To meet demand, the Paris Mint made silver and bronze restrikes starting in the 1790s, and in 1861 the mint shipped 20 bronze restrikes to U.S. Mint director James Pollock for sale to American collectors. Pollock hubbed gunmetal copy dies from one of them, and restruck more pieces in copper as needed. The latter specimens lack Dupré's signature on the reverse exergue.

After the war, Commodore Jones went to Russia to command a Black Sea squadron for Catherine the Great. In 1790, he moved to Paris, where he died in 1792 at the age of 45. In 1905 General Horace Porter discovered the location of his Paris burial, and in 1906, with great ceremony, he brought Jones's remains home. Jones now rests in a massive sarcophagus of veined marble set on the backs of four bronze dolphins, in a crypt beneath the chapel of the U.S. Naval Academy.[55] Here, Jones's own gold medal is on display.

Actual Size: 55.7 mm

John Paul Jones in a circa-1890 portrait by George Bagby Matthews after Charles Willson Peale.

ESTIMATED MARKET VALUES

ORIGINAL SILVER STRIKING
PF-60 to 62: .... $20,000 to $30,000
PF-50 to 58: .... $15,000 to $20,000

ORIGINAL BRONZE STRIKING
PF-60 to 62: .... $5,000 to $10,000
PF-50 to 58: .... $2,500 to $5,000

19TH-CENTURY U.S. MINT COPPER RESTRIKE
PF-63 to 65 (choice to gem): .... $300 to $500
PF-60 to 62: .... $200 to $300
PF-50 to 58: .... $125 to $200

COMMENTARY ON VALUE

Commentary: Nineteenth-century copper U.S. Mint restrikes made from the copy dies lack Dupré's signature. When buying any Jones medal, you should consult a recognized professional expert. Modern Mint restrikes have relatively little value.

No. 36

EARLY NEW YORK CITY STORE CARDS
1794 AND 1795 TALBOT, ALLUM & LEE TOKENS

Breen-1028 to 1039 • Several thousand known of each

At 241 Water Street in lower New York City, the firm of Talbot, Allum & Lee engaged in the East India trade, importing goods by ship. Formed in 1794, the partnership operated only until 1796. Principals of the firm included William Talbot, William Allum, and James Lee. This district of the city was a beehive of activity, with vessels continually arriving and departing. Numerous ships' chandlers, grog houses, cheap lodging places, and other establishments for the convenience of sailors did a lively business.

Although the Talbot, Allum & Lee firm earned just fleeting mention in newspapers and directories of the era, in numismatic circles its tokens have been favorites with collectors for many years. Indeed, in autumn 1858 they were discussed at length in the first American book written on the subject, Charles I. Bushnell's *An Arrangement of Tradesmen's Cards, Political Tokens, also, Election Medals, Medalets, Etc. Current in the United States of America for the Last Sixty Years, Described from the Originals, Chiefly in the Collection of the Author, With Engravings.*

Copper tokens dated 1794 and 1795, bearing the image of the standing goddess of Commerce on the obverse and a fully rigged sailing ship on the reverse, were struck to order for Peter Kempson & Co., Birmingham, England. The quantity has been estimated at more than 200,000 pieces, but no original records have ever been located.

The first tokens, dated 1794, were put into circulation, where they served at the value of 1¢ in local and regional commerce. Today, nearly all such pieces in collections show signs of wear. Pieces dated 1795 seem to have been less popular, with few reaching circulation. Fortunately, enough Mint State tokens were saved as souvenirs or otherwise that they are seen with some frequency today.

Undistributed tokens piled up at the waterfront store. What should be done with the hoard? The Philadelphia Mint was in need of copper to make half cents and cents, so on April 23, 1795, the firm sold 1,076 pounds of the tokens to the Philadelphia Mint for 18¢ per pound, or $193.68. On December 10, 1796, the remainder of the token stock, amounting to 1,914 pounds of copper, was purchased by the Mint from William Talbot for 16.6¢ per pound, or $319. These tokens weighed in at about 46 to 50 per pound, putting the quantity acquired in the Mint's two purchases at around 140,000 to 150,000 pieces.

Actual Size: 29 mm

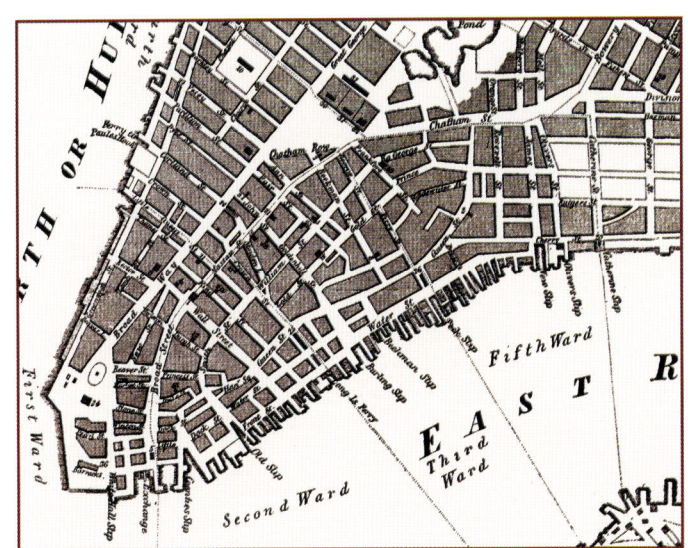

Detail of a 1789 map of the lower part of New York City, showing Water Street running along the East River. This district was the most active in American maritime trade at the time.

ESTIMATED MARKET VALUES	COMMENTARY ON VALUE
Standard 1795 Issue With Standing Figure and Ship	*Commentary:* The 1795 issue priced here is readily available in AU and Uncirculated grades. Pieces dated 1794 are much scarcer, especially in Uncirculated grade, and are worth more.
MS-63 to 65 (choice to gem): $1,200 to $2,500	
MS-60 to 62: $700 to $1,200	
EF-40 to AU-58: $350 to $700	
VF-20 to 35: $200 to $350	

No. 37
IDEAL FOR THE COLLECTION PLATE
1790 ALBANY CHURCH PENNY

Breen-1169 and 1170 • 8 to 12 known

Actual Size: 29.3 mm

Just as they do today, in the 18th century churches depended upon the contributions of members to remain in operation. The problem for the treasurers of the First Presbyterian Church of Albany, New York, was the scarcity of small change in the area. Many parishioners had either no change at all or only worn-out coppers and counterfeit cents to drop into the Sunday offering plate. On January 4, 1790, the church elders hit on a novel solution:

> Resolved: That one thousand coppers be stamped Church Penny, and placed with the treasurer to exchange with members of the congregation, at the rate of twelve for one shilling, in order to add respect to the weekly collections.[56]

Two different variations were produced. The first has CHURCH in block letters with PENNY in script. The second variety bears the script letter D above CHURCH, perhaps because "d" (from *denarium*) is the abbreviation for *penny* in the English monetary system. Today, these pieces are exceedingly rare: fewer than a dozen exist of each variety. (The neighboring congregation at Troy issued paper scrip for the same purpose in 1792.)[57]

The First Presbyterian Church was organized in 1763 and erected its initial building in 1764. For more than 50 years it was the only place for Presbyterians to worship in the city. Alexander Hamilton was a member in 1782 while he read law at Albany. When Hamilton was killed by a bullet from the dueling pistol of political rival Aaron Burr in 1804, pastor Eliphalet Nott penned his eulogy, "On the Death of Hamilton." In this most celebrated sermon ever to come from the First Presbyterian pulpit, Nott condemned the practice of dueling:

> I am called to attack, from this place, a crime, the very idea of which almost freezes one with horror—a crime, too, which exists among the polite and polished orders of society, and which is accompanied with every aggravation; committed with cool deliberation, and openly in the face of day!

This popular oration was published and circulated nationwide.

The church pennies of Albany were likely superseded by federal issues as soon as the Philadelphia Mint began coining the real thing in 1793. By the end of the century, church councils across the country were striving to discourage the traditional practice of giving only a penny as offering. In the words of one writer, "such an offering is an insult to God and to His church, and the sooner people see the matter in this hard, true light, the better."[58]

Eliphalet Nott was named pastor of the First Presbyterian Church of Albany in 1798. A powerful orator, as well as a mathematician and inventor, he later became president of Union College in Schenectady.

ESTIMATED MARKET VALUES	COMMENTARY ON VALUE
EITHER OF THE TWO TYPES	
EF-40 to AU-58: .... $17,500 to $25,000	*Commentary:* Grading is determined by the sharpness of the counterstamp.
VF-20 to 35: .... $12,500 to $17,500	

No. 38

"OPUS FRASER"
1925 NORSE-AMERICAN OCTAGONAL MEDAL

Rulau V-30 • Gold, 31 mm: several known • Silver, 31 mm: thin planchet, 200 to 400 known; thick planchet, 3,000 to 5,000 known

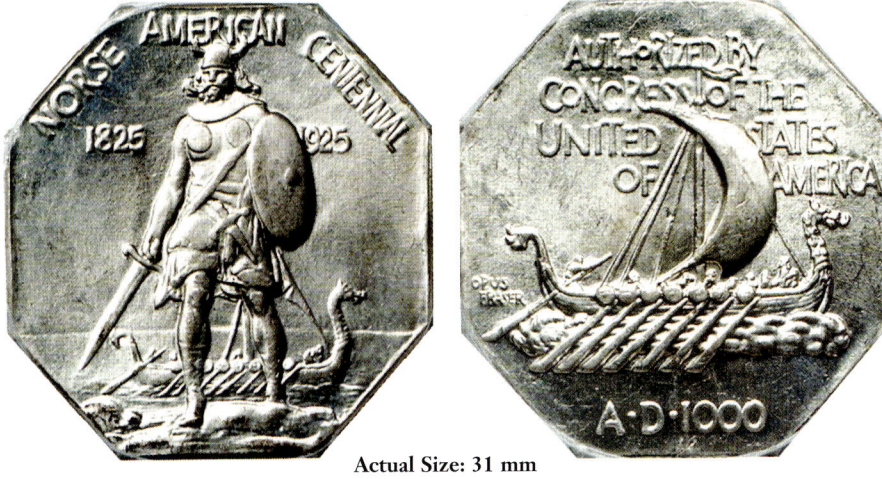

Actual Size: 31 mm

It is no surprise that a medal by sculptor James Earle Fraser (1876–1953) achieved a place in our top 100. Famed designer of the 1913 Buffalo / Indian Head nickel and the first recipient of the Saltus Medal Award (see No. 97), Fraser was a Beaux Arts master at the pinnacle of his medallic career when he created the Norse-American Centennial medal in 1925. His use of sans-serif lettering and bold, simply modeled forms gave a modern look to the piece, appropriate to the sensibilities of the Roaring Twenties, when world war was considered a thing of the past, and the future was as filled with possibility as a ship touching a newfound shore.

During World War I, President Woodrow Wilson had suggested that all "hyphenated" Americans (German-Americans, Italian-Americans, Norwegian-Americans, etc.) demonstrate their loyalty by speaking only English and abandoning their "foreign" traditions. At the same time, at the height of wartime nationalistic hysteria, many native-born Americans displayed hostility toward all immigrants. In the large Norwegian-American community of the upper Midwest, a divide arose between those who wanted to retain Norse language and customs, and those who wished to become fully Americanized. With the upcoming centennial of the first arrival of Norwegians on the ship *Restauration* in 1825, Minnesota legislators saw a grand opportunity to step beyond these differences and, at the same time, to improve the Norwegian public image: they would host a four-day national exposition of Norwegian culture and showcase the many contributions the Norse had made to American life. A massive publicity campaign drew contributions of memorabilia, costumes, tools, furniture, crafts, fine art, and inventions for display at the Minnesota State Fairgrounds in Minneapolis. The festival featured Norse cooking, Viking parades, performances of Norse music and drama, and a 1,000-actor historical pageant. Almost 80,000 visitors attended the closing ceremonies, in which President Coolidge acknowledged that Leif Ericsson had been the first European to land on America's shores.

Fraser's official medal was but one of many beautiful medals struck to commemorate ethnic arrivals in America. The Norse medal stands out, perhaps because Wayte Raymond placed an octagonal socket for it in one of his cardboard U.S. coin holders, making acquiring the piece a goal for an entire generation of collectors. Shown is the 31 mm silver medal, the style widely sold in thick-planchet and thin-planchet (scarcer) versions. A few were struck in gold. Related 69 mm (nickel) and 76 mm (silver-plated bronze) medals were also made.

The 1925 Norse-American commemorative postage stamps, in 2¢ and 5¢ values. These were voted No. 65 among the *100 Greatest American Stamps* (Whitman, 2007).

ESTIMATED MARKET VALUES

Silver, Thick Planchet		Silver, Thin Planchet	
MS-63 to 65 (choice to gem):	$225 to $350	MS-63 to 65 (choice to gem):	$350 to $450
MS-60 to 62:	$175 to $225	MS-60 to 62:	$250 to $350
EF-40 to AU-58:	$125 to $175	EF-40 to AU-58:	$150 to $200

No. 39

USA MONOGRAM
CIRCA 1785 BAR COPPER

Breen-1145 • 60 to 100 originals known

In the 16-year period between the colonies' declaration of independence in 1776 and the opening of the U.S. Mint in 1793, the numbers of foreign coins circulating as small change were never quite sufficient for the purposes of day-to-day business. The now-forgotten New York City merchant who commissioned the cent-sized "Bar copper" tokens for use in his postwar trade must have wanted to make it clear that he was no loyalist. The *New Jersey Gazette* of November 12, 1785, gave the rationale for their patriotic design:

Actual Size: 29.6 mm

> A new and curious kind of coppers have lately made their appearance in New York. The novelty and bright gloss of which keeps them in circulation. These coppers are in fact similar to Continental buttons without eyes; on the one side are thirteen stripes and on the other U.S.A., as was usual on the soldiers' buttons.[59]

The buttons described were one of many types of Continental Army uniform buttons, and usually were cast in pewter, although examples have been noted of wood covered with a shell of pressed brass or tin. The highest-quality pewter examples—intended for the jackets and vests of officers—were likely manufactured in France,[60] even though many colonial-period households possessed molds for making their own buttons.[61]

Nineteenth-century numismatist and collector Charles Ira Bushnell attributed the engraving work on the 1785 Bar copper to George Wyon III of Birmingham, but researchers in 2004 attributed it to Thomas Wyon.[62] In any case, the quality of the Bar coppers was too high for attribution to any American manufacturer of the era.

Any numismatic rarity with a link to colonial or federal-period America is subject to copying, and during the spike in collecting interest of the early 1860s, some of the country's most respected diesinkers engaged in the practice. (See also Nos. 7 and 30.) In 1862, John A. Bolen made a fresh pair of Bar copper dies, from which he struck 65 look-alikes in copper, identical except that in the Bolen copy the "S" of USA is over the left side of the "A." Bolen also struck 10 in silver. Using Bolen's dies in the 1870s, George H. Lovett produced another short run in nickel, brass, and tin. These copies are highly collectible in their own right.

John A. Bolen's copy of the Bar copper. In the monogram the S is *over* the left side of the A.

Estimated Market Values	
MS-60 to 62:	$10,000 to $15,000
EF-40 to AU-58:	$7,000 to $10,000
VF-20 to 35:	$4,500 to $7,000

Commentary on Value

Commentary: Beware of Bolen copies in copper that are offered as originals. These copies have the S in the monogram passing over the A instead of under, as on the original; copies also lack a tiny spine of metal that connects the two middle bars on the center of the reverse on the original.

No. 40
PLANTERS BANK OF NOUVELLE ORLEANS
1812–1815 P.B. COUNTERSTAMP ON CUT COIN SEGMENT

Rulau HT-124 to 126 • 75 to 100 known

Numismatists have been tantalized for the better part of a century by curious pieces counterstamped "PB NOUVELLE ORLEANS." These pie-shaped pieces are cut quarters from round Spanish-American silver 8-real or dollar coins. Howland Wood described such a piece in the July 1902 *American Journal of Numismatics*, but ventured no suggestions as to its origin.

It seems that when coins of 2 reales were scarce, the Planters Bank of New Orleans cut dollars into wedges worth 25¢, then stamped them with its mark to assure the public that they were worth fully as much as a coin. To judge by the multiple die varieties and the quantity of pieces that exist today (perhaps as many as 100), in that busy river port these pie-shaped little counterstamps must have been a very familiar sight in their time.

Then a new generation of researchers, led by R.W. Julian, Robert D. Leonard, and Gregory Brunk, took up where Wood had left off.[63] Today, it is virtually certain that PB stands for the Planters Bank and that the pieces were issued for a few years beginning about 1812, when the city was generally referred to as Nouvelle Orleans. Julian learned that silver quarter dollars were struck at the Philadelphia Mint in 1815, when Bailly Blanchard, cashier of the Planters Bank, shipped more than 14 thousand dollars' worth of cast, struck, and cut Spanish-American dollars with the specific request that quarter dollars be minted from the metal.[64]

According to Karl Moulton, the next-smallest Spanish coin denomination, 1 real, was known as a "bit" and had a value of 12-1/2 cents. It was Blanchard's large order for "two-bit" pieces that effectively entrenched the U.S. quarter dollar in circulation.

Regarding Blanchard in later times, *Niles' Weekly Register*, November 20, 1819, included this item:

Actual Size: 27–29 mm (varies)

> Planters Bank at New Orleans. The cashier of this bank, Mr. B. Blanchard, who seems to have been a very amiable man, having strangely disappeared and now believed to have been assassinated, a report spread that he had absconded with a large sum of money. The affairs of the institution were immediately investigated and all found to be right; but there was a press for the payment of specie, and as fast as the tellers could count out the dollars everybody was satisfied.

The further news was not good: a week later the same periodical reported that Blanchard's body had been found, and that an inquest held that he "fell under the blows of some assassins, and was afterwards thrown into the river."

His legacy is these curious PB pieces, the Planters Bank version of a twenty-five-cent piece—by far the most popular silver denomination circulating in America at a time when regular coins were scarce.

Moulton states that the earliest auction appearance of the P.B. counterstamp on 8-real segments was at the Lorin Parmelee sale by New York Coin & Stamp Co. in June of 1890. Only two lots appeared at this offering, with one identified as "bad" (i.e., counterfeit), but Parmelee owned a total of five pieces in all. A set of the five photographic plates made for the sale was sold, in turn, at the Armand Champa II sale of 1995.

ESTIMATED MARKET VALUES

EF-40 to AU-58:	$4,000 to $7,500
VF-20 to 35:	$2,500 to $5,000

No. 41

FOUNDATION OF ANY HARD TIMES COLLECTION
1832 ANDREW JACKSON PRESIDENTIAL CAMPAIGN MEDALET
Rulau HT-1 to 3, DeWitt-AJACK 1832-1 • Several dozen known of all varieties combined

Actual Size: 28 mm

It was during the nation's 10th presidential election in 1824, which pitted Andrew Jackson against John Quincy Adams, that diesinkers first began striking medalets to publicize the virtues and goals of a candidate. Three varieties of brass medalets sported busts of Jackson, dubbing him the "Hero of New Orleans" and linking him to "the nation's pride" and "the nation's good" (all inscribed on the medalets). His supporters wore these suspended from pins at their lapels, and although Jackson lost the election, a precedent had been set and a series launched.

The 27 mm copper and brass medalets issued for Jackson's third run at the presidency, in 1832, are the items our voters placed at No. 41. They rank high with campaign-series and Jacksoniana collectors; and for Hard Times token collectors, they have been No. 1 ever since Lyman Low first cataloged them as such in 1899. All cent-sized (27 and 28 mm) supportive and satirical campaign medalets of the 1830s belong to the Hard Times series, because they circulated as money during the specie shortage of 1837 through 1844. (See No. 34 for a discussion of the satirical pieces.)

In 1832, incumbent Andrew Jackson's opponent was Henry Clay, a Whig advocate of the so-called American system and of the lending practices of the Second Bank of the United States. Since 1816, this bank had issued extensive credit to land buyers, and sometimes printed paper currency to finance its loans. Jackson's supporters, the Democrats, advocated hard-money banking and opposed the credit system. One of these was New York City Indian contractor Daniel Jackson,[65] of the firm Suydham & Jackson, issuer of our token. He placed his president's famous unequivocal statement, "The bank must perish," around its rim.

The second slogan on the token is a reference to a critical issue of Jackson's first term: the controversial Tariff of 1828. Jackson had alienated many Southerners with its passage, because it imposed on imported raw materials duties that were favorable to the industrial North but damaging to the agricultural South. The state of South Carolina voted to nullify the tariff's provisions within its borders. With his saying "The Union must and shall be preserved"—repeated on the token—Jackson took a strong stand against any state's right to nullify a federal law or secede from the Union.

The Second Bank of the United States. (Bartlett's *American Views*)

One of the most famous and desired of all Hard Times tokens is HT-1, alongside two of its obverse variations, HT-2, the "scowling head," and HT-3, the "aged head," depicting Andrew Jackson. Inscriptions on the reverse related to a statement he had made in 1830 and to his declared stance against the renewal of the charter of the Second Bank of the United States.

ESTIMATED MARKET VALUES	
HT-1, THE MOST AVAILABLE VARIETY	
EF-40 to AU-58:	$7,500 to $10,000
VF-20 to 35:	$3,500 to $7,500
F-12:	$2,000 to $3,500

No. 42

CONTINENTAL DOLLAR-STYLE REVERSE
1783 FELICITAS BRITANNIA ET AMERICA MEDAL

Betts-614 • 12 to 20 known

The major hostilities of the American Revolution ended in autumn 1781 with the surrender of British general George Cornwallis after the Battle of Yorktown, Virginia. Scattered skirmishes and battles continued into 1783, however. In February of that year, King George III issued his Proclamation of Cessation of Hostilities, which led to the signing of the Paris Peace Treaty on September 3, 1783—the event commemorated on this medal.

The medal, rare today, is one of the most interesting items listed in C. Wyllys Betts's *American Colonial History Illustrated by Contemporary Medals* (1894). It also brings down the curtain on Betts's extensive listing of colonial pieces, as the treaty marked the official end of the colonial period (although Americans considered it terminated with the signing of the Declaration of Independence on July 4, 1776!).

The reverse of this medal immediately attracts attention and has projected it into the forefront of pieces desired by American collectors. It is a close copy of the famous Continental dollar, with names of various states arranged around the border, with AMERICAN CONGRESS and WE ARE ONE within. Perhaps as a tribute to the Continental dollar, it is even struck in pewter, the same metal.

The obverse is allegorical, expressing, per the legend, the anticipation of felicity or friendship between Britain and America: a standing Indian queen represents our side of the Atlantic, and Britannia is seated to the right with her shield. A dove holding an olive branch is perched above, the symbol of peace. In the background is a city view of London, with St. Paul's Cathedral to the left. The date in Roman numerals below is September 4, 1783, the date that the news of the September 3 signing of the treaty in Paris reached London.

When the Betts publication was issued, the editors noted:

> Of this medal only two impressions are at present known, and it seems to be a mule—the reverse of the well known "Continental currency: combined with the obverse described. The execution, like the Latin of the legend, is poor. The engraving

Actual Size: 39.6 mm

is not quite correct. Dr. Clay's impression was sold in New York in December 1891 for $31. . . .

The Betts book and the acceleration of interest during the century since its publication have brought additional specimens to light, and today more than a dozen are known. A particularly nice example, described as About Uncirculated and the second-finest known, was offered in Part I of the Ford Collection sale, October 2003, cataloged by Michael Hodder, and offered in a section of Continental dollars.

1776 Continental Currency dollar in pewter. The reverse of the 1783 Felicitas Britannia et America medal was inspired by this. Shown actual size, 39.6 mm.

ESTIMATED MARKET VALUES	
EF-40 to AU-58:	$25,000 to $50,000
VF-20 to 35:	$15,000 to $25,000
VG-8 to F-15:	$10,000 to $15,000

No. 43

MEDALS OF AMERICA'S "FORGOTTEN CONFLICT"
WAR OF 1812 CONGRESSIONAL MEDALS

Julian MI-11 to 21, NA-4 to 17, and NA-22 to 23 • Originals: 6 to 8 known in gold (1 struck for each awardee), 35 to 50 in silver, 20 to 30 in white metal • 19th-century restrikes and copies in copper: 50 to 100 of each type

Few realize that 27 congressional medals were awarded for the War of 1812. America's "second war of independence" marked a growing national identity and sense of economic and military power. Despite misadventures that included an abortive invasion of Canada, American military victories gained concessions and a measure of respect from Britain.

While today's Medal of Honor is awarded for individual valor, early congressional medals recognized those in command and bore their portraits. The reverses featured battle or allegorical scenes. A single medal was struck in gold for the honoree; for naval battles, copies were struck in silver for subordinate officers. In some cases navy enlisted men may have received versions in copper, but there is scant evidence for this.

For history lovers, War of 1812 congressional medals preserve a dazzling array of portraits, battle scenes, and symbolism. Medal recipients include Isaac Hull, commander of the USS *Constitution* at the time when she earned the nickname "Old Ironsides." Here too are future presidents Andrew Jackson and William Henry Harrison, as well as naval heroes Stephen Decatur and Oliver Hazard Perry. Representative of lesser-known recipients is George Croghan. While in command of Fort Stephenson in Ohio, 21-year-old Croghan and his men repelled repeated attacks by numerically superior British forces.

The medals were struck at the Philadelphia Mint, which experienced difficulties in producing them because of their large size. Assistant Mint engraver John Reich managed to cut usable dies for only one—Isaac Hull's—before his eyesight failed. Dies for the remaining 26 were created by immigrant engraver Moritz Fürst.

In the mid-19th century the Mint began to restrike War of 1812 medals in copper for collectors, using both original and copy dies. These bronzed copper medals are popular with collectors today, but an expert eye is sometimes needed to distinguish original

Actual Size: 65 mm

from copy dies. Rare gold and silver originals are usually identified by a collarmark (a ridge on the edge from a segmented collar). Nearly all surviving original gold medals and many original silver ones are in institutional collections.

Some army commanders received white-metal copies of their gold medals to present as keepsakes. Shown is a white-metal version of Brigadier General James Miller's medal.

ESTIMATED MARKET VALUES

ORIGINALS IN GOLD
PF-63 to 65 (choice to gem): Lieutenant Robert Henley's gold medal sold in October 2004 for $103,500 in Part V of Stack's Ford Collection sales (lot 170).

ORIGINALS IN SILVER
PF-63 to 65 (choice to gem):	$35,000 to $45,000
PF-60 to 62:	$30,000 to $35,000
PF-50 to 58:	$25,000 to $30,000

ORIGINALS IN WHITE METAL
PF-63 to 65 (choice to gem):	$4,000 to $5,000
PF-60 to 62:	$2,500 to $4,000
PF-50 to 58:	$1,500 to $2,500

COPPER RESTRIKES, 19TH CENTURY
PF-63 to 65 (choice to gem):	$600 to $1,200
PF-60 to 62:	$400 to $600
PF-50 to 58:	$200 to $400

COMMENTARY ON VALUE

Commentary: Nineteenth-century copper specimens were struck with bronzing powder and are of chocolate color, with mirror Proof fields. Those from copy dies may sell for somewhat less. Modern bronze copies with sandblast finish sell for nominal amounts.

No. 44
BY CHRISTIAN GOBRECHT
1836 FIRST STEAM-COINAGE MEDAL

Julian MT-20 and 21 • Feb. 22 die, copper: 5 to 10 known • Overdated die, copper: 50 to 100 known
• New dies (1862 and later), various metals: common

Actual Size: 27mm

When the Philadelphia Mint opened in 1792, coins were struck by means of a screw-type press with weighted arms at the top. One or two men would tug on the weights at the end, and the screw would force the upper die down upon a planchet resting on the bottom die. The process was slow, and the finished coins often differed in the sharpness of details. In the meantime, by 1789, Matthew Boulton of the Soho Manufactory in Birmingham, England, had devised a steam-powered press that could be attended by a lone boy and that produced coins of uniform diameter (using a collar, which could be lettered or ornamented) at high speed. In 1792, in a visit to Philadelphia, Jacob Perkins suggested that steam be used for coinage.

Ignoring such opportunities, the Philadelphia Mint continued the use of hand-operated presses for another 40 years and more. In 1833 the Mint moved into a vastly enlarged and improved building, but continued to use the older coining technology. In the early 1830s, Franklin Peale, a son of museum owner Charles Willson Peale (see No. 55), went to Europe and visited several mints, making sketches and obtaining models of machines used in coinage, including a steam-driven, knuckle-action press made by Thonnelier in Paris.

In 1835, Mint director Robert Maskell Patterson commissioned Merrick, Agnew & Taylor, local makers of heavy equipment, to construct a Thonnelier-type press for the Mint. This was done, and a special ceremony for its inauguration was set for Washington's birthday, February 22, 1836. Christian Gobrecht, hired as second engraver in September 1835, cut the dies for a commemorative medal with a liberty cap and rays on the obverse and an appropriate inscription on the reverse, including the date as Feb. 22.

Problems arose, and the press was not ready. Finally, on March 23 the ceremony was held. Medals were struck, now with the date of Mar. 23 punched over the earlier inscription on one of the dies. Soon, copper cents were made on the press, and on November 10, silver coins were made.

Today, copper impressions of the medal with the Feb. 22 date (Julian MT-20) are very elusive, but this is often overlooked in descriptions, and the market price is not consistent with its true rarity. Medals with the overdated inscription were widely distributed and, while elusive, are collectible today. In 1862 Anthony C. Paquet made a new die pair. Impressions from these dies were made in quantity.

The first steam-coining press of 1836, a knuckle-action press patterned after that made by Thonnelier in Paris.

Estimated Market Values	
Copper, Feb. 22 Date	
PF-63 to 65 (choice to gem):	$1,000 to $1,300
PF-60 to 62:	$600 to $1,000
PF-50 to 58:	$300 to $500
Copper, Mar. 23 Over Feb. 22 Date	
PF-63 to 65 (choice to gem):	$300 to $450
PF-60 to 62:	$225 to $300
PF-50 to 58:	$135 to $175

Commentary on Value

Commentary: Those with the Feb. 22 date (not overdated) are much rarer and are more valuable, although their rarity is not widely appreciated. Those with the Mar. 23 date, with traces of the earlier date, sell for less. Modern restrikes from copy dies have only nominal value.

No. 45
Masonic Issue
1797 WASHINGTON MEDAL BY GETZ

Baker-288 • Silver: 2 or 3 known • Brass: 10 to 12 known

The medal that silversmith Peter Getz of Lancaster, Pennsylvania, struck in 1797 honoring George Washington as a General Grand Master of the United States Masons is the oldest piece in the Masonic series, as well as being one of the rarest. This extensive fraternal category includes many portraits of Washington, the country's most famous Freemason, who was initiated in 1752 at the age of 20 in Fredericksburg, Virginia. The rituals of Masonry often involved the conferring of medals, orders, and decorations, and individual chapters loved to strike commemorative pieces for building dedications, anniversaries, and special gatherings, and sell them to raise funds for Masonic charities. The lodges were also prolific issuers of "mark pennies" struck well into the 20th century, which members carried as pocket pieces to mark them as brothers when visiting other chapters. E.A. King cataloged nearly 10,000 varieties in his 1930 work, *Masonic Chapter Pennies*. The majority of these types were made of copper and white metal, but their granddaddy, our No. 45, was struck in silver and brass.

As described in the volume introduction, Washington congratulated Peter Getz on the quality of his portrait work, and the likeness seen on the Masonic piece resembles the ones Washington liked: those on the half dollar patterns made in 1792 at the request of Robert Morris, head of the Senate Committee on Coinage (Baker-23 to 25). Getz's patterns never resulted in coins, because Washington objected to the placement of his portrait on currency as too "monarchical."

The arcane symbols on the Getz medal, such as the all-seeing eye, globe-topped pillars, burning candles, compasses, plumb, level, and square, have special meaning to those initiated into the Masonic rites. As pointed out by Rulau and Fuld in *Medallic Portraits of Washington*, however, the irony of the piece is that there is no genuine Masonic rank of General Grand Master of the United States Masons. The invented degree was an honor conferred on Washington by the Grand Lodge of Pennsylvania in 1780, and was not endorsed by the wider Masonic populace, although this medal, struck 17 years later, implies that the office existed.

Actual Size: 34.8 mm

Getz submitted this Washington portrait as a potential design for a federal half dollar in 1792.

Estimated Market Values	Commentary on Value
Brass Strikings	
EF-40 to AU-58: .... $20,000 to $30,000	*Commentary:* Most examples have irregular surfaces and show wear. Some are holed for suspension.
VF-20 to 35: .... $15,000 to $20,000	

No. 46
THREE CENTS; WASHINGTON ON HORSEBACK
ATWOOD'S RAILROAD HOTEL TOKEN

HTT-221, Low-201, Miller NY-45 • Copper: 25 to 50 known • Fire gilt: 2 to 3 known • White metal: 2 to 3 known

It was the height of the Washington portrait medal craze in 1861 when William Cowper Prime published a price list indicating there was already strong interest in the Atwood's Railroad Hotel merchant tokens. Prime noted that the cent-sized copper tokens could be found "in three varieties, now highly prized, each $5."[66] The diesinking team of James Bale and Frederick B. Smith had struck them in 1836, and they bore the same equestrian portrait of Washington seen on their Hard Times–era store card. The reason the tokens were scarce is simple: Atwood was only in business at 243 Bowery for one year.

Henry Clinton Atwood, familiarly known as Harry, chose a difficult era in which to set up a public house. Born in Connecticut on March 13, 1802, Atwood first appears in New York business directories in 1835, listed as a hatter working on Stanton Street. The great fire of December 1835 likely destroyed that business, as it did more than 700 others in the area bounded by Bond Street, South Street, Wall Street, and Coenties Slip. In 1836, Atwood opened his new hotel within the fire-razed district. His merchant tokens, which were surely struck to entice customers to the establishment, were good for 3¢ in trade (perhaps the price of a pitcher of beer). In 1837, however, Atwood relocated to 85 First Street, and in the next five years he moved five more times, returning at least once to the hatter's trade. It is likely that the Panic of 1837 hit him hard, depressing his finances throughout the Hard Times era, because in 1845 he took the post of gauger in the New York Custom House.

By 1852, Atwood's fortunes had recovered enough for him to open a new hotel/liquor establishment on Division Street, which he operated through 1859. On September 20, 1860, he died suddenly in the town of Seymour, Connecticut, where he was either visiting or living after a relocation. Today, Atwood is remembered less for his work as a hotelier and more for his contributions to Freemasonry. As Master of the St. John Lodge, Atwood gave his heartfelt participation to the brotherhood. He founded a New York City mystic chapter patterned on the ways of his mentor, Jeremy Ladd Cross, "Father of the Mystic Rite." In 1846 he penned a 360-page book explaining the rituals and procedures of his order, entitled *The Master Workman: or The True Masonic Guide*. It saw a second printing in 1851.

Actual Size: 25 mm

This Union Square statue of George Washington by Henry Kirke Brown was unveiled 13 years after the issuance of Atwood's token. (*A Centennial View of Our Country and Its Resources*, James D. McCabe Jr., 1876)

Estimated Market Values	Commentary on Value
Copper Strikings	
MS-60 to 62: $2,000 to $4,000	*Commentary:* Electrotypes are common; beware. Strikings in other metals sell for higher prices than those listed.
EF-40 to AU-58: $1,000 to $2,000	
VF-20 to 35: $400 to $1,000	

No. 47

GEORGE H. LOVETT'S NOD TO COIN COLLECTORS
1860 "WE ALL HAVE OUR HOBBIES" MEDALET

Rulau/Miller NY-491A to 491C • White metal (491A): 100 to 200 known • Brass (491B): 75 to 125 known
• Copper (491C): 125 to 250 known

The motto on our No. 47 piece plays on the multiple meanings and connotations of the word *hobby* that were familiar at the time. In 1831, for example, a Kentucky editor accused a fellow journalist of making up news by saying, "He never sits down to write without having a swarm of visible lies buzzing around his pen. . . . Let him but once get fairly mounted on his hobby of blackguardism, and away he goes like a Lapland witch, astride of a broomstick!"[67] A hobbyhorse was a child's toy: a stick with a wooden horse's head attached. To "ride a hobby" meant to follow a passion to the exclusion of everything else.

An 1867 editorialist could have been referring to token and medal collectors when he commented: "There are people who ride the high horse and some who mount their hobbies, and the last are quite as likely to run down other people's patience as those who sit astride the loftier animal. Hobbies are a headstrong race, and go their length they will. The rider does best to sit firm, give a slack rein, and avoid a fall."[68]

Clearly, when George H. Lovett separated from his father, seal engraver Robert Lovett, and set up shop on his own at 131 Fulton Street in New York in 1858, he aimed to attract collectors with some amusing new designs. His own store card featured a cupid figure bouncing on the back of a sea serpent, and the rest of his tokens from 1858 through 1860, such as "The Antiquary," "The Smoker," and the Atlantic Cable medalet, feature an appealing silliness not seen in the rest of his vast body of work. He struck brass, copper, and white-metal varieties of the witch/hobby medalet, and muled both the witch obverse and collector-themed reverse with other dies in his possession, including F.C. Key's "Pater Patriae" Washington portrait, William Bridgens's "Boy and Dog," his own store-card obverse and reverse, and, for good numismatic measure, his "Mobile Jockey Club" obverse. One die combination, that of the witch obverse mated to a Daniel Webster portrait, fooled numismatist Gustav Kobbé, who included the piece in an 1888 discussion of political campaign tokens of 1836![69]

The sight of a witch flying beneath the motto "We all have our hobbies" may have been commonplace by 1860, as it can be found

Actual Size: 28 mm

on British postal-wafer seals of 1844 through 1852. The significance of the crutch or cane the witch carries in Lovett's version remains a mystery.

1864 photographs of George H. Lovett, at the age of 40.

Estimated Market Values	Commentary on Value
Copper, Brass, or White Metal	
PF-63 to 65 (choice to gem): . . . . $75 to $150	*Commentary:* These were sold to collectors and tend to be in high grades when seen today.
PF-60 to 62: . . . . $50 to $75	
PF-50 to 58: . . . . $30 to $50	

No. 48

HONORING "THE NATION'S GUEST"
1824 WASHINGTON/LAFAYETTE COUNTERSTAMPS

Baker-198 to 198G • On copper cents: 30 to 40 known • On half dollars: 6 to 10 known

In 1824, the Marquis de Lafayette, French hero of the American Revolution, revisited America and was proclaimed by Congress "the Nation's Guest." Numerous tributes—in print, in the form of medals, and in other media—were created during his stay in the United States, which extended into the year 1825. He arrived at Staten Island in New York harbor on August 15, stayed overnight, then disembarked at Castle Garden the next day. For the next three weeks he was feted throughout the city, and a ball in his honor was held at Castle Garden.

The collecting of counterstamps has been popular for a long time. Among the most famous and most desired are coins from this event, with the portrait of Washington stamped at the center of one side and that of Lafayette on the other. These are from dies created by Joseph Lewis for striking small (9 mm) medalets or tokens, but here applied to half dollars, copper cents, and a few other issues.[70] Most of these coins were holed at the top to permit wearing on a chain or cord, as was done with the 1800 Washington funeral medals (No. 11). These were ready by September 2 and were endorsed as official for the special ball and celebration at Castle Garden. Later, they were sold and distributed widely across America.

A contemporary writer recalled:

> [Lafayette] landed at Castle Garden amidst the acclamations of many thousands, the ringing of bells, and the firing of cannons. All the merchant and coasting vessels in our harbour hoisted their colors, and the ships of war, packets and numerous steam boats, were decorated with flags of different nations in the most elegant manner. In short, no demonstration of joy, which the ingenuity of our citizens could invent, was wanting to express the pleasure which was so generally felt on the arrival of this veteran hero, this distinguished Guest of the Nation, at our metropolis.
>
> . . . During his short residence amongst us, he visited our navy yard and garrisons, our public institutions, theatres, &c., and was every where received with that gratitude, to which, from his eminent services, he was so justly entitled. He daily kept a levee, at certain hours, in the City Hall, where he was incessantly visited by crowds of citizens, with whom he conversed with great familiarity, and readily shook hands with everyone, who came forward for that purpose.[71]

Actual Size: Depends on host coin

Lafayette arriving at Castle Garden, New York City, in August 1824, as "the Nation's Guest." (Devens, *Our First Century*, 1881)

ESTIMATED MARKET VALUES		COMMENTARY ON VALUE
ON A COPPER CENT	**ON A HALF DOLLAR**	*Commentary:* Cents are most often seen, but are rare. Only a few half dollars exist. Scattered strikings exist on other coins. A 9 mm medalet struck from the counterstamp dies is worth about $500 to $1,000 in Very Fine grade or thereabouts.
EF-40 to AU-58: . . . . . . $3,500 to $6,000	MS-60 to 62: . . . . . . $15,000 to $25,000	
VF-20 to 35: . . . . $2,250 to $3,500	(1 known, ex Roach Collection 1944)	
F-12: . . . . $1,750 to $2,250	EF-40 to AU-58: . . $10,000 to $15,000	
VG: . . . . $1,250 to $1,750	VF-20 to 35: . . . . . . $5,000 to $10,000	

No. 49

HONORING THE CAPTAIN OF "THE SHIP OF GOLD" IN 1858
MEDAL FOR THE 1857 LOSS OF THE SS *CENTRAL AMERICA*

Silver: 2 or 3 known • Copper: 3 to 5 known • White metal: 1 or 2 known

The 57.5 mm SS *Central America* medal was commissioned by the Commonwealth of Virginia to honor its fallen son, William Lewis Herndon, captain of the ill-fated side-wheel steamer SS *Central America*, who went down with his ship. Bronze examples were presented to the governor of the state and others, but the medal was never restruck, as the dies were held by the commonwealth as soon as striking was completed and later disappeared while in state hands. Of the 20 to 30 struck, only a handful can be accounted for today.

Struck from dies cut by F.B. Smith, the obverse illustrates the ship in distress, with Captain Herndon standing on top of the paddlewheel box, the sails in tatters, and a lifeboat struggling nearby in mountainous waves. The reverse bears an inscription to Herndon and is dated 1858, the year the medal was made.

In early September 1857, several hundred passengers in Panama boarded the SS *Central America* for its 44th trip between Panama and New York City. Captain Herndon welcomed all aboard, and verified that treasure comprising nearly $2 million in gold ingots, freshly minted 1857-S double eagles, and other coins was safely secured.

Under sunny skies, the ship steamed forward at about 12 knots. After a stop in Havana, the *Central America* continued north. Soon a gale came up, which quickly developed into an equinoctial storm (as tropical hurricanes were then called). By noon on Friday, September 10, the holds were flooded and the ship was without power. Disaster was imminent. Captain Herndon and his crew held on as best they could, and on the next day most of the women and children escaped in lifeboats to two passing ships. Herndon fired a rocket to signal distress and flew the flag upside down, but conditions went from bad to worse. On Saturday evening, as Herndon stood precariously on the starboard paddle box, the ship slipped beneath the waves, carrying with it 438 men and the gold treasure. A few survived, but Herndon was not among them.

In the 1980s, a team of explorers led by Bob Evans and Tommy Thompson located the wreck of the ship in 7,200 feet of water off the coast of North Carolina. More than 6,000 double eagles (mostly of the 1857-S variety) and several hundred gold

Actual Size: 57.5 mm

ingots were recovered, creating a sensation in numismatic circles when they were brought to market beginning in 2000. *Coin World* editor Beth Deisher called it "the story of the year."[72]

Commander William Lewis Herndon of the SS *Central America*.

ESTIMATED MARKET VALUES	COMMENTARY ON VALUE
SILVER STRIKING	
PF-60 to 62: .... $15,000 +	*Commentary:* Values are highly conjectural due to the great rarity of these medals.
COPPER STRIKING	
PF-60 to 62: .... $7,500 to $10,000	

No. 50
THE CAMPAIGN FOR NEWPORT
1778–1779 RHODE ISLAND SHIP TOKEN

Betts-561 to 563, Breen-1138 to 1142 • 400 to 600 known of all varieties and metals combined

Actual Size: 31.5 mm

In his *Complete Encyclopedia of U.S. and Colonial Coins*, Walter Breen called our No. 50 object a token, because so many examples are found in a worn and circulated condition. In the 2007 edition of *A Guide Book of United States Coins*, Kenneth Bressett classifies the piece as a medal, because its original purpose was believed to be commemorative or political. Exactly what that purpose was has been a mystery ever since the piece first appeared before American collectors in a W.E. Woodward sale of June 1864 (where it sold for $40).

Since no contemporary references have yet been located, the coiners' intent must be guessed from the pictorial content and legends (in Dutch). The obverse shows an island covered with soldiers marching toward the right, with three British warships off the left shore and 13 small boats (representing Continental forces) departing from the right shore. Since the legend translates to THE FLEEING AMERICANS OF RHODE ISLAND, AUGUST, 1778, it would seem that this is a British commemorative piece exulting over Admiral Richard Howe's successful campaign for Newport, Rhode Island, when 10,000 American militia retreated before him across Conanicut Island in 1778. Numismatists William T.R. Marvin and Lyman Low suggested that the pieces were struck in England for export to Holland, as propaganda to discourage Holland from signing the Treaty of Armed Neutrality in 1780.

The 19th-century expression "the other side of the coin" (meaning "the other side of the story") certainly applies in this case. The Dutch word *vlugtende* ("fleeing") was used on both sides of the medal. On the reverse appeared a three-masted vessel under a legend that translates to THE FLAGSHIP OF ADMIRAL HOWE 1779, and beneath it, FLEEING. Numismatist Charles I. Bushnell felt this meant the piece was satirical, and had a pro-Continental message: although the Americans were indeed routed in 1778, Howe himself did the fleeing in 1779. In 1880, collector George T. Paine speculated that the piece was struck in Holland by an American sympathizer.

Such mysteries to contemplate! To add to the confusion, certain people filled in the VLUGTENDE lettering on the reverse die and replaced it with a wreath ornament, eliminating any satirical interpretation. On many struck specimens the lettering has been filed away, evidence that the altered pieces circulated in Great Britain. There is no evidence of either variety circulating in North America.

Earlier state of the die with VLUGTENDE below the ship. This word was later effaced from the die, and a wreath ornament put in its place.

Estimated Market Values	Commentary on Value
Striking in Brass, Typical Variety EF-40 to AU-58: .... $2,500 to $4,000 VF-20 to 35: .... $1,200 to $2,500	*Commentary:* Rare die varieties sell for more. Pewter strikings are scarcer and sell for more. Horace M. Grant of Providence, Rhode Island, had copies made in 1936; his initials, HMG, appear on the crest of the wave below Howe's battleship.

No. 51
"JETONS DE PRÉSENCE"
1796 CASTORLAND MEDALS

Breen-1058 to 1061, Rulau NY-30 to 52 • Silver: 8 to 12 originals known • Copper: 6 to 10 originals known
• Restrikes and modern copies: plentiful

In the developing United States, the decade of the 1790s saw a sharp increase in fascination with all things French—not just with the ideals of the French Enlightenment and Revolution, but also with French artistic culture. French literature, music, architecture, and medallic design all became highly fashionable, and of course French investment capital was equally well received on this side of the Atlantic.

Meanwhile in France, in the aftermath of the violent overthrow of Louis XVI's ruling monarchy in 1789, the uncertain situation for people of wealth and property prompted many to consider investing their money in America. A Parisian stock company was formed on June 23, 1793, to create a colony in the state of New York. It purchased a tract of sugar maple forest in what is now Jefferson and Lewis counties, divided into 4,000 farms of 50 acres each, along the watershed of the Beaver River.[73] The "Compagnie de New York" drew up an elaborate constitution designating director Pierre Chassanis as head of government, to be assisted by six commissaries. Two of the six would reside at the settlement seat, known as Castorville (*castor* being the French word for beaver). Four would remain in Paris. Chassanis and commissary Rodolphe Tillier were the only members to receive a salary; those remaining in France would be paid in silver tokens.

> In recognition of the care which they may bestow upon the common concerns, there shall be given them an attendance fee for each Special or General Assembly where they may meet on the affairs of the Company. The fee is fixed at two jetons of silver, of the weight of four or five gros. They shall be made at the expense of the company, under the direction of the commissaries, who shall decide on their form and design.

Benjamin Duvivier, a stockholder in the company, executed the handsome jetons in 1796. Their intrinsic worth was near 50¢, and they were the same size and weight as a 1796 U.S. half dollar. The veiled female on the obverse is thought to represent France in America, while on the reverse, Ceres, goddess of agriculture, stands guard over a sugar maple atop the symbol of the colony, the

Actual Size: 32 mm

beaver, in exergue. The Latin SALVE MAGNA PARENS FRUGUM translates to HAIL, GREAT MOTHER OF FRUIT, a truncation of a phrase from Virgil. In early 1919, Theophile E. Leon exhibited a gold Proof strike at a meeting of the Chicago Coin Club, and modern restrikes in silver, copper, and bronze may still be purchased from the Paris Mint.

The Castorland settlement did not endure as long as its jetons: losses from harsh winters and the theft of company funds, combined with improvements in the situation in France, provoked most settlers to return home by 1818. The region remained sparsely populated for many years after.

Official seal of the Compagnie de New-York.

Estimated Market Values	
Silver Strikings, Original	
EF-40 to AU-58:	$4,000 to $7,000
VF-20 to 35:	$2,500 to $4,000

Commentary on Value

Commentary: The Paris Mint issued restrikes from original dies and, later, from copy dies. Copper restrikes made from mirror-surface dies in the early 19th century may sell for several hundred dollars and upward; later issues sell for less. Modern strikings are still being made. Consult an expert before buying any piece offered as an original silver striking.

No. 52

A NATION COMMEMORATES ITS FIRST CENTURY
OFFICIAL U.S. 1876 CENTENNIAL MEDAL

Julian CM-10 and 11, HK-20 to 22, Loubat-82 and 83 • Silver, 38 mm: 10,133 struck • Bronze, 38 mm: 13,000 struck • Gilt, 38 mm: 10,500 struck

Actual Size: 38 mm

The year 1876 was not without its problems. It was the third year of a severe economic depression that had begun with the Panic of 1873; General George Custer and all of his men fell at Little Bighorn; and recurring conflicts with Native Americans prompted the government to order the entire population onto reservations. Pennsylvania's Molly Maguires, a group of Irish miners outraged by squalid housing and working conditions, conducted a reign of terror in the anthracite district. In New York, scandals surrounding William Marcy "Boss" Tweed and his cronies tinged the era with the shame of rampant political corruption. But 1876 is remembered as well for its great triumph: a century of existence for the world's first fully democratic republic. This was the beginning of the Gilded Age, when the fabulous wealth of the barons of industry and the benefits of the machine were ushering in a new way of life at breakneck speed. It was the perfect time for an international exposition to emphasize the wonders of the day: the gigantic Corliss steam engine, the transcontinental railroad, the telephone, and even the typewriter.

Congress authorized the official souvenir medals of the U.S. Centennial Exposition on June 10, 1874, whereupon Chief Engraver William Barber made the dies at the Mint, and striking began in October. By May 10, 1876, when President Ulysses S. Grant opened the expo in Philadelphia before a crowd of international dignitaries, nearly 10,000 large (57 mm) versions in silver, bronze, white metal, copper, and gilded copper, and more than 33,000 smaller (38 mm) versions in silver, bronze, and copper were ready for sale to visitors. The prices ranged from 50¢ to $1 for the small medal and $2 to $5 for the large. A case including four different specimens was available for $11. The souvenir medals (not to be confused with the bronze Centennial Commission award medals by Henry Mitchell) commemorated not only the anniversary but also the progress in manufacturing and the arts of nearly 40 countries, featured at more than 30,000 exhibits on 250 acres. The obverse bears a quotation from the first resolution of the Continental Congress of June 10, 1776. America, who won her liberty with a sword, raises a reverent hand to the original colonies, shown as a ring of 13 stars.

Today the 38 mm versions are widely collected by enthusiasts of "so-called dollars." Quantities of the 57 mm size vary by metal—gold (unique), silver (9 struck), bronze (7,000 struck), white metal (583 struck), or gilded copper (2,100 struck). It is likely that the majority of the 57 mm medals did not find buyers and were melted.

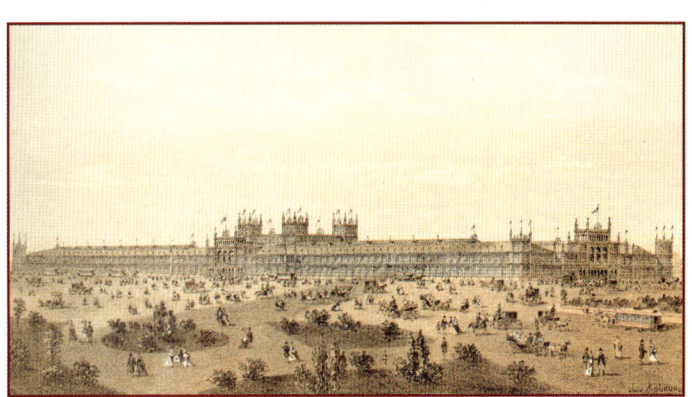

Main Building at the Centennial Exhibition held in Fairmount Park, Philadelphia, 1876. (Thomas Hunter, *Centennial Portfolio*, 1876)

Estimated Market Values	
Gilt or Bronze Strikings, 38 mm	**Silver Strikings, 38 mm**
PF-63 to 65 (choice to gem): .... $75 to $100	PF-63 to 65 (choice to gem): .... $225 to $400
PF-60 to 62: .... $50 to $70	PF-60 to 62: .... $175 to $225
EF-40 to 58: .... $30 to $50	EF-40 to 58: .... $100 to $175

No. 53

Obverse by Augustus Saint-Gaudens
1893 Columbian Exposition Award Medal

HK-223 • 400 to 600 known in copper

Actual Size: 76.4 mm

In the chronicle of world's fairs, America has many notable entries, including the 1876 Centennial Exhibition, the 1915 Panama-Pacific International Exposition, the 1926 Sesquicentennial Exposition, the 1933 Century of Progress, and those of later years. However, not one ranks with the 1893 World's Columbian Exposition in importance. Constructed at the dawn of the age of electricity, its ornately decorated white buildings were a heavenly sight at night.

Planned to open in 1892 to observe the 400th anniversary of Christopher Columbus's discovery of America (never mind the Norsemen who had arrived centuries earlier), the event was to showcase the ultimate in American technology, art, and science, in good company with exhibits from around the world. Construction took longer than expected, and it was not until 1893 that the fairgrounds were ready to receive the public. President Grover Cleveland was on hand to signal the opening.

It was envisioned that Augustus Saint-Gaudens, one of America's most accomplished and lauded sculptors, would create the official award medal. Offered a fee of $5,000, a remarkable sum for the era, the artist demurred at first, as he was busy with another commission, the Shaw Memorial (today an attraction in Boston Common). He suggested that the work be placed with an artist in France, where medallic engraving was a high form of art.

Finally, he consented to do the work, if only to keep it out of the hands of Charles E. Barber, the chief engraver at the Mint. (Saint-Gaudens and other sculptors of the time viewed Barber's work as mediocre at best.) Having relented, Saint-Gaudens prepared suggestions for the design, the obverse featuring Columbus reaching shore in the New World, in a triumphant pose with his cape flared and hand outstretched. The reverse depicted a nude boy holding a torch and several small wreaths against a background of lettered inscriptions.

The depiction of a nude male, however, was considered obscene by some observers, while in the same era nude *females* in paintings and statues were perfectly acceptable. After much wrangling, an insipid reverse design by Barber was mated with the Saint-Gaudens obverse. The process took a long time, and the medals and accompanying certificates were not awarded to recipients until 1896. It was planned at first that 20,000 medals would be struck, but final production fell far short of that figure.[74]

The rejected Saint-Gaudens reverse design depicting a nude boy. (*Century Magazine*, June 1897. Image reduced)

 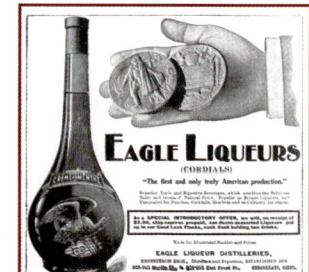

Product advertisements featuring the Columbian Exposition award medal.

Estimated Market Values	Commentary on Value
Copper Strikings MS-63 to 65 (choice to gem): .... $150 to $200 MS-60 to 62: .... $100 to $150	*Commentary:* The surface is chocolate brown as made. These typically come with the name of the awardee on the back, added with an insert into the die. The prices are for medals without the original aluminum boxes, which could add $50 to the estimate.

No. 54

USED ON THE BATTLEFIELD
SUTLERS' TOKENS OF THE CIVIL WAR

Schenkman describes several hundred varieties • 5,000 to 10,000 known in copper and brass

Sutlers' tokens constitute one of the scarcest and least understood specialties in exonumia, especially for Civil War history buffs. One book, however, tells all: *Civil War Sutler Tokens and Cardboard Scrip* (1983), by David E. Schenkman.

In 1861 the War Department set up a system of sutlers—appointed individuals or partnerships who sold goods to soldiers. At a permanent post, the sutler would operate a store, whose shelves were lined with stationery, pens, ink, cards and games, clothing, utensils, tobacco, patent medicine, knives, books, newspapers, toiletries, and more. Liquor was officially prohibited, but as patent medicines such as Drake's Plantation Bitters were essentially made of alcohol, spirits were available in abundance. Schenkman mentions that sutlers also received frequent shipments of regular liquor, often marked as "milk" or "tonic." In traveling companies and on the battlefield, sutlers would set up in tents or operate from the rear of wagons.

Actual Size: 19.1 mm

As each post or regiment was allowed just one sutler, he could charge about what he pleased. There was little regulation of the quality of goods. Resentful soldiers felt that the government, not private individuals, should be in charge of selling supplies, and that in any event the prices should be fair and the quality above reproach. Sometimes disgruntled soldiers would raid sutlers' supplies in reparation, with officers often looking the other way. After the Civil War, the sutler system was replaced by government-operated post exchanges.

During the war, sutlers also made loans to soldiers between paydays, giving them tokens or scrip that could be used to purchase goods. The tokens were primarily made by John Stanton in Cincinnati (his tokens are usually of brass, very thin, and with his name in a small backstamp on the reverse), but also by S.D. Childs (Chicago), William K. Lanphear (Cincinnati), Joseph H. Merriam (Boston), and other makers of Civil War tokens. For some sutlers' tokens, a Civil War token die was used for one side.

All sutlers' tokens are highly collectible today. More than 500 varieties are known, but few extensive collections have ever been formed. Indeed, a holding of 100 different ones would be a good showing. Adding to the supply in numismatic hands are continuing discoveries by people with metal detectors who comb battle sites. Tokens found in this manner are usually heavily oxidized.

A sutler's tent serving Captain Geary's division at Harper's Ferry. (*Frank Leslie's Illustrated News*, November 29, 1862)

ESTIMATED MARKET VALUES	
BRASS, TYPICAL VARIETY	
EF-40 to AU-58:	$350 to $600
VF-20 to 35:	$250 to $350
F-12:	$150 to $250
VG-8:	$100 to $150

COMMENTARY ON VALUE

Commentary: Tokens excavated from battlefields usually show oxidation, sometimes extensive. In addition to the above pieces, which were made for use by troops, various numismatic strikings and die combinations were sold at a premium to collectors and exist today in Uncirculated grade. These can be very rare and expensive.

No. 55
Admission Medal by Gobrecht
1821 Peale's Philadelphia Museum

Rulau-397 and 398, Julian UN-23 • Silver: 3 to 5 known • Copper (a few gilt): 40 to 60 known

In the annals of American museums, the name of Charles Willson Peale (1741–1847) looms large. In 1786 he founded the Philadelphia Museum, through which he sought both to turn a profit and to educate and entertain the public. It was an era of wonderment, and curiosities and relics of natural history, foreign lands, and science attracted a lot of attention. Newspapers and magazines of the era had few illustrations, and what things looked like was left largely to the imagination. Peale's friend Robert Patterson (later director of the Mint) donated the first specimen for display, a *Polydon spathula*, or paddlefish. In the next decade, George Washington sent a pair of stuffed pheasants from Mount Vernon.[75]

In time, Peale assembled a marvelous display of paintings, silhouettes of famous people, stuffed birds and animals, coins and medals, and more. By 1799 he had more than 100 mammals, 700 birds, and thousands of fish, reptiles, amphibians, and insects. Care was taken to have "moral" displays, so as to be uplifting in spirit and not offend public sensibilities. Unable to obtain funding from the city or state, Peale sought patrons and sold annual admission tickets. A later pass was created in medal form and is our No. 55—a tangible link to a remarkable man and a storehouse of treasures.

Like similar entities, the Philadelphia Museum advertised extensively in local papers, telling of its attractions and also of special displays. At the time, the city was one of America's most important cultural centers; in the 1790s it was the U.S. capital.

As described by historian Oliver Jensen,

> Peale was one of the universal men of the 18th century, a man whose talent and interests ran in a hundred different directions—inventor, mechanic, silversmith, watchmaker, millwright, patriot, soldier, politician, and naturalist. His hands could make anything his brain devised, from moving pictures to a new type of bridge. He practiced every branch of the graphic arts—oils, watercolors, etching, mezzotint—and he was also a sculptor. . . . He was on friendly, sometimes intimate terms with most of the great figures of his age: men like Franklin, Lafayette, Jefferson, Madison, and Thomas Paine.

Actual Size: 32 mm

Peale was not only what today we would term an intellectual, but a painter of renown as well. He studied under such artists as John Singleton Copley and Benjamin West. He and his first wife, Rachel, had 10 children, four of them boys and named after famous artists: Raphaelle (or Raphael), Rembrandt, Rubens, and Titian. With his second wife, Elizabeth, he had another six children, including Franklin, who was born in the hall of the American Philosophical Society, and Titian (the first Titian had died of yellow fever in 1789). Rembrandt achieved fame as an artist. Numismatically, Titian is remembered as the designer of the eagle on the reverse of the 1836 Gobrecht dollar, while Franklin was chief coiner at the Mint for many years.

After Peale's death, the assets of the museum were sold. Among the buyers were Moses Kimball and P.T. Barnum.

Peale's Philadelphia Museum. (Print published by Fenner Sears & Co., London, 1831)

Estimated Market Values	Commentary on Value
Copper Strikings	*Commentary:* Some have numbers engraved on the back to identify the original persons to whom they were distributed. These are much rarer, are usually seen in Uncirculated state, and are worth double the estimates at left.
PF-60 to 62: . . . . $100 to $200	
EF-40 to PF-58: . . . . $50 to $100	
VF-20 to 35: . . . . $30 to $50	

No. 56
THE COMITIA AMERICANA SERIES
HORATIO GATES AT SARATOGA MEDAL

Julian MI-2 and related • Originals (MI-2): a few known in silver, 10 to 20 known in white metal, 10 to 20 known in copper • Restrikes, 19th-century copper (MI-2): 10 to 20 known

Knowing that the fame, importance, and high artistic quality of America's 17 Revolutionary War medals might place the entire lot in the top 100, our nominators included "Comitia Americana medals as a class" as a separate candidate on our ballot. The individual medal to receive the most votes after Washington Before Boston (No. 2) and become our class representative was the award to General Horatio Gates for his victory at Saratoga, New York, in October 1777. Because this success emboldened the French to enter the war on the American side, it is considered a major turning point of the Revolution. Although generals Daniel Morgan and Benedict Arnold may deserve more credit for the outcome at Saratoga than Gates, who spent much of the engagement in a tent two miles from the scene,[76] it was Gates who accepted the sword of Britain's General John Burgoyne and entered the schoolbooks as the hero of the day.

The three Parisian engravers who executed the Comitia Americana medal dies—Pierre Simon Duvivier, Nicholas Marie Gatteaux, and Augustin Dupré—had the benefit of the metallurgical experience, artistic training, and advanced minting capability of both the richest court and the oldest mint in Europe. Dupré and Duvivier came from families that had dominated French medallic art for much of the 18th century. These young artists rejected the serene, stately forms of their fathers' era, which reflected the tastes of the Sun King's court,[77] for designs that were filled with the movement and energy appropriate to the new spirit of enlightenment and revolution taking seed in France as well as in America. Their horses rear, cannons belch smoke and flame, and ships lean before the wind. As in the Libertas Americana medal (No. 1) and the naval medal of John Paul Jones (No. 35), all of the Comitia Americana designs exude action and life.

Aaron Burr delivered the Gates medal dies to the Mint in 1801, where they would be used first to strike silver and white metal copies for Gates's family, and then on a larger scale to strike bronze copies for collectors of the 1860s. Gates's original gold medal now resides at the New-York Historical Society. Shown is an original

Actual Size: 50.5 mm

impression of the Gates medal in silver from an early die state. This is from a set of Comitia Americana medals presented to George Washington, later the property of Daniel Webster.

Treasury Department proof of a proposed 1862 design for a $1 note. The art, *Surrender of Gen. Burgoyne at Saratoga, N.Y., Oct., 1777*, is by John Murdoch. At times it was proposed that federal paper money include scenes from American history, making the notes appealing and familiar in motif to those who used them. This was continued in practice, often with historical scenes on both sides, but not as panoramic as on this early proof.

ESTIMATED MARKET VALUES

COPPER STRIKINGS, ORIGINAL		COPPER RESTRIKES, 19TH CENTURY	
PF-63 to 65 (choice to gem):	$2,000 to $3,000	PF-63 to 65 (choice to gem):	$400 to $600
PF-60 to 62:	$1,200 to $2,000	PF-60 to 62:	$200 to $400
PF-50 to 58:	$600 to $1,200	PF-50 to 58:	$125 to $200

No. 57

THE "SCALPING MEDAL"
ABRAHAM LINCOLN INDIAN PEACE MEDAL

Julian IP-38 (76 mm) and 39 (62 mm), Loubat-70, Prucha Plate 51 • Silver originals: 76 mm, 20 to 30 known; 62 mm, 15 to 20 known • Bronze restrikes: 76 mm, 100 to 150 known; 62 mm, 100 to 150 known

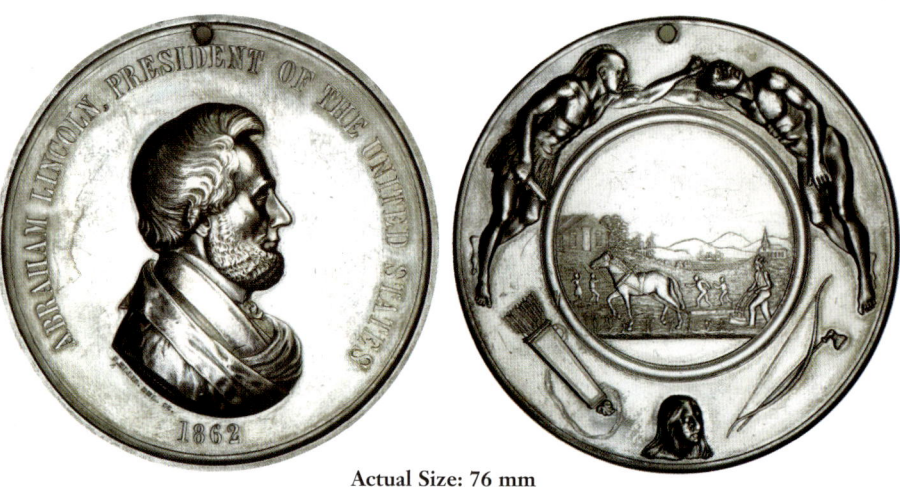

Actual Size: 76 mm

Whenever a medal belongs to more than one series, it achieves heightened fame. The Lincoln Indian peace medal of 1862 is a must-have for both Lincoln portrait and peace-medal collectors, in spite of its somewhat unsavory pictorial content. The example shown here is the finest of several in the John J. Ford Jr. collection.

Salathiel Ellis, a New York City cameo cutter, and Joseph Willson, his protégé, had been the U.S. peace-medal design team since 1850. Ellis had engraved the obverse portraits, and Willson the reverse scenes, for the medals of Millard Fillmore, Franklin Pierce, and James Buchanan. For the Fillmore and Pierce medals, the pair departed from the handshake/peace pipe design used since 1802 (No. 3) in favor of a scene of an Indian and a settler facing each other in front of the American flag. This device retained the usual symmetry seen on peace medals, showing Indian and settler, hand in hand or eye to eye, occupying equal space within the circular field. The reverse Willson conceived in 1857 for the Buchanan and Lincoln medals, however, departed radically from that format. According to one historian, this reflected the changing status of Indians and their role in the political life of the nation.[78] Literally and figuratively, Indians were being pushed to the outside.

The symbolic content was based on the same philosophy as that of the Seasons medals (No. 6), but instead of merely indicating the benefits of domestic life, it also contrasted them with the "barbarity" of Indian ways. Robert Julian believes that the scalping motif (also used on Buchanan medals) may have derived from Henry Rowe Schoolcraft's popular books on Indian life published in 1851, one of which featured a scalping scene on the cover.[79] As pointed out by Rita Laws, the Indian tradition was to remove a scalp only as a trophy from an opponent killed in battle, and the practices of paying bounties for scalps and scalping living people were European modifications.

A more entertaining error on the Buchanan/Lincoln reverse die was detected by both Buchanan and his Secretary of the Interior when they reviewed the design, but it was too late in the production process to do anything about it. The Indian operating the plow in the foreground is wearing a feathered headdress. The Sioux were the only tribe to wear this type of headgear, and only on ritual occasions or when riding into battle. The illustration on the medal must have seemed ridiculous to its recipients.

Detail from another medal (Massachusetts Historical Society) showing four children playing baseball, a design first used on Buchanan peace medals in 1857. Note that the brave operating the plow wears a peace medal.

Estimated Market Values	Commentary on Value
Silver Originals, 76 mm	
PF-60 to 62: .... $20,000 to $25,000	*Commentary:* Copper restrikes are seen with some frequency in the marketplace, and Proof-60 to 62 examples are valued at about $500 to $1,000.
EF-40 to PF-58: .... $15,000 to $20,000	
VF-20 to 35: .... $10,000 to $15,000	

No. 58
PROMINENT 19TH-CENTURY NUMISMATIST
CHARLES I. BUSHNELL MEDALET

Sage's Numismatic Gallery No. 1 • 75 to 100 known

Actual Size: 31 mm

On May 25, 1857, the new Flying Eagle cents made their debut. Small in diameter and made of copper-nickel, these replaced the copper "large" cents that had been a familiar part of the American scene since 1793. Soon a wave of nostalgia spurred hundreds if not thousands of people to check their coins and pick out as many different dates of cent as they could. There was much interest in coins that were rare and valuable. As there were no books on American coins and their values, articles about numismatics were published in city newspapers and in *The Historical Magazine*, founded in January of that year.

Several dealers in artifacts and curiosities dealt in coins as well. In New York City, teenager Augustus B. Sage was prominent. Imbued with energy and an innovative spirit, in March 1858 he was instrumental in founding the American Numismatic Society, which held its first meeting in the Sage family home at 121 Essex Street. In the same year, local diesinker George H. Lovett issued a medalet relating to the Atlantic Cable, which was a sensation in August when the first cable communication was received from England. Sage thought that collectors might like to buy a *series* of medalets, and contacted Lovett to create such pieces. The first issue in what he titled Aug. B. Sage's Odds and Ends Series featured on the obverse the New York Crystal Palace in flames, and on the reverse the legend ALL IS VANITY. This immense structure of steel and glass, a great attraction when it opened in 1853, was destroyed by fire in 1858.

In early 1859 Sage launched his Numismatic Gallery series, depicting prominent numismatists. The first subject was Charles I. Bushnell, a New York City attorney who enjoyed numismatic research and had published a study of tokens the year before. He and Sage had participated in a series of articles about coins published in the *New-York Dispatch* in 1857.

Sage's Numismatic Gallery extended to include nine subjects: Charles I. Bushnell, Henry Bogert, Jeremiah Colburn, James R. Chilton, Winslow Lewis, Frank Jaudon, William H. Chesley, Frank Jaudon, Horatio N. Rust, and Robert J. Dodge. Although the Chilton medalet was advertised, the authors are not aware that any example was produced. The other eight were made to the extent of up to several hundred of each, mostly in copper, but some later issues in white metal. See Nos. 98 and 100 for other Sage items.

Henry Bogert, a partner in the coin business with Sage, was aptly chosen to be the second honoree in the Numismatic Gallery series.

Jeremiah Colburn was probably the most knowledgeable American numismatist in 1859 when Sage honored him on Numismatic Gallery No. 3.

ESTIMATED MARKET VALUES	
BUSHNELL MEDALET IN COPPER	
PF-63 to 65 (choice to gem):	$100 to $150
PF-60 to 62:	$75 to $100
PF-50 to 58:	$40 to $75

COMMENTARY ON VALUE

Commentary: Other medalets in the series include some strikings in white metal. Whether in copper or white metal, these usually sell for less than the Bushnell medals, as the men depicted are not as well known.

No. 59

With Fictitious Portrait: The First Struck Washington Medal
1778 Washington "Voltaire" Medal

Betts-544, Baker-76B • Silver: 6 or 7 known • Bronze: 200 to 250 known

The 1778 medal of Washington published by Voltaire is the first of what would become a very extensive medallic and numismatic series. Never mind that it did not depict the title subject!

Modern catalog entries sometimes note that the obverse portrait used here may be of British jurist and philosopher Jeremy Bentham (1748–1842). In March 1861, the "Queries" editor of *The Historical Magazine* stated, "I have heard that when [the medal] was designed, the parties to save expense took a hub . . . containing a head of Bentham, and from it struck the die on which the inscription 'Washington &c' was then cut."[80] We inquired of Catherine Fuller of University College London, editor of *The Old Radical: Representations of Jeremy Bentham*, a 1998 publication cataloging all known Bentham portraits. She informed us that the only contemporary medal of Bentham was made by Pierre Jean David (better known as David d'Angers) in 1828. Viewing a picture of the Voltaire medal, she stated, "This medal does not portray Bentham at any age."

Our next step was to examine the suggestion of numismatist and Washingtoniana scholar George Fuld, who pointed out that the portrait looks very much like Julius Caesar.[81] The subject's hair is short and combed toward the face in Roman style, and the features match those on a famous marble bust of Caesar from the Vatican Museums. It is likely that the medal's designers, not knowing how Washington actually looked, had good reason to equate him with Caesar, history's most brilliant general.

Voltaire, a.k.a. François-Marie Arouet (1694–1778), was the leading writer of the French Enlightenment. He advocated individual liberty and freedom of religion, and opposed the tyranny of monarchs and courts—all subjects that were at issue in the American Revolution. A confidant of Benjamin Franklin, who was in Paris in the spring of 1778 trying to enlist French aid for the colonists' cause, Voltaire followed the progress of the revolution with deep concern, lamenting the Continental Army's reverses and celebrating its victories. According to *Dunlap's Pennsylvania Packet* of July 18, 1778, the medal he issued bore a reverse legend in Latin that translated as follows: "General Washington has reunited, by an uncommon assemblage in his character, the talents of the warrior with the virtues of the philosopher." Clearly, Voltaire hoped to inspire confidence in the Revolution's leadership, and to instill

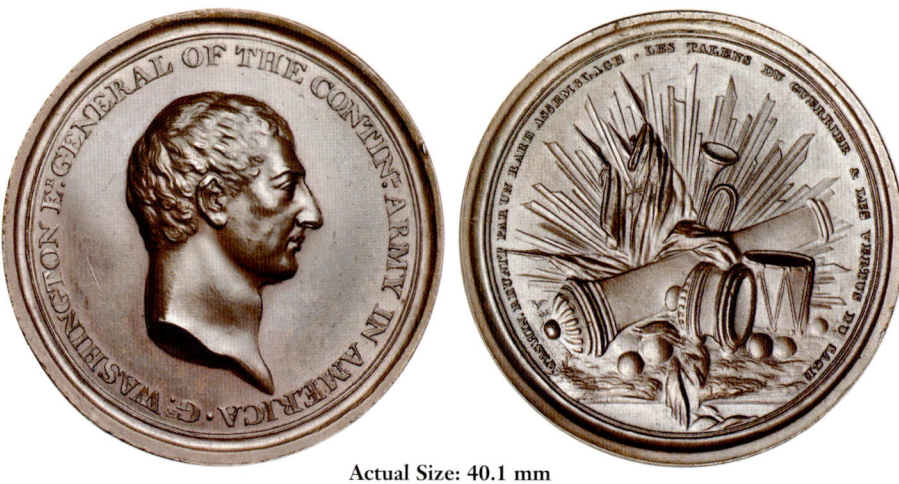

Actual Size: 40.1 mm

the hope that Washington would fare as well as Caesar in history. Voltaire died in May 1778, just a month before France signed a formal alliance with the Continental Congress.

"Paper money eventually returns to its intrinsic value—zero," Voltaire declared. Here he is depicted on the 1964 French 10-franc note.

Estimated Market Values
Bronze Strikings

MS-60 to 62:	$600 to $900
EF-40 to AU-58:	$400 to $600

No. 60
NATIONAL REFORM ASSOCIATION POLITICAL MESSAGE
1844 "VOTE THE LAND FREE" COUNTERSTAMP
Rulau HTT-833, DeWitt MVB 1848-3 • On cents: 250 to 400 known • On silver coins: 5 to 10 known

During the early 19th century, inscriptions counterstamped on large copper cents were often used to carry messages relating to merchants, politicians, and events. These coins were omnipresent in American commerce. For many collectors, counterstamped coins have formed an interesting specialty, one delineated in Gregory Brunk's *Merchant and Privately Countermarked Coins: Advertising on the World's Smallest Billboards*, and in Russell Rulau's essential *Standard Catalog of United States Tokens 1700–1900*.

Among the more interesting and significant of these are cents counterstamped VOTE THE LAND / FREE. For many years these were believed to have been issued by the Free Soil Party for the election of 1848. However, modern research indicates that all known cents with this marking are dated 1844 or earlier. Now they are attributed to the National Reform Association (NRA), a group initiated by George Henry Evans from the membership of the Loco Focos, the National Trades Union, and the Workingmen's Party. Evans held that property is something that is produced by labor, and that land, therefore, could not be property in the same sense that a plow or other manufactured item could. In his eyes, one could "own" land only by investing one's labor in it; the fact that the labor invested could not be separated from the land itself provided the basis for ownership (a view similar to that of English philosopher John Locke). Evans is credited with coining the popular 1844 slogan "Vote yourself a farm," which was later taken up by others (including in the 1860 election).

On March 13, 1844, a meeting of working people, under the name of the National Reform Party, was held in New York City. A committee was appointed to investigate "a depression of labor, and a social degradation of the laborer." The committee filed a report that was accepted at the next meeting. Resolutions included encouraging Congress to allow workers and others to acquire public lands free of charge, to protect land from being seized in debt collection, and to restrict the ownership of large parcels by wealthy individuals. The land belonged to the people, and legislators should vote that it become so.

The National Reform Party soon disappeared, but the efforts of Evans and others lived on in the 1862 Homestead Act. By allowing individuals to claim, work, and eventually own parcels of government land, this act played an important role in the settlement of the West. Several hundred counterstamped "Vote the land free" cents remain as reminders of that time. The counterstamp is usually seen on the obverse of copper cents, such as the 1841 coin shown above left. Rarer are stamps on other denominations, such as the 1843 quarter dollar, above right.

Actual Size: Depends on host coin

Pioneers like those in this engraving may never have heard the words "Vote the Land Free"—but the Homestead Act of 1862 that drew thousands of settlers westward shared a history with that slogan. (Ca. 1869 engraving by Henry Bryan Hall; Library of Congress, LC-USZC4-2634)

Estimated Market Values	
On Large Copper Cent	
EF-40 to 45:	$175 to $250
VF-20 to 35:	$125 to $175
F-12:	$100 to $125

No. 61
FOR EXTRAORDINARY VALOR
CONGRESSIONAL MEDAL OF HONOR

More than 3,400 awarded

Tales of Medal of Honor recipients and their deeds are the highlights of U.S. military lore, recounted in scores of magazines, books, and even video games. The award is the nation's highest, because it is the only one given by Congress for acts deemed to be of extraordinary valor, and bestowed personally by the president. Since the decoration was established in December 1861, 3,460 men and one woman have received it.[82] Numismatists may refer to it as a *badge*, but official decree designates it as a medal.

Anthony C. Paquet engraved the original design by Philadelphia silversmiths William Wilson & Son (1858–1884), one of five submitted by Mint director James Pollock to the award's chief proponent, Secretary of the Navy Gideon Welles. The reverse of the star-shaped medal was left blank for inscribing the recipient's name. Pollock described the "Minerva repelling discord" theme as follows:

> The foul spirit of Secession and Rebellion is represented by a male figure in crouching attitude holding in his hands, serpents, which with forked tongues are striking at a large female figure, representing the Union or Genius of our country, who holds in her right hand a shield, and in her left, the fasces. Around these figures are 34 stars, indicating the number of states in the Union.

The Civil War medal illustrated above is cataloged by the Massachusetts Historical Society as "Five-pointed star with trefoil terminals, suspended fouled anchor. Minerva repulsing Discord within a circle of 34 stars. . . ." It is engraved on the reverse: "Personal Valor / Lewis A. Horton / Seaman / U.S.S. Rhode Island. / Loss of the Monitor / Dec. 31 / 1862."

The army Medal of Honor was struck from the same dies, but employed a different suspension bar. Today, the navy's medal is unchanged from the original, save for the ribbon color and suspension elements. The army's medal went through a redesign in 1904, which replaced the Minerva scene with the profile of a helmeted goddess of war and added a green-enameled ring of leaves around the star. The Air Force medal, instituted in 1965, bears a head of the Statue of Liberty in place of the war goddess.

Actual Size: 102 mm

According to the 1998 book *Stolen Valor* by B.G. Burkett and Glenna Whitley, due to the wide availability of costume reproductions of U.S. decorations (like those George C. Scott wore in the movie *Patton*), medals fraud is on the rise. The "Stolen Valor Act," which makes it a crime to impersonate a decorated veteran, was signed into law in December 2006. Many knowledgeable collectors and dealers buy and sell authentic decorations, but not Medals of Honor, as trading in them is illegal. Title 18, Section 4 of the United States Code prohibits the sale, trade, barter, "or exchange for anything of value" of the Medal of Honor, effectively rendering it noncollectible.

Army Medal of Honor design of 1904, featuring a helmeted bust of Minerva and a ring of enameled leaves. This example was awarded during World War II. (Library of Congress, LC-USW36-952)

COMMENTARY ON VALUE

Commentary: Noncollectible due to prohibition by federal law (see text).

No. 62

PORTRAIT OF "OLD FUSS AND FEATHERS"
1848 CONGRESSIONAL MEDAL TO WINFIELD SCOTT

Julian MI-26 • Gold: 1 known • Silver: 2 to 3 known • Bronzed copper (19th century): 150 to 175 known

Charles Cushing Wright (1796–1854) enjoyed renown as an engraver after he created the Erie Canal medal (No. 8) in 1826, but it was the U.S. Mint assignment of the Winfield Scott, Zachary Taylor, William Bliss, and Somers Rescue congressional medal dies in 1848 that propelled him to the apex of his career. By 1850 Wright could practically name his commission, and Mint director Robert Patterson proposed him for the Mint engraver's job, although James B. Longacre, who held the position at the time, could not be unseated. (It was just as well, for within four years, Wright would be dead of tuberculosis.) Wright's medal for Winfield Scott, which attempted to convey every detail of the great general's Mexican War campaign, had personal meaning—his son Charles Washington Wright had fought under Scott from the siege of Vera Cruz to the storming of Chapultepec.[83]

Scott's military career began when he joined the army as an artillery captain in 1808. During the War of 1812 he achieved the rank of major general, and earned the nickname "Old Fuss and Feathers" for his strict insistence on discipline and attention to detail. During the nullification crisis of 1832 he commanded the force sent to Charleston, South Carolina, to make sure the state's repudiation of federal law didn't snowball into a civil war. He led the field against Sauks and Foxes in the Black Hawk War (1832) as well as Seminoles and Creeks in Florida (1835), and negotiated an important truce in the Aroostook War with Canada in 1839. By 1841 he had been named general-in-chief of the army, and he remained in that post until his retirement 20 years later. His orchestration and successful waging of the campaign for Mexico City in 1848 made him the first person since George Washington to attain the rank of lieutenant general. Basking in the glory of that success, he ran for president against Franklin Pierce in 1852, but apparently couldn't translate his military prowess to the political sphere.

Scott's congressional medal was a milestone in American medallic art, not only for its design and execution, but for its size, a huge 90 mm, and the quantity of gold it required. Today it reposes in the National Numismatic Collection in the Smithsonian Institution. Although its busy reverse design by C.C. Humphries is not aesthetically pleasing to some, it makes the piece a standout among all medals of the period.

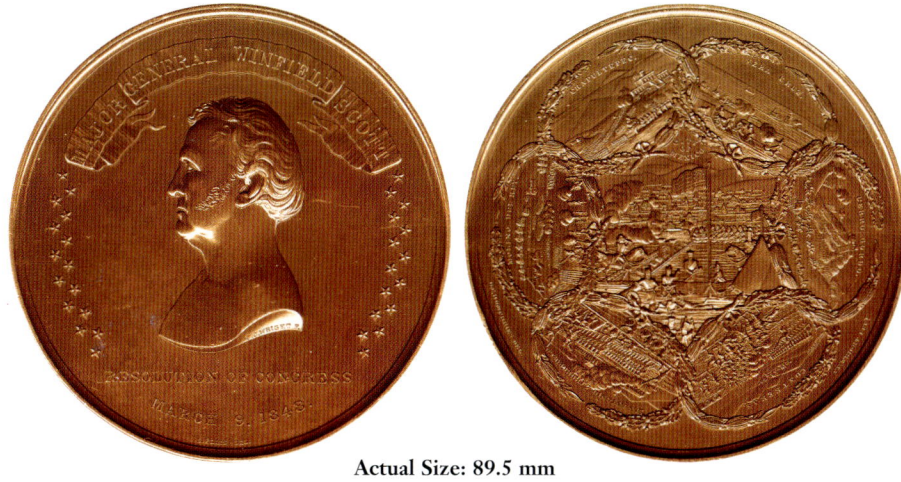

Actual Size: 89.5 mm

"Winfield Scott." Bureau of Engraving and Printing proof vignette.

"Scott Entering the City of Mexico." Bureau of Engraving and Printing proof vignette.

ESTIMATED MARKET VALUES

BRONZED COPPER STRIKINGS

PF-63 to 65 (choice to gem):	$500 to $1,000
PF-60 to 62:	$400 to $500

No. 63

THE "PLEASURE OF THE WEED"
1860 "THE SMOKER" MEDALET

Rulau/Miller NY-426 to 429 • Estimated 100 to 200 known in brass (NY-429)

"The Smoker" has been a numismatic favorite for a long time. Although collectors of tokens know it well from Russell Rulau's *Standard Catalog of United States Tokens 1700–1900* and auction catalogs, most other numismatists are unaware of its existence. Whenever such a token is displayed at a convention, it often attracts buyers who never collected tokens before. This is the "I didn't know it existed, but now that I do, I want one!" syndrome.

The obverse depicts a happy old duffer holding a cigar and exhaling a cloud of smoke. Around the border is inscribed NO PLEASURE CAN EXCEED / THE SMOKING OF THE WEED. The obverse was designed and made for Joseph N.T. Levick (usually given as J.N.T. Levick), who was in the tobacco business at 904 Broadway. The token was struck in silver, brass (the style usually seen), copper, and white metal.

In the 1850s he lived in or near Philadelphia and was active in coin-collecting circles there, while serving as the chief bookkeeper for Freeman & Simpson. Apparently, he first visited New York City in 1859, in which year he attended auction sales, including Augustus B. Sage's Whitmore event in November.[84] Levick moved to New York later in the year, and in 1860 he seems to have commenced the issuing of tokens made by local engraver and diesinker George H. Lovett. These consisted of advertising cards as well as improbable mulings and different metals, most made for the numismatic market rather than to increase his tobacco business. He also collected early copper cents with a passion, building a remarkable display of rarities of the 1793 date.

Levick was a man of varied talents. In the early 1860s he was a banker, a dealer in government securities, and a broker at 44 Wall Street. Among his many activities, he also traded in gold and silver specie, which at the time sold at a sharp premium in terms of federal "greenback" notes. During the Civil War, as Lieutenant Levick of Sickle's Brigade, New York, he served as an observer in a reconnaissance balloon.

On December 14, 1865, he joined the American Numismatic and Archaeological Society and rapidly became active in its projects. On March 8, 1866, he made a proposal that eventually led to the publication of the *American Journal of Numismatics*.

Actual Size: 27.4 mm

Coins from Levick's collection appeared in many auction sales from 1859 to 1886.[85] When Levick died in 1908, his library was given to the American Numismatic Society.

"The Smokers" vignette, from a specimen book issued by the Treasury Department in 1876.

ESTIMATED MARKET VALUES	
BRASS STRIKINGS	
PF-63 to 65 (choice to gem):	$200 to $400
PF-60 to 62:	$150 to $200

No. 64

"NO SUBMISSION TO THE NORTH"
1860 WEALTH OF THE SOUTH TOKENS

Fuld obverse 511, Rulau and DeWitt various • 1,000 to 2,000 known across different varieties

"Wealth of the South"—the rhythmic phrase evokes the era of *Gone With the Wind*, "Dixie," and the plantation songs of Stephen Foster.

In 1860 in Cincinnati, diesinker Benjamin True prepared tokens that featured on the reverse a suite of agricultural products, with the inscription THE WEALTH OF THE SOUTH above, and a listing of four crops below: RICE TOBACCO SUGAR COTTON. This sturdy die was combined with at least five obverses inscribed NO SUBMISSION TO THE NORTH and dated 1860. These were advertised for sale in Southern newspapers that summer. The tokens were struck and issued by the shop of John Stanton. The Wealth of the South die is known today as Fuld-511, combined with the five No Submission dies plus various other political and commercial dies.

The sentiment "the wealth of the South" is explained in a December 1857 comment in *DeBow's Review*: "The wealth of the South is permanent and real, and that of the North fugitive and fictitious."[86] That is, the South drew its wealth from the land, which would forever endure. In contrast, the North took its wealth from banking, manufacturing, and related enterprises.

Around the time that these tokens were being made in Ohio and sold in the South, nominees were selected for the forthcoming presidential election. Accordingly, the Cincinnati diesinker made obverse dies portraying the four nominees—Stephen Douglas, Abraham Lincoln, John Bell, and John Breckinridge—and two reverse dies lettered PRESIDENTS HOUSE and showing a front view of the White House. The dies picturing certain candidates cracked, and new dies were made up.

Adding to the above dies, by now numbering over a dozen, were dies bearing the names of merchants or, in one instance, a steamship. The workmanship on all of the dies was excellent, and examination indicated that they emanated from a single source.

The maker of the political tokens was no fool, and after the presidential campaign ended, in November 1860, he combined the dies with others, creating many different rarities for the numismatic trade. Such pieces were instantly popular. Many die combinations were scarce enough to merit individual listings in auction catalogs soon after they were issued. The passion continues to the present day for collectors who have discovered this fascinating niche in numismatics. A token struck from the related PRESIDENTS HOUSE die is illustrated below.

Actual Size: 21.7 mm

Fuld 507/510A

Estimated Market Values	Commentary on Value
Typical Die Variety in Brass	*Commentary:* Some brass pieces are zinc plated and resemble silver. These prices are for the more readily available die combinations; other die combinations and metals are worth more, sometimes much more. Some examples are holed for suspension.
PF-63 to 65 (choice to gem): . . . . $700 to $1,250	
MS-60 to 62: . . . . $450 to $700	
EF-40 to AU-58: . . . . $300 to $450	
VF-20 to 35: . . . . $250 to $300	

No. 65

REWARD FOR SKILL AND INGENUITY
1824 FRANKLIN INSTITUTE AWARD MEDAL

Julian AM-17 to 22, Fuld RR.M.FR.1 to 11 • Silver: 150 to 200 known • Copper: 100 to 150 known

Bound up in every Franklin Institute award medal is the tale of some extraordinary individual who rose above the crowd to achieve something. These pieces, from dies engraved by Christian Gobrecht in 1825, and similar versions struck at the U.S. Mint through 1860, constitute a remarkable material record of American achievement in science, invention, and the mechanic arts.

Publisher Matthew Carey, Mint director Robert Patterson, geologist William Keating, and other prominent Philadelphians established the institute in 1824 as a memorial to Benjamin Franklin. Their aim was to preserve his writings and belongings, and perpetuate his quest to expand human knowledge through scientific inquiry. For their first competition in 1825, the directors laid out specific goals toward this end. They hoped to develop the Northeast's vast reserves of iron, and offered a gold medal to anyone who could produce 20 tons of iron from ore using anthracite coal as fuel, or 100 tons using bituminous coal. Silver medals could be earned by the best treatise on dying cloth, by American-made writing paper "equal to the best imported," or by the best method of preventing rot in ship timbers, among others. Individuals and companies displayed their efforts at annual public expositions in Philadelphia, concluded by elaborate award ceremonies. Apparently the gold-medal objectives were seldom met in the 19th century, for though some references to gold strikes can be found in Mint records, no gold examples from the Gobrecht dies are known today.

As the expositions grew in scope and importance, the Mint cut new dies for a second premium (1845). Through the years, dies with a fur-hat bust of Franklin on the obverse came into use (and gold strikes of this are known), along with dies for various special medals, such as the Elliot Cresson Medal (1848), the Scott Premium (1850s), and the gold Samuel Insull medal for "signal and eminent service in science" (1914). By the turn of the 20th century, the institute had abandoned large expositions and focused its efforts exclusively on the encouragement of scientists. In 2006, Franklin's tercentenary year, his thriving institute bestowed the Benjamin Franklin medals (instituted in 1998) and the Bower medals (1990), and awarded substantial cash endowments to pioneers joining the ranks of former recipients like Marie Curie, Albert Einstein, and Stephen Hawking.

Actual Size: 50 mm

Madame Schmidt featured the Franklin Institute medal in her advertising. (*Gurley's United States Centennial Guide and Gazette*, 1876)

ESTIMATED MARKET VALUES			
SILVER STRIKINGS		**COPPER STRIKINGS**	
PF-60 to 62:	$250 to $350	PF-60 to 62:	$125 to $200
PF-50 to 58:	$150 to $250	PF-50 to 58:	$75 to $125

NO. 66
ILLUSTRATING AMERICA'S DEFINING MOMENT
DECLARATION OF INDEPENDENCE MEDAL BY C.C. WRIGHT

Baker-53 • Washington reverse: bronze, 10 known; white metal, unique; copper electrotype, 10–15 known • Tablet reverse: silvered copper electrotype, unique; copper electrotype, 2 known; bronze, 2 known • Signature reverse, copper electrotype: 2 known

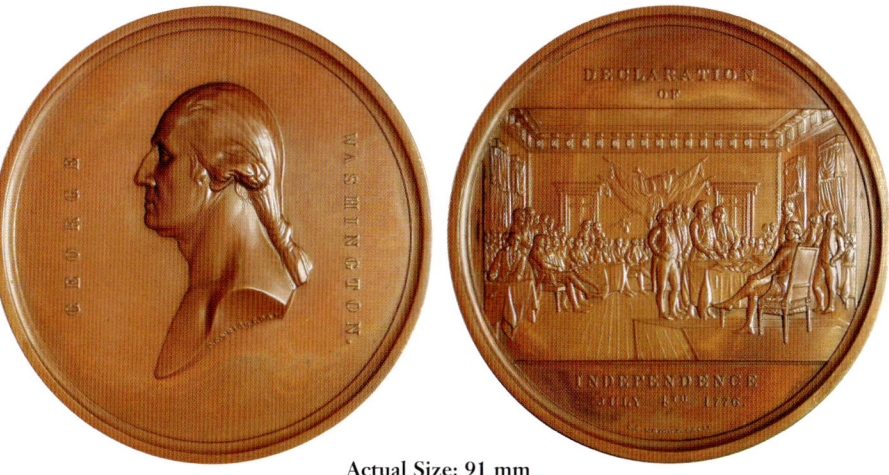

Actual Size: 91 mm

Charles C. Wright first gave artistic consideration to America's defining moment, the signing of the Declaration of Independence, in 1824. Joining Asher B. Durand, Peter Maverick, James B. Longacre, and other engravers, he contributed bookplates to John Sanderson's nine-volume *Biography of the Signers to the Declaration of Independence*, published between 1823 and 1827.

As a highly regarded diesinker in 1851, Wright returned to the theme of the Declaration with a spectacular 75th-anniversary commemorative medal based on John Trumbull's painting, *Declaration of Independence*, which was made for the U.S. Capitol rotunda. Wright paired this obverse die with a beautifully crafted reverse die bearing exact facsimile signatures of the founding fathers, and his inclusion of all 59 signatures was probably the reason this medal was struck at a huge 91 mm. Because examples of the signatures reverse are known only in electrotype versions made by George Segebaden of New York around 1880, it can be supposed that the huge die failed early in the striking operation, and that the electrotypes were made from struck medals.

Interestingly, Trumbull's painting is often misdescribed as the *signing* of the Declaration of Independence, but it in fact depicts the presentation by the "Committee of Five" (who drafted the document) to the Continental Congress. The five committee members standing at the table are, from left to right, John Adams, Roger Sherman, Robert R. Livingston, Thomas Jefferson (presenting the document), and Benjamin Franklin. The seated figure behind the table is John Hancock, president of the Continental Congress.

In 1854, Wright mated this same scene with an exquisite George Washington portrait based on the Houdon bust (Baker 53). Baker himself rated this medal as second in importance only to the Washington Before Boston medal (our No. 2).

A third reverse for the presentation scene is known. It shows a tablet with a 14-line inscription describing major events in American history prior to 1776. Above and below the tablet are scenes of ships and harbors.[87] Examples of this are quite rare as well.

John Trumbull's famous painting *Declaration of Independence*, the basis for Wright's design.

ESTIMATED MARKET VALUES	COMMENTARY ON VALUE
COPPER STRIKINGS	
PF-63 to 65 (choice to gem): . . . . $6,000 to $8,000 PF-60 to 62: . . . . $4,000 to $6,000	*Commentary:* Issued with a bronzed (chocolate-colored) surface. Electrotypes exist and are collectible in a price range of $300 to $500 in Proof-60 to 62.

No. 67

MORE POPULAR NOW THAN IN 1825
JOHN QUINCY ADAMS INDIAN PEACE MEDAL

Julian IP-11 to 13, Prucha Plate 42 • Silver originals: 76 mm, at least 14 known; 62 mm, 4 known; 51 mm, 3 known from auction records, none traced today

Actual Size: 76 mm

When Bureau of Indian Affairs chief Thomas L. McKenney first commissioned engraver Moritz Fürst to create a set of John Quincy Adams peace medal dies, he wrote, "I would prefer your taking the likeness, in person, to any you could get from any painting, or print." In May, 1825, the president obliged the artist with two half-hour sittings, and Fürst sketched his profile with a pencil. It was the beginning of a bumpy ride for everyone concerned with the medals' production, which turned out to be, in the words of John Quincy Adams Jr., "a tedious and disagreeable business."

Moritz Fürst had risen to prominence as an engraver of U.S. Mint medal dies during the War of 1812, when John Reich did not complete the order for congressional medals for the army and navy (see No. 43). In addition to the war medals, Fürst created a peace medal for president Monroe in 1819 which employed Reich's handshake reverse dies.

Knowing his past output was well received, Fürst was indignant when McKenney and members of the Mint staff rejected his first set of Adams portrait dies. McKenney told him, "The second size is esteemed a good likeness but the largest and the smallest are not so. There is too much projection on the point of the nose, the head and shoulders are too big, and look to belong to a very fat man.... [T]he impressions, I fear, will not do you credit." Fürst penned an immediate angry rebuttal: "[T]he folts [sic] you have been pleased to find with those two dies, it does not strike me so.... [P]erhaps the sizes of the larger and smaller deceive your judgment.... I beg you to consider that the great artists in the world are not able to make one likeness exact like the other ... specially in this art which is considered the most difficult of all the arts."

After more delay and wrangling, Fürst made some slight revisions to the dies, which McKenney accepted with reservation. The president was not pleased with the final result, calling Fürst a "wretched medalist and a half-witted man."[88] Nevertheless, the German went on to create peace medals for Jackson (1831), Van Buren (1837), and—to fill a gap in the series—John Adams (whose medals were struck in the 1850s). He returned to Munich in 1841,[89] and disappears from historical records as of 1847.

John Quincy Adams as featured in *The National Portrait Gallery*, Volume 4, 1840. Engraving by J.W. Paradise after a painting by Asher B. Durand.

Adams portrait from a Treasury Department book of vignettes presented in 1876.

ESTIMATED MARKET VALUES	
76 MM SILVER ORIGINAL STRIKINGS	
PF-40 to 58:	$15,000 to $30,000
VF-20 to 35:	$12,500 to 15,000
F-12:	$10,000 to $12,500

No. 68

CURE-ALL FROM BALTIMORE
HOUCK'S PANACEA COUNTERSTAMP

Rulau HT-140 to 145 • On silver dollars: 5 or 6 known • On half dollars: 200 to 300 known
• On other U.S. and foreign coins: a few known

Actual Size: Depends on host coin

Nineteenth-century America was flooded with patent medicines—pills, potions, and lotions that promised to cure any ailment known to mankind. Throughout the century, advertisements for these products were a mainstay for newspapers and magazines and often formed their greatest source of revenue except for local services and goods.

More than just a few of these have numismatic connections, including Drake's Plantation Bitters, French Cognac Bitters, and Ayer's Pills on encased postage stamps; Seward's Cough Cure, Atherton's Pills, French's Hair Restorative, and Cary's Cough Cure on Civil War store cards; and Egyptian Hair Coloring, Romaine's Crimean Bitters, and Perry's Pain Killer on scrip notes, for example.

Counterstamps advertising cures are a class of collectibles that has drawn much interest. Gold Pile Salve, G.G.G. & G.G.G.G., Shattuck's Water Cure, Kidder's Family Pills, and Houck's Panacea are but a short list. It is Houck's that forms the focus of No. 68 among the 100 Greatest.

Jacob Houck, born in Frederick, Maryland, came to Baltimore in 1828 and set up a dry-goods store at 121 West Baltimore Street, opposite Peale's Baltimore Museum (of which Rembrandt Peale was the curator). Although Peale's Philadelphia Museum (see No. 55) was best known, Charles Willson Peale's family operated similar businesses in Baltimore and New York City—all together, three leading centers of culture and the arts in the early 19th century.

By 1834, then at the corner of German and Hanover streets, Jacob was advertising Houck's Panacea, "prepared solely from vegetable matter," and said to be a veritable drugstore in a bottle, a cure for "dyspepsia, loss of appetite, indigestion, inflammation of the stomach, heartburn, diarrhoea, dysentery, piles, fistulas, obstructed menstruation, ague, smallpox, yellow fever, gout, rheumatism, venereal disease," and a long list of other ailments. A bottle of the stuff, about pint size and with an aqua tint to the glass, cost $1.50.

In the early 1830s, the largest U.S. silver coins regularly seen in circulation were half dollars, the style called the Capped Bust type by numismatists today. Silver dollars had not been struck since 1804 and were not often seen. Likely, tens of thousands of half dollars were stamped HOUCK'S / PANACEA / BALTIMORE, as implied by the survival of at least two or three hundred today. In addition, a lesser number of quarters and foreign silver coins were so marked.

An advertisement from *Matchett's Baltimore Director* for 1835.

ESTIMATED MARKET VALUES	COMMENTARY ON VALUE
ON HALF DOLLARS	
EF-40 to AU-58: . . . . $800 to $2,000	*Commentary:* The typical grade encountered is Very Fine.
VF-20 to 35: . . . . $450 to $800	

No. 69
Commissioned by Sansom in 1807
1807 "1776" American Beaver Medal

Betts-549, Baker-54, Julian CM-4 • Silver: 5 to 7 known • Copper: 125 to 175 known

Actual Size: 40 mm

Few American medals depict characters and themes so recognizable that no legends whatsoever are necessary. No anepigraphic medal is better known than the 1776-dated American Beaver medal depicting Benjamin Franklin and George Washington. Their portraits, engraved by John Reich, are shown jugate, or with overlapping profiles facing the same direction. Washington, depicted as a general, wears the epaulets of his rank; the portrait is a near duplicate of Reich's bust of Washington on the 1783-dated Washington CCAUS medal (see No. 71). The bust of Franklin shows him in everyday dress. Both images show the men as they led the nation in the American Revolution: Franklin as the citizen-politician and Washington as the military leader.

Struck as one of four completed issues in Joseph Sansom's planned "Medallic History of the American Revolution," the medal showcased Sansom's patriotic fervor. In an 1807 newspaper advertisement, Sansom described the image on the reverse of this medal as "The American Beaver nibbling at the Overshadowing Oak of the British Power on the Western Continent. Date—1776." To Americans of the era, the beaver represented perseverance, industriousness, teamwork, and other classic virtues associated with the national character. The beaver had been depicted on some issues of Continental Currency, together with the motto "Perseverando," or "by perseverance." No single man embodied these virtues in the eyes of popular America more than Benjamin Franklin. Sansom apparently agreed, as he muled the American Beaver reverse to both this Franklin obverse and another Franklin medal in his series, Betts-546.

Sansom's ambitious "Medallic History of the American Revolution" would end with the Franklin medals. Sansom, in a way, had doomed it through his own support of engraver John Reich. His recommendation to President Thomas Jefferson helped Reich land a job, thereby limiting his future potential to do private medal projects like Sansom's. The life of this medal, however, continued for years. The dies were restruck at the Mint for collectors well into the 19th century, with various rim breaks and the appearance of bronzed patinas helping to identify those later strikings. Silver medals were apparently struck only early on, though, as specimens in that metal remain very rare today. Bronze examples are relatively easy to obtain with some patience.

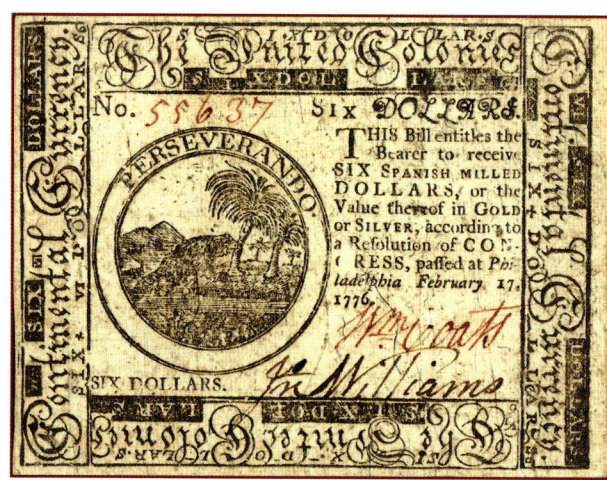

Continental Currency $6 note of February 2, 1776, with the motif that possibly inspired the American Beaver medal. In this instance a palm tree is at risk.

Estimated Market Values	
Strikings in Copper	
PF-63 to 65 (choice to gem):	$2,000 to $2,500
PF-60 to 62:	$1,750 to $2,000
PF-50 to 58:	$1,200 to $1,750

No. 70

HE TOOK PORTO BELLO "WITH SIX SHIPS ONLY"
1739–1741 ADMIRAL VERNON MEDALS

Betts-171 to 337 • 1,500 to 3,000 known across all varieties

In 1739, British politician Admiral Edward Vernon spoke to a rapt Parliament, ascribing cowardice and laziness to the administration of Sir Robert Walpole in its interactions with Spain. While Spain had been a rival in the 200 years since the first settlement of the New World, the previous decade had been marked by heightened friction in the Caribbean between the two powers. The tense interaction had reached critical mass a year earlier, when a British captain named Robert Jenkins displayed his pickled, preserved ear in Parliament and told the story of its severing at the blade of a Spanish sword aboard his own ship.

Vernon deftly capitalized on the anger that followed. When he declared in Parliament that he could take the Spanish port of Porto Bello in what today is Panama, a main staging area for trans-shipment of metals from South America, "with six ships of the line," most thought it was typical grandstanding. Vernon, however, let his actions speak for him: he arrived in the British island of Jamaica in October, and by November Porto Bello was in English hands. He had captured the entire city with just six ships. Vernon became an instant hero.

Among the many ways Vernon was feted, none were as diverse as the series of medals struck to celebrate his exploits. Birmingham's "toymakers"—metal workers who made miniatures and cheap souvenirs like medals—mass-produced these inexpensive brass baubles. Dies were often amateurishly executed, planchets were of indifferent quality, and the portraits bordered on cartoonish, but the pieces still sold well. By the large number of dies and mulings, many thousands must have been struck, and the wear seen on most specimens confirms their popularity as pocket pieces. Today, nearly all known are in brass (pinchbeck), although a few exist in white metal and silver.

As Vernon's campaign against the Spanish progressed through 1740 and 1741, the medalists of Birmingham found a wide variety of subjects for the Admiral Vernon medal series. Among the most interesting medals are those struck to commemorate the victory of Cartagena, Colombia, which never actually happened despite the presence of thousands of American troops—the first to fight in a foreign war. Among those who served was George Washington's half-brother Lawrence, who was so taken with Admiral Vernon that he named his new Virginia home *Mount Vernon* for him.

Actual Size: 37–38 mm

A 19th-century print depicting Washington's Mount Vernon home.

Estimated Market Values		Commentary on Value
Typical Variety in Brass		*Commentary:* Most examples are in lower grade and have poor eye appeal. These fit into the G to VG category given at bottom left.
EF-40 to AU-58:	$500 to $1,250	
VF-20 to 35:	$200 to $500	
F-12:	$100 to $200	
G-4 to VG-8:	$20 to $75	

No. 71

COMMANDER IN CHIEF OF THE ARMIES OF THE UNITED STATES
1783 WASHINGTON C.C.A.U.S. MEDAL

Baker-57 • 8 or 9 known in silver

It is a testament to the American experiment that a man who was born in a foreign country could arrive in the United States as a bonded servant, have his expertise recognized, make a lasting memorial to one president, and in so doing win a job from another president. This was the exact circumstance of John (Johann) Reich, the German-born engraver whose private contract work for Philadelphia merchant Joseph Sansom would help earn him a decade-long appointment at the U.S. Mint.

Washington's resignation as commander was likewise unique; stepping down from the pinnacle of power in a peaceful fashion was all but unheard of in world history. Washington's last circular, authored in 1783 as Commander in Chief of the Armies of the United States (or CCAUS), ended with his "last farewell to the cares of office, and all the employments of public life." King George III is said to have remarked that if Washington indeed yielded power peacefully, he would be "the greatest man in the world." It is sentiments such as these that yielded the Washington CCAUS medal.

Joseph Sansom envisioned his "Medallic History of the American Revolution" as a long series of medals, struck to commemorate every important battle and personage of the conflict. In a letter to Thomas Jefferson dated December 28, 1805, he projected "an intended series from the discovery of America to the retirement of Washington." He began his undertaking in 1805, but only four medals were ever issued, two of which shared the reverse of this one. All the dies were accomplished by John Reich. Joseph Sansom was eager to recommend the engraver to President Jefferson, who was given a specimen of each of Sansom's medals. (Jefferson's specimen of this medal remains at Monticello.) Sansom's plea to Jefferson to give Reich a permanent job at the U.S. Mint, which arrived on the same day in 1807 as a letter from Mint director Robert Patterson on the same subject, found an appreciative ear. Reich was appointed to the Mint staff less than a week later!

Reich signed the Washington CCAUS medal under the shoulder. The reverse, showing an eagle with an olive branch, commemorates the Treaty of Paris (which ended the American Revolution in 1783), along with the date of Washington's resignation as commander in chief. A detailed map of the United States, including the recently acquired Mississippi district, is seen below.

Actual Size: 40 mm

Specimens of this medal are known only in silver, including two worn specimens that were likely pocket pieces.

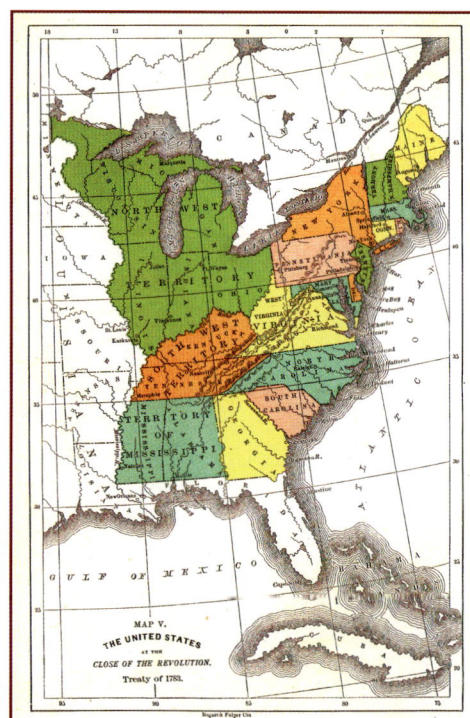

Map of the United States illustrating the boundaries as per the Treaty of 1783.

ESTIMATED MARKET VALUES	
SILVER STRIKINGS	
PF-60 to 62:	$25,000 to $30,000
PF-50 to 58:	$20,000 to $25,000

No. 72
Celebrating Washington's Birth and Acts
1792 Washington "Born Virginia" Medal

Baker-60, Breen-1238 and 1239 • 50 to 60 known (mostly Breen-1239)

Actual Size: 31 mm

The Washington Born Virginia copper has been numismatically famous for a long time. The obverse legend has the inscription GEO. WASHINGTON BORN VIRGINIA FEB. 11. 1732, while the reverse has a biographical inscription in 10 lines: GENERAL / OF THE / AMERICAN ARMIES / 1775. / RESIGNED / 1783. / PRESIDENT / OF THE / UNITED STATES / 1789. As with certain other Washington tokens and medals (for example, our No. 11), the inscriptions are educational to anyone examining the piece. The date of February 11, 1732, is correct for the old-style calendar then in use. Later, the calendar was revised and dates were moved forward by 11 days, yielding the February 22 date that is familiar to us now. Nearly all known examples show signs of circulation, often extensive.

The Washington Born Virginia copper (unlisted in Baker, but a variation of B-22) and the related Washington President 1792 copper (Baker-59), which shares the same reverse, were struck in Birmingham, England, by Obediah Westwood. The portrait closely resembles copper cents made on speculation in Birmingham, some examples of which were sent to America unsolicited for distribution among members of Congress, with the thought that this group, instead of establishing a federal mint, might want to obtain coins through an overseas contract. In addition, there is another reverse die for the Washington Born Virginia, with a similar inscription but with the letters arranged slightly differently. The most often encountered reverse is the second, with "I" (AMERICAN) over the "1" in the date 1775 (Baker-22), while the rarer style (four or five known) has the "I" under the "C" (reverse of Baker-59).

John Gregory Hancock (precocious teenaged prodigy according to some accounts, an engraver "with the character of a dissipated man" according to another[90]) is said to have cut the dies (also see No. 92). The plentiful 1791 Washington Large Eagle and Small Eagle cents have a related obverse portrait and are also attributed to Hancock and Westwood. Breen creates this scenario:

> The pieces with inscriptions on reverse and/or the BORN VIRGINIA obverse [are] medals, but as they were not fancy enough to please British token collectors, they were dumped into a keg and shipped to the USA.... In the 1790s federal cents were seldom seen, but the size of these Washingtons surely means the two passed side by side....[91]

Although this account is presented as fact, it is completely unsubstantiated. Moreover, the approximately 31 mm diameter of the Washington pieces does *not* match the 27 mm size of early federal cents.

Gutzon Borglum and superintendent inspecting work on the face (nose) of Washington on Mt. Rushmore. Borglum's profile is remarkably similar to that on the Born in Virginia copper. (Library of Congress, LC-USZ62-3648)

Estimated Market Values	
MS-60 to 62:	$15,000 to $25,000
EF-40 to AU-58:	$10,000 to $15,000
VF-20 to 35:	$7,000 to $10,000
F-12:	$5,000 to $7,000

Commentary on Value

Commentary: On circulated examples the center area of the reverse is usually worn away, as this area bulged outward.

No. 73
"PEACE AND COMMERCE"
THE DIPLOMATIC MEDAL

Julian CM-15, Loubat-10 • 50 to 75 known in copper (copy dies)

Long before the diplomatic medal was struck in Paris in 1792, Native Americans had been used to symbolize America. In 17th-century world atlases, cartographers placed drawings of women with appropriate features and costumes on each continent, and North America was invariably represented as a native princess carrying a bow and arrow, and often tinted a fire-engine red.[92] For the U.S. diplomatic medal (bearing the date 1776, but ordered in 1790 and first struck in 1792), Parisian engraver Augustin Dupré employed an Indian princess to represent the United States. He augmented her feathered skirt and headdress with flowing classical drapery, and his princess extends a cornucopia as a peace offering to Europe, represented by the god Mercury. With her empty hand, she indicates the wealth of goods America has to offer, and the legend PEACE AND COMMERCE indicates the diplomatic direction she wishes to pursue.

The medal was struck a few times in gold for presentation to certain European diplomats. Thomas Jefferson, in Paris in 1790, was instrumental in obtaining the first few strikes of this medal in gold. An April entry from George Washington's diary recalls the thinking behind the medal:

Actual Size: 73 mm

> Fixed with the Secretary of State on the present which (according to the custom of other Nations) should be made to Diplomatic characters when they return from that employment in this Country and this was a gold Medal, suspended to a gold Chain—in ordinary to be of the value of about 120 or 130 Guineas. Upon enquiry into the practice of other Countries, it was found, that France generally gave a gold Snuff-box set with diamonds; & of differt. costs; to the amount, generally, to a Minister Plenipotentiary of 500 Louisdores—That England usually gave to the same grade 300 guineas in Specie—And Holld. a Medal & Chain of the value of, in common, 150 or 180 Guineas the value of which to be encreas'd by an additional weight in the chain when they wished to mark a distinguished character. The Reason why a medal & Chain was fixed upon for the American present, is, that the die being once made the Medals could at any time be struck at very little cost, & the Chain made by our own artizans, which (while the first should be retained as a memento) might be converted into Cash.[93]

Soon after the gold strikings, the dies were lost. A pair of white metal clichés, or trial impressions from the original dies, is shown here. In 1876 the Philadelphia Mint began issuing copies from newly made dies engraved by Charles Barber.

Britain and her colonies duke it out in this anonymous American etching of 1776. (Courtesy of The Lewis Walpole Library, Yale University)

Estimated Market Values
Striking From 19th-Century Copy Dies
PF-63 to 65 (choice to gem): . . . . $400 to $600
PF-60 to 62: . . . . $250 to $400

No. 74
ONLY OFFICIAL C.S.A. MEDAL
STONEWALL JACKSON MEDAL OF 1864

Bertram MBR 863W6-7901 • 200 to 300 known in white metal

Remarkably, only one Confederate commemorative medal was struck during the entire Civil War, and it was to honor the South's short-lived military genius, General Thomas Jonathan "Stonewall" Jackson. As a corps commander of Robert E. Lee's Army of Northern Virginia, Jackson orchestrated the successful Shenandoah Valley Campaign in 1862, as well as what is considered Lee's greatest victory, the battle of Chancellorsville. Ironically, Jackson was hit by friendly fire during that May 1863 engagement, and died a few days later.

A prominent Georgian named Charles Augustus Lafayette Lamar commissioned Jackson's medal. Son of wealthy Savannah banker Gazaway Bugg Lamar (who was the intermediary when the CSA ordered paper money from the National Bank Note Co. of New York before the war), Charles served as director of his father's bank and a number of important Savannah businesses.[94] An avid secessionist and slavery proponent, Lamar purchased the schooner-yacht *Wanderer* in 1858, outfitted her as a slaver, and began shipping people from Africa's Slave Coast to be sold at Jekyll Island. There was a federal law against importing slaves, and in November 1859 Lamar was charged, tried, fined $500, and confined to house arrest for 30 days. In 1862, he joined the Confederate army and captained the Lamar Rangers, a mounted rifle unit.[95] He traveled to France on official business for the state of Georgia in 1863, and there heard that Jackson had fallen at Chancellorsville. He commissioned the medal from Parisian Armand Auguste Caqué, engraver to Emperor Napoleon III, but returned home before the order was completed. Lamar was killed in Columbus, Georgia, during Union general James Wilson's April 6, 1865, attack on that city.

The 1,000-plus 50 mm white-metal medals, meanwhile, could not enter the port of Savannah due to its capture by Union forces, but made it to Wilmington, North Carolina, some time in 1864. Lamar's cotton-business associate, Antoine Poullain of Augusta, received and stored them on behalf of Lamar's widow until after the war. The case of medals eventually became submerged in Lamar's Savannah cotton warehouse. In 1894, thirty years too late to award to members of Jackson's "Stonewall Brigade" as originally intended, they were discovered and donated to the Ladies' Auxiliary of the Confederate Veterans Association, which sold them for $1 apiece to benefit disabled veterans.

Actual Size: 50.3 mm

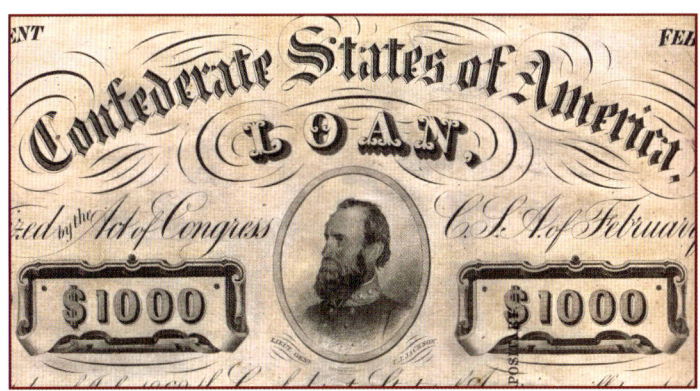

Authentic portrait of "Stonewall" Jackson on $1,000 CSA bond (detail), variety Criswell-122. Issued February 20, 1865, late in the life of the Confederacy.

Estimated Market Values	Commentary on Value
MS-60 to 62: .... $400 to $600 EF-40 to AU-58: .... $250 to $400	*Commentary:* Like as not, the typical example bears scuffs and marks from careless handling.

No. 75
Display at the Philadelphia Mint
1860 Washington Cabinet Medal

Baker-326 and 326A, Julian MT-23 • Silver: 25 to 50 known • Copper: 200 to 400 known

One of the most impressive and numismatically oriented of all medals struck at the Philadelphia Mint in the 19th century is this 59.8 mm piece, struck from dies by assistant Mint engraver Anthony C. Paquet. The date was February 22, 1860, and the occasion for its presentation was the dedication of the Washington Cabinet of Medals as part of the Mint Collection. Specimens in copper and silver were made available for sale to the public.

The obverse presents the profile of President George Washington, designed after the famous bust by Jean Antoine Houdon—the image found on nearly all Washington tokens and medals issued during this era by the Mint as well as by private medalists. Years later, in 1932, it would be adapted for use on the Washington quarter dollar.

The reverse features the Washington Cabinet and illustrates a bust of Washington atop a four-sided, slightly pyramidal display case. Some 35 medals and tokens are shown on the side of the case facing the viewer, and another 20 are on the side angling away to the right—giving this "medal about medals" a special niche in numismatics and making it a longtime favorite.

On June 4, 1853, James Ross Snowden was confirmed as the new director of the Mint, after the death of Judge Thomas Pettit, who had served in the position for less than two months. Perhaps more than any of his predecessors in the post, Snowden developed an interest in numismatics. Under his watch, in 1858 the sales of Proof coins and sets as well as patterns were vastly expanded.

In 1859, when contemplating the Mint Cabinet display of coins, which had been inaugurated in June 1838, Snowden noticed that it contained only four or five medals depicting George Washington. Upon inquiry to other numismatists he learned that at least 60 varieties were known to them. Information was scarce, and to that point there were no generally used reference books on either medals or coins to which he could refer.

With a passion, Snowden set about adding pieces to the cabinet, trading Proof coins, freshly made restrikes, and other

Actual Size: 59.8 mm

coins for them. By 1860, he had gathered 138 specimens. The Washington exhibit in the Mint Cabinet remained an attraction long thereafter. In 1861, Snowden's 203-page book, *Medallic Memorials of Washington*, was published. Illustrated by fine steel engravings, it was widely acclaimed in its time.

The Mint Cabinet as it appeared in the 1880s. Today, the Washington Cabinet specimens are in the Smithsonian Institution. (Engraving by D.A. Schiller, 1885)

Estimated Market Values	
Silver Strikings	
PF-63 to 65 (choice to gem):	$600 to $800
PF-60 to 62:	$400 to $600
EF-40 to 58:	$250 to $400
Copper Strikings	
PF-63 to 65 (choice to gem):	$200 to $300
PF-60 to 62:	$125 to $200
EF-40 to 58:	$75 to $125

Commentary on Value

Commentary: Copper strikings have bronzed surfaces as made. Most surviving pieces in both medals are choice to gem Proof.

No. 76

GREGOR MACGREGOR ISSUE
1817 AMELIA ISLAND "GREEN CROSS" MEDAL

Rulau Fla-10, BHM-957 • 15 to 20 known in bronze

Actual Size: 33 mm

If Gregor MacGregor (1786–1845) had one great guiding force in life, it was his hatred of Spain—although some would suggest his search for glory was a close second. Inspired by the battles for independence in South America, but perhaps even more by the chance to make a name for himself, he left Scotland in 1811, already a veteran officer of the Black Watch. He quickly rose to a position of stature in the army of Simon Bolivar; by 1816, he was a general. He married Bolivar's niece, returned to Great Britain, and began the first of his schemes against Spanish power—schemes that, if successful, would have the added benefit of making him a rich man.

He arrived in the United States in 1817, when optimism about American power ran high. MacGregor appealed to the contemporary hope for further expansion and promised profits to those who would back him: he would capture Spanish Florida, win the residents over to "the protection of wholesome laws," and annex the province for the United States. His idea was unpopular in Philadelphia, but played better in the South. More than $100,000 was raised, and he was able to outfit ships in Charleston and pay troops in Savannah.

The "invasion" occurred on June 29, 1817, as given on the medal. His 55 men took the small Spanish fort on Amelia Island, Florida, without opposition and sent the Spanish troops back to St. Augustine. The tiny spit of land, north of modern Jacksonville, had few other residents. He unveiled a "Proclamation of the Liberating Army" and raised a flag, the Green Cross, which is copied on the obverse of the medal. The peripheral legend translates to "Under the Leadership of MacGregor, the Liberty of Florida."

As Laurence Brown notes in *British Historical Medals*, "His occupation was relatively short-lived since he was turned out by naval and military forces sent by the president of the United States after some six months." The official orders to the U.S. troops in Charleston were to "remove from Amelia Island the persons who have lately taken possession thereof . . . to the great annoyance of the United States."

MacGregor returned home and planned his next conquest, this time of modern-day Nicaragua. After raising funds and being introduced to King George IV as "His Serene Highness Gregor I, Prince of Poyais," he arrived with 200 settlers in a mosquito-infested jungle. Most died, but MacGregor escaped to France, where he began another colonizing expedition. After a prison stay, he retired to Venezuela, where he was buried with military honors in 1839. This medal was likely struck as a present to investors in the two adventures that followed his Florida "conquest."

Artist's depiction of the Green Cross design. The emblem was displayed on the fifth flag to fly over Amelia Island, which would become known as "the isle of eight flags."

Estimated Market Values	
EF-40 to AU-58:	$2,500 to $3,500
VF-20 to 35:	$2,000 to $2,500

No. 77
CALIFORNIA GOLD RUSH DRUGGIST
1850S J.L. POLHEMUS COUNTERSTAMPS

Rulau/Miller Calif-1 and 2, Brunk P-563 • On mostly U.S. and foreign silver coins: 150 to 250 known • On $20 coin: 3 known

The silver and gold coins counterstamped by Gold Rush druggist John L. Polhemus were scarcely known to collectors a generation ago. Then on December 14, 2000, in a catalog guest-written by Q. David Bowers, the art auction house Christie's offered an 1855-S double eagle with such a stamp, recovered from the lost treasure aboard the SS *Central America* (see No. 49). The price soared to $48,300 amid much excitement, and the fame of Polhemus was assured.

It seems that John L. Polhemus, born in 1825 in Ohio, spent much of his early life in Wyckoff (also spelled Wykoff), New Jersey. Eliza Catherine Van Voorhies lived in the same community and later became his wife. Imbued with an adventurous spirit, the young couple moved to Wisconsin, then Michigan, then Ohio, where John caught Gold Rush fever. He went to New York City and departed for the land of fortune on Tuesday, January 26, 1849, aboard the German ship *Orpheus* under Captain Freeman.[96] Arriving in San Francisco, he traveled to Sacramento and set up in business as a druggist. Eliza joined him in due course. His first location was across from the Magnolia Saloon. In December 1850 he moved to the address used on his counterstamps.

In 1850s California there was no paper money in circulation. Indeed, the state constitution forbade its use. Silver and gold coins were the mainstay of commerce. Seeking to advertise his business, Polhemus stamped coins ranging from dimes (which barely accommodated his imprint) to double eagles with the inscription J.L. POLHEMUS / [mortar and pestle emblem] / DRUGGIST / 180 J. ST. COR. 7TH / SACRAMENTO CAL. Quarters were his favorite denomination.[97]

One can envision Polhemus behind his counter, stamping all of the coins that came his way, stopping now and then to sell products, which included his own patent medicines (J.L. Polhemus Sarsaparilla Bitters and J.L. Polhemus Stomach Bitters) as well as fireproof paint, kerosene, toilet articles, "perfectly pure" bottled water, sealing wax, and an extensive line of pills and potions. By

Actual Size: Depends on host coin

1857 his counterstamps were familiar in circulation throughout the state. In August of that year, a handful were among the thousands of gold double eagles and other coins and hundreds of freshly cast gold ingots that were taken aboard the SS *Sonora* on its voyage from San Francisco to Panama and ultimately placed aboard the ill-fated *Central America*.

The J.L. Polhemus counterstamp was always the same size, regardless of the size of the host coin. To demonstrate, the coins illustrated in our "place of honor" are repeated here at actual size (for the 1856 Liberty Seated dime, at left, 17.9 mm; for the 1850 British half crown, at right, 30.5 mm).

Estimated Market Values	Commentary on Value
On a Silver Coin **EF-40 to AU-58:** $300 to $600 **VF-20 to 35:** $225 to $300 **F-12:** $125 to $225	*Commentary:* Counterstamps are known on a wide variety of foreign and American coins, the latest ones usually Liberty Seated coins struck at the San Francisco Mint. A counterstamp on a $20 double eagle sold for more than $48,000.

No. 78

KEEPSAKE FOR MEMBERS
1808 WASHINGTON BENEVOLENT SOCIETY MEDAL

Baker-327, Julian RF-23 • 100 to 125 known

Actual Size: 42.3 mm

The 1808-dated medal of the Washington Benevolent Society observes the year that the New York City branch was opened. The obverse illustrates the standing goddess Liberty, with a liberty cap on a pole held in her right hand, placing a wreath upon a portrait bust of George Washington. The reverse is drawn in concept from the parable of the Good Samaritan, except with a temple as the backdrop instead of a roadside in the Holy Land.

The obverse bears the initial R, for John Reich, a German immigrant who did extensive medal and coin die work of a high order of excellence for the Philadelphia Mint from 1800 to 1817. He had hoped to gain the post of engraver, but he never rose above assistant, working under John Scot. Reich was also an accomplished engraver of bank-note plates in the private sector. Today he is best remembered for the Capped Bust design inaugurated on half dollars and half eagles in 1807 and continued in use through the 1830s. The John Reich Collectors Society, a numismatic special interest group, bears his name.

The Washington Benevolent Society medals have been popular for a long time. Augustus B. Sage's June 1859 fixed-price catalog, one of the earliest such lists published in America, offered such a piece, described as "Bust of Washington on a pedestal. *Fine and very rare*" and priced at $5. Ever since, these medals have been a standard item for any cabinet of Washingtoniana.

The Good Samaritan motif and the name of the organization notwithstanding, the Benevolent Society was more political than benevolent or altruistic. The tenets of the Federalist Party served as the guidelines for the group, which had branches in various cities. Political and patriotic orations by Daniel Webster, Gulian C. Verplanck, and others were the order of the day, especially on the fourth of July. Pro-Americanism was a focus, with emphasis on the improvement of the election process and resistance to the influence of foreigners and distant countries. The benefits of democracy for its members were showcased, including employment, fair laws, and health care. In the year that the New York branch opened, relations were tense with England and France, and the group maintained a strong stance for American rights while many politicians and others were wavering. The Washington Benevolent Society continued for some years afterward, but its importance ebbed after about 1820.

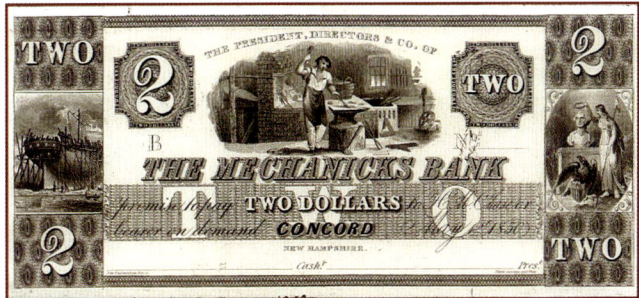 

The apotheosis or honoring of Washington motif appears on the 1850 illustrated $2 note of the Mechanics Bank of Concord, New Hampshire, near the margin.

Detail of a $20 note issued by the Franklin Bank of New Jersey, Jersey City, in 1827.

ESTIMATED MARKET VALUES	
PF-63 to 65 (choice to gem):	$2,000 to $3,500
PF-60 to 62:	$1,200 to $2,000
PF-50 to 58:	$900 to $1,200

No. 79
AUDREY MUNSON MODELS FOR AITKEN
1915 PAN-PACIFIC EXPOSITION MEDAL

Hibler-Kappen 400 • Silver: 100 to 200 known • Brass: 500 to 800 known • Gilt brass: 300 to 500 known

Today the official medal for the 1915 Panama-Pacific International Exposition is well known to specialists, but for most numismatists this medallic sculpture by Robert Ingersoll Aitken (1878–1949) exists in the shadow of the famous octagonal and round $50 gold coins he designed for the same event. It was not always so. In the January 1918 issue of *The Numismatist* Farran Zerbe, who headed the Department of Coins and Medals at the event, took issue with the artistry of the $50 gold coins, noting:

> With everything so favorable there were great expectations, hence the greater the disappointment. Robert Aitken, deservedly noted sculptor that he is, had and lost his opportunity. Had Mr. Aitken essayed to place the class of art and relief on the $50 gold pieces that he gave the souvenir medal . . . it would have been more fitting.

Actual Size: 38 mm

Art is in the eye of the beholder, and not everyone would agree today. The fame of the $50 coins has achieved heroic proportions. However, by any standard Aitken's official medal ranks high in the pantheon of medallic art of the early 20th century and richly deserves its niche in the 100 Greatest. As the Pan-Pacific showcased more sculptures, paintings, and works of art than any American world's fair before or since, it can be inferred that his medal is all the more important for its context.

Audrey Munson (1891–1996) was the model for the figures on the reverse. In 1916 she appeared in the Thanhouser Company film *Inspiration*, the first American motion picture showing frontal nudity.[98]

For the fair Aitken also created the *Fountain of the Earth*, a monumental production involving many figures, including a colossal Hermes with outstretched arms grasping reptiles—"suggestive of earliest forms of earth life, from the mouths of which streams of water are thrown all over the globe; steam clouds shrouded by night." Aitken's bust of William Howard Taft and statue of Michelangelo were located near the Palace of Fine Arts. His sculptures of heroic proportions, *Earth*, *Air*, *Fire*, and *Water*, were displayed in the sunken gardens.

The fair was situated on 635 acres in Golden Gate Park. Its themes were the rebuilding of San Francisco after the 1906 earthquake and fire, and the celebration of the 1914 opening of the Panama Canal. Open from February 20 to December 4, 1915, it attracted about 19 million visitors. It was one of most successful such events ever held.

Commemorative $50 Pan-Pacific gold coin (actual size 44 mm) by Aitken, not lauded in its time, but very popular today.

The Palace of Fine Arts at the Exposition, where commemorative coins and medals were sold. Today this is the only building surviving from the fair. (2001 photograph)

Audrey Munson in the 1916 film *Inspiration*, about the life of an artist's model.

ESTIMATED MARKET VALUES

SILVER STRIKINGS		BRONZE AND GILT BRASS STRIKINGS	
MS-63 to 65 (choice to gem):	$150 to $350	MS-63 to 65 (choice to gem):	$80 to $100
MS-60 to 62:	$150 to $175	MS-60 to 62:	$40 to $80

No. 80

EARLY AMERICAN USE OF LIBERTY POLE AND CAP
1746 ANNAPOLIS TUESDAY CLUB MEDAL

Betts-383 • Gilt silver: 4 known • Copper: 1 known

One of the rarest objects in our top 100, the membership medal of the Tuesday Club is a piece that revives the memory of life in the beautiful port city of Annapolis at the middle of the 18th century. On the Severn River near its entrance to the Chesapeake, the small village first settled in 1649 became the colonial capital in 1694. By the time the Tuesday Club formed in 1746, the city had become an economic hub of Maryland with a population surpassing 25,000. An 1886 essay in *Frank Leslie's Popular Monthly*[99] recalls the era:

Actual Size: 43.9 mm

> In the halcyon days of the colonies, when tobacco returned a handsome profit, fashion, wit and learning found a centre here. The wealthy planters built substantial and embellished mansions framed in verdure, and with grounds terraced to the water, where their barges and boats, manned by liveried servants, were ready for ceremonial visits or exciting sport. . . . The presence of official authority, the sharp definition of rank, and the existence of Negro slavery gave an aristocratic tone to society. . . . At the "Tuesday Club" were gathered the wits and classical scholars, who mixed their punch with Latin quotations, and conducted themselves with state and ceremony, all of which was duly recorded and illustrated.

The group held biweekly meetings called *sederunts* in each other's homes, applying a set of exacting but lighthearted laws. One law made it mandatory to toast the health of the members' wives and ladies, "immediately after supper and before any other toasts or healths go round." Another, called the "Gelastic Law," stated:

> That if any subject of what nature soever be discussed, which levels at party matters, or the administration of the government of this province, or be disagreeable to the Club, no answer shall be given thereto, but after such discourse is ended, the Society shall laugh at the member offending, in order to divert the discourse.[100]

In May of 1748, the members authorized the striking of a gilded silver keepsake that holds the record as America's earliest club medal. Dr. Alexander Hamilton of Scotland, a founding member who later would write the 1,900-page *History of the Tuesday Club*, created the design. The medal's legends indicate what was most important to the group: CONCORDIA RES PARVAE CRESCUNT roughly translates to "happily joining like-thinking fellows," and LIBERTAS ET NATALE SOLUM means "liberty and homeland only." The "Carolus Cole" of the obverse legend was Charles Cole, the club's first president. The dies were cut in London, possibly by John Kirk (according to C. Wyllys Betts), at a cost of 6-1/2 guineas. The Tuesday Club disbanded in 1756.

ESTIMATED MARKET VALUES	COMMENTARY ON VALUE
EF-40 to AU-58: . . . . $40,000 to $60,000	*Commentary:* In March 2001, a gilt-silver specimen sold in the Lucien LaRiviere offering for $57,500, and in May 2006 the unique copper example from the John J. Ford Jr. collection, Part XIV, fetched $46,000.

No. 81
CURRENCY OF RATIONING
1944 O.P.A. RED AND BLUE POINT TOKENS
Many thousands known

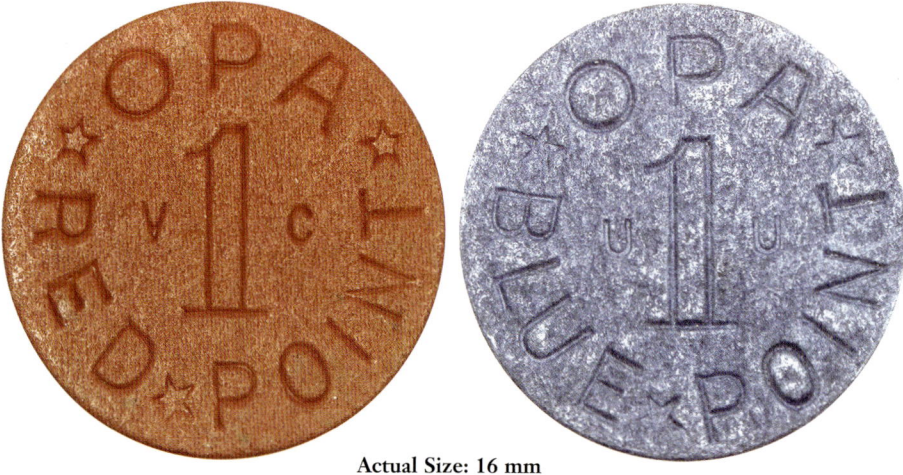

Actual Size: 16 mm

Some readers may be surprised to see the humble little vulcanized-fiber ration tokens of the U.S. Office of Price Administration (OPA) in our top 100. On reflection, their placement made sense to our voters, as nostalgia pieces from the most cataclysmic event of the 20th century—the Second World War. Every man, woman, and child not employed by the U.S. military overseas was familiar with this currency of sacrifice in the closing years of the war.

America began supplying war matériel to its European allies in 1939, but did not commit troops to the conflict until the formal declaration of war after the Japanese surprise attack on Pearl Harbor in on December 7, 1941. From that point on, the immensity of the supply mission made conservation of metals necessary, and producers of all kinds of tokens were asked to switch from copper and brass to fiber, vulcanite, cardboard, or wood. (The Mint made its own effort with its zinc-coated steel cent of 1943.) Commodities such as coffee, sugar, and gasoline were also in short supply and were the first items to be rationed under a coupon system in 1942. By early 1943, the OPA had switched to a point system, assigning ration point values to a greatly expanded list of goods. Every household was allotted a booklet of ration stamps commensurate with its estimated monthly need. Citizens still paid for their goods using U.S. paper money and received U.S. coins in change; but now, at the same time, they turned in their ration stamps and received tokens in change.

The OPA tokens were slightly smaller than a dime and came in two colors: blue for canned and processed foods, and red for meat, fish, dairy products, and cooking oils. By the end of the war in 1945, 1.75 billion red and 1 billion blue tokens had been made by Cincinnati's Osborne Register Company, a leading national distributor of transit, gambling, amusement, and sales-tax tokens since 1920, with antecedents dating back to the 19th century. Each token was worth one point, and had two letters stamped on its obverse. These letter pairings had no relation to what could be purchased, but were a security coding used to identify and track token shipments. The blue tokens offer a possible 24 letter combinations to collect. The red points offer 30, and the significant rarity of the series is the red MV.

A ration poster from World War II.

ESTIMATED MARKET VALUES	COMMENTARY ON VALUE
EF-40 to AU-58: .... 25¢ to $5	*Commentary:* The significant rarity, the red MV is worth about $100 to $200 in EF-40 to 58. It is a testimony to the diversity of numismatics that an item listed among the 100 Greatest Tokens and Medals can be purchased for 25¢! (Also see No. 82.)

No. 82
"BLOOD MONEY"
SALES-TAX TOKENS

Listed in token references for individual states • Availability ranges from very common to rare, depending on variety

Actual Size: 24 mm

As seen during the Hard Times era, the Civil War, and World War II, national crises could result in token issues. The most devastating economic emergency in U.S. history, the Great Depression of the 1930s, generated tokens as well. After the infamous stock market crash of 1929, banks closed, agricultural prices and manufacturing wages fell, and by 1932 more than 13 million American workers, with 30 million dependents, were unemployed. Nearly every U.S. citizen was living in greatly reduced circumstances, and many states found it necessary to support their residents with employment programs and welfare assistance. To fund these programs, they instituted general taxes on sales, sometimes calling them "emergency relief taxes" or "public welfare taxes."

Many of the assessed tax rates resulted in extra amounts being paid on small purchases, due to rounding up of fractional amounts less than 1¢. Yet in those difficult times shoppers resisted paying fractions of cents they did not owe, and merchants did not want to be stuck for the difference. In Kewanee, Illinois, the Chamber of Commerce came up with the solution: fractional-cent tokens that merchants could give out as change, and would accept in payment of sales tax. The idea caught on, and other municipalities began issuing local "provisional" sales-tax tokens or paper tax scrip. This unofficial currency concerned state governments, and 12 of them decided to outlaw it and issue official state sales-tax tokens. These were Alabama, Arizona, Colorado, Illinois, Kansas, Louisiana, Mississippi, Missouri, New Mexico, Oklahoma, Utah, and Washington. In Utah, the tokens were popularly known as "blood money" because it was Governor H.H. Blood who had instituted the tax.

Most states made a concerted effort to ensure that their tokens did not look like coins. They made some of colored vulcanized fiber, and placed holes in the center of metal issues. Missouri created a series made out of cardboard. Because these tokens come from a dozen states in various denominations, there are numerous issues for collectors to pursue today. The use of sales-tax tokens ended with the Depression. Many states specified a time period during which they could be redeemed for cash, but it is estimated that fewer than 40% of the total populations were ever turned in.

Unlike the Arizona and Washington State sales-tax tokens (top and middle, respectively), the tokens for some states had identical obverse and reverse designs. The Louisiana (bottom left) and Colorado (bottom right) tokens were among the latter.

COMMENTARY ON VALUE

Commentary: Values vary widely, depending on the location, age, composition, and rarity of each token. Many are available for 25¢ to $5 each in grades from EF to Uncirculated.

No. 83

MERRIAM'S CLASSIC WITH DOG'S HEAD
"GOOD FOR A SCENT" CIVIL WAR TOKEN

Fuld MA-115-D and E • MA-115-D: 1 known in copper, 10 to 15 known in white metal, 5 to 7 known in brass
• MA-115-E: 250 to 400 known in copper

Humor never goes out of style, and when a bit of fun is reflected on a token or medal it is cause for numismatists first to take notice, and then to want to own one. How else can we account for "The Smoker" (No. 63) and "We All Have Our Hobbies" (No. 47)?

During the Civil War quite a few diesinkers produced tokens that looked and spent like cents, but, as only Uncle Sam could make official cents, they were denominated something else. NOT ONE CENT was a popular inscription. Taking the cake, however, was the punning "Not One Scent" token issued by Joseph H. Merriam in Boston.[101] The obverse pictured a dog's head with this inscription surrounding it. These were immensely popular in their own time, and today they are even more so. In the 1869 *American Stamp Mercury and Numismatist*, "Nemo" (probably Charles Chaplin) contributed this:

Actual Size: 19 mm

> We have a "copperhead" issued by our friend Merriam, of Brattle Square. This medal bears a dog's head, with the inscription, "Good for a scent," and is the "head scenter," both in design and execution, of all the mushroom crop of tokens that sprang up during the latter part of the war, nine-tenths of which are a disgrace to the die-sinking profession. . . .

sutlers' tokens had removable circular sections that could be replaced with others to change a part of the description, such as the denomination! The same modular inserts for the denominations of 5, 10, 25, and 50 were used for the C.F. Tuttle's Restaurant series (Fuld MA-115-G) as well as tokens for Harvey Lewis, sutler of the 23rd Massachusetts Regiment (David Schenkman's MA-B).

Merriam was in business in Boston from 1850 to about 1870. He made punches for letters and numbers, created dies, and also sold a line of seal presses (a desktop lever device that embossed corporate seals or other devices on paper). His work reflects exceptional artistry and skill, and the devices on his dies are unusually boldly impressed. Beginning in 1860 he was caught up in the passion for medalets for the numismatic trade. As did George H. Lovett, he combed magazines and newspapers for timely subjects, including the famous 1860 Heenan-Sayers boxing match and the visit of the Prince of Wales to the United States.

Merriam also may have been the first U.S. token manufacturer to make extensive use of *modular dies*, as noted by one of the authors (Bowers).[102] The dies Merriam employed for Civil War tokens and

One of several tokens issued by Merriam for C.F. Tuttle's Restaurant, each with a common obverse die and with the reverse from a common modular or compound die (called a *slip die* in the trade today), in which plugs for the denominations 5, 10, and 50 were inserted.

ESTIMATED MARKET VALUES	COMMENTARY ON VALUE
MA-115-E, STRIKINGS IN COPPER	
MS-63 to 65 (choice to gem): . . . . $1,000 to $1,500	*Commentary:* While this is not a rare token, its great popularity has made it quite valuable.
MS-60 to 62: . . . . $700 to $1,000	
EF-40 to AU-58: . . . . $400 to $700	
VF-20 to 35: . . . . $300 to $400	

NO. 84
INAUGURATING THE J.A. BOLEN SERIES
1861 PIONEER BASE BALL CLUB MEDAL

Musante JAB-1, Rulau Mass-528 and 529 • Copper: 75 struck • Tin: 125 struck

Actual Size: 31.6 mm

The Pioneer Base Ball Club medal, struck in 1861, is generally regarded as the first medal issued to commemorate America's national game, although a baseball scene formed a part of the Indian peace medal of 1857 for President James Buchanan, a design continued on Lincoln peace medals. John Adams Bolen, of Springfield, Massachusetts, cut the dies to the order of Charles A. Vinton, a numismatist and a clerk at the local Massasoit House hotel. Bolen stated that he made 75 in copper and 125 in white metal (actually tin).

The obverse depicts a uniformed player at bat, standing on grass in Hampden Park, where home games were played. The Pioneer Base Ball Club played its first games in 1857, but was not officially organized until April 30, 1858, the date on the reverse of the medal. At the time the club had about 40 members. The players acquitted themselves in fine form, and by autumn 1860 had become the champions in the western part of the state, adding to their success in October by beating the Boston Bowdoins, champions of eastern Massachusetts.

Although the Pioneer Base Ball Club medal is the earliest piece positively attributed to Bolen today, he was listed as a "die sinker" for the first time in the May 1859 *Springfield Directory*. By the early 1860s, in time to ride the ebb tide of the medalet craze, he was into diesinking full swing. His products were numerous and varied. From an artistic viewpoint, most of his dies were very well cut. It has been noted that Bolen and Joseph H. Merriam, a Boston diesinker (and maker of our No. 83), employed the same bold style of die preparation and may have had some type of relationship, including the sharing of punches and the use of each other's dies. Although no citations have been found in numismatic literature to prove such a relationship existed, it is known that certain Bolen and Merriam dies were extensively combined to create specimens for collectors.

Bolen's output was modest, and only a handful of varieties were made to the extent of several hundred pieces. Thus, it seems his tokens were made as a sideline, not as a serious business. While Bolen signed dies for pieces that were popular in numismatic circles, it is likely that he did unsigned work on contract for others. He seems to have had his own coining press, for in December 1864 he set one up at the Soldiers' Fair in Springfield and used it to strike 350 medalets in soft tin or white metal.

Today, well over 100 varieties are known of Bolen medals, including an illustrious series of copies of colonial coins from superbly crafted dies. When Bolen pieces cross the auction block there is always a lot of interest.[103]

Token or store card (actual size 39 mm) by Bolen, 1865, with his own portrait.

Estimated Market Values		Commentary on Value
Copper Strikings		*Commentary:* Strikings in tin, a volatile metal, sometimes show oxidation. The popularity of this token has extended far beyond numismatic circles.
PF-60 to 62:	$800 to $1,200	
PF-50 to 58:	$600 to $800	
Tin Strikings		
MS-63 to 65:	$500 to $650	
PF-60 to 62:	$400 to $500	
PF-50 to 58:	$300 to $400	

No. 85

GOOD FOR A RIDE
1835 NEW YORK AND HARLAEM RAIL ROAD

Rulau HTT-298 to 300 • 75 to 100 known

In reminiscences given to the American Numismatic and Archaeological Society in 1887, Andrew C. Zabriskie commented on the tokens created by the firm of Bale & Smith, including this one:

> A very interesting little token is that which bears on its obverse a representation of an extremely antique railroad car, the reverse being inscribed NEW YORK HARLAEM RAILROAD CO. At the time of its issue that corporation was in its infancy, and probably some persons present remember when its locomotives came down as far as Union Square. To still larger numbers the mention of this railroad reminds them how often they have been brought down Fourth Avenue in one of its passenger cars by a four-in-hand team to the old 26th St. Depot, since the scene of so many slugging matches and circus shows. A specimen in copper of this little token, which I show, is I believe extremely rare.[104]

The line was incorporated on April 25, 1831, as the New York and Harlaem Rail Road. This may have been the first street railway in the United States, or at least among the first. Although the form "Harlem" was in popular use then, and is today preferred by railroad historians, "Harlaem" is the spelling used on the tokens. Likely, these octagonal tokens were ordered early in the company's life.

The line was authorized to operate on rails to be laid in Manhattan, with a franchise "to construct a single or double railroad or way from any point on the northern boundaries of Twenty-Third Street to any point on the Harlem River by the power and force of steam or of any mechanical or other power or any combination of them." In this era railroads, most of which used steam locomotives, were attracting much attention as a growth industry, soon to render obsolete many of the canals then in use. Most companies were formed with a lot of imagination but little business sense, and soon failed. The New York and Harlem

Actual Size: 18 mm

Rail Road was an exception. It started with horses and evolved into steam operation, years later joining the New York Central system.

The first run took place on November 26, 1832, at which time the rails ran north from the Bowery (a center of commerce and entertainment) to 14th Street. On October 26, 1837, the line reached Harlem, via a tunnel at Yorkville. In time, locomotives were used on the northern trackage, but horses remained the motive power downtown for a long time, due to objections to noise.

Horse-drawn rail car of 1832 used on the New York and Harlaem Rail Road. (*Harper's Weekly*, October 24, 1891)

Estimated Market Values	
MS-60 to 62:	$1,000 to $2,000
EF-40 to AU-58:	$600 to $1,000
VF-20 to 35:	$400 to $600
F-12:	$300 to $400

Commentary on Value

Commentary: Some bear small counterstamps, seemingly a part of a system of tracking or registration.

No. 86
CLASSIC OF THE 1840S
BECK'S PUBLIC BATHS TOKEN

Rulau HTT-441 to 441B • Copper: 150 to 200 known • White metal: 3 to 6 known • German silver: 3 to 6 known

While today we may think that, per the saying, "cleanliness is next to godliness," it was not always so. In the period from about 1832 to 1844, when Charles Beck distributed his Beck's Public Baths tokens in Richmond, Virginia, bathing was an occasional experience at best.[105] Houses did not have indoor plumbing, and for most people in the city the closest thing to a bath was wiping with a soapy wet cloth. Across the country, some academies and boarding schools forbade bathing in the colder months, a practice deemed unhealthy.

For those who desired to bathe, public baths were operated in most of the larger cities. Records show that in 1832 Charles Beck was a confectioner and the operator of a bathing facility. The baths were in operation until at least 1844. These tokens, about the size of a quarter dollar, may have circulated locally as currency; more likely, they were used as admission checks.

In 1858, New York City numismatist Charles I. Bushnell published *An Arrangement of Tradesmen's Cards, Political Tokens, also Election Medals, Medalets, &c. Current in the United States of America for the Last Sixty Years, Described from the Originals, Chiefly in the Collection of the Author.* This engendered an interest in collecting such pieces. Soon, the Beck token became a favorite.

A December 1859 letter from Philadelphia collector J. Ledyard Hodge to R. Alonzo Brock, a Richmond numismatist, mentions these:

Actual Size: 28.5 mm

> . . . I have delayed acknowledging your last two favors—expecting every day to do so—and be able to send with my answer a larger set of pieces than I do—However as they turn up rather slowly I have concluded to send what I have and forward by Adams Express of this day a package containing sixteen pieces, which I find cost altogether exactly $2. One of these is one of the Washington medalets you wanted, which I was unable to procure till the other day; the others are American tokens of various kinds. . . .
>
> I enclose also one of the circulars issued by our Committee asking for information regarding our proposed works. We intend getting up the volume on store cards, tokens etc., first leaving the one on Medals till afterwards. If you have any pieces not mentioned in the Bushnell work, we would like to have rubbings and descriptions. Probably before answering, you had better wait for the catalogue of this coming sale. . . .
>
> Can you procure any more of the card you sent me, "Beck's Public Baths"? I will take any you can get with pleasure, as I have three or four friends here who want them. . . .

With its somewhat risqué depiction of a nude woman, this token is a favorite today, just as it was a century and a half ago.

ESTIMATED MARKET VALUES
COPPER STRIKINGS

MS-60 to 62:	$1,250 to $2,000
EF-40 to AU-58:	$500 to $1,250
VF-20 to 35:	$300 to $500

No. 87
OFFICE IN NEW YORK, FACTORY IN CONNECTICUT
1850S SCOVILL MANUFACTURING CO. TOKEN

Rulau/Miller-802 and 803 • 250 to 300 known

The Scovill Manufacturing Co. of Waterbury, Connecticut, was the American equivalent of the Soho Manufactory in Birmingham, England: a factory staffed by innovative management that turned out a wide line of metal goods, including tokens, medals, badges, buttons, and housewares. While the Soho facility was liquidated in 1850, at that time the glory years of Scovill were yet to come.

For numismatists, the Scovill firm is especially important. Its products included Hard Times tokens, campaign tokens, ferrotypes, Civil War tokens, encased postage stamps, game counters, and oddities such as copies of the 1787 Fugio cent. By 1829 a full-time engraver was on staff.[106]

W.E. Woodward's May 1884 sale of the J.N.T. Levick Collection described this item:

Actual Size: 28 mm

> [Token with] view of the old factory of the Scovills at Waterbury, Conn. "Established 1804, enlarged 1812, burnt down March, 1830, rebuilt July, 1830"; rev., a wreath of oak leaves and acorns. "J.M.L. & W.H. Scoville [sic], Waterbury, Conn., manufacturers of naval, military, crest, fire, plain, gilt and plated, and all kinds of fancy buttons." Tin. Very Fine, indeed; *excessively rare, but one other known.*

During the 1850s Scovill was a prolific maker of store cards. Many varieties were restruck in various metals, making them easily collectible today. Again we turn to Woodward, who in his sale of the Twining Collection in April 1886 included this preface to Lot 1257:

> About 30 years ago a number of gentlemen of New York, interested in numismatics, discovered at Waterbury, Conn., a large number of original dies of store cards and mercantile tokens. From these they obtained a number of impressions, struck in various metals, with which they supplied their own cabinets, and those of their friends. Mr. Levick then purchased the remainder, with the object of destroying, and thus rendering them scarce. In the purchase of the Levick Collection, the lot came into my hands. Very few of them have since been sold. . . . They are all in beautiful Proof or bright Uncirculated condition, and the dies have all since been destroyed by fire, at the burning of the die room at the Scovill Co.'s factory. As no more exist, and none can be struck in the future, they must become very rare. . . . Nearly all are of old red cent size, and of the "Hard Times" period.

Actually, most were of the 1850s, a decade after the Hard Times era ended (in 1843).[107]

Scovill Manufacturing Co., Waterbury, Connecticut. (*Great Industries of the United States*, 1871)

ESTIMATED MARKET VALUES	
BRASS STRIKINGS	
MS-63 to 65 (choice to gem):	$80 to $150
MS-60 to 62:	$50 to $80
EF-40 to AU-58:	$30 to $50

COMMENTARY ON VALUE

Commentary: Most examples are Uncirculated and seem to have been struck for collectors.

No. 88

FOR SELFLESS CIVILIAN ACTION
1904 TO DATE, CARNEGIE HERO MEDAL

• Gold: 19 issued • Silver: 617 issued • Bronze: 8,000+ issued

Actual Size: 76 mm

In 1904 in the little coal-mining village of Harwick, Pennsylvania, a horrific underground explosion and fire killed 181 people, among them several who had attempted to rescue survivors. Newspaper coverage of the event gave retired industrialist Andrew Carnegie an idea for yet another way to put his fortune to benevolent purpose. The Scottish-born steel baron had become the richest man in America in 1901 by selling his companies to J.P. Morgan and Henry Frick. By the time of his death in 1919, he had handed out $350 million toward the establishment of free libraries, universities, research institutes, and museums, and his Carnegie Trusts "for the improvement of mankind" received a final bequest of $125 million to ensure their survival into the 21st century. In terms of the purchasing power of his gifts, Carnegie may well still retain the title of the most generous private benefactor to citizens of America.

Knowing that the widows and children of the rescuers killed at Harwick would have no means of support, Carnegie set up a fund of $5 million to assist anyone disabled during a selfless or heroic act, or the dependents of anyone killed during such an act. The Carnegie Hero Fund Commission, with its well-publicized award ceremonies, emphasized spontaneous acts of bravery by ordinary people, America's "heroes of peace." By the time of the fund's 100th anniversary in 2004, it had awarded 8,900 medals and $28 million in assistance. It recognized heroism in the aftermath of the San Francisco earthquake, the *Titanic* disaster, and the September 11 attacks. The history of its medals program is the history of disaster in America.

The award medals were first struck in gold, silver, and bronze by J.F. Caldwell & Co. of Philadelphia. Most recipients earned bronze medals; silver and gold awards were reserved for the most outstanding acts, as determined by the awards committee.

For the fund's centennial in 2004, sculptor Luigi Badia redesigned the medals. Today, they are made by Greco Industries of Danbury, Connecticut, in a blend of 85% copper and 5% each of tin, lead, and zinc. Also in 2004, the fund struck commemorative silver proof medals for collectors. These are similar in design to the award medals but bear legends relating to the anniversary.

Portrait of Andrew Carnegie in the early 20th century. (*Century Magazine*, October 1902)

Estimated Market Values	Commentary on Value
Matte PF-60 to 62: .... $800 to $1,200	*Commentary:* These medals are quite rare, but demand for them is limited.

No. 89

Depicting the Park Theatre
THE THEATRE AT NEW YORK TOKEN

Rulau E NY-982, Breen-1055 • 14 to 18 known

The decade of the 1790s was an exciting time in New York City. A revolution in France and political repression in the British Isles had driven thousands of well-educated, highly skilled, and some very cultured people to Manhattan, to the extent of doubling its population from near 30,000 in 1790 to more than 60,000 in 1800. The city offered the freedoms the refugees sought, but little else. Leading citizens began opening private libraries, museums, and music rooms, and broke ground for a number of large structures to be financed by public subscription: among them were the Tontine Coffee House, the City Hotel, and the subject of our No. 89, the Park Theatre. This 2,000-plus-seat edifice, erected on Park Row across an open square from the new City Hall, rivaled the best houses in Europe, featuring a full orchestra and three tiers of box seats.[108] For more than 30 years it would remain the city's most important entertainment venue, first under proprietor William Dunlap (1798–1824) and later under William Price and Edward Simpson (1825–1848).

Actual Size: 34 mm

The Park Theatre offered fare for all tastes and budgets, from the homegrown popular musical play or rowdy farce, to the lilting arias of "La Signorina" (Italian soprano Maria Garcia Malibran) or the virtuoso performances of violinist Ole Bull of Norway. It witnessed the American premiere of many famous compositions, including Mozart's *Don Giovanni* in 1826 and Beethoven's *Fidelio* in 1843. Proprietor Simpson's business plan contributed greatly to the development of the "star system" in American theater, because he studied the prior successes of productions in Europe and sought to book only performers with established fame and drawing power.

The handsome copper New York Theatre token, struck in England, was not an admission pass but a tradesman's token (part of the Conder series described in the volume introduction). It was one of a group of penny-sized pieces bearing views of famous buildings published by Peter Skidmore and engraved by Benjamin Jacob. On most specimens, the edge reads I PROMISE TO PAY ON DEMAND THE BEARER ONE PENNY. Admission passes were eventually struck for use at the Park Theatre: they are the well-known "Admit" and "Paid" tokens of 1817, cataloged by Rulau as NY-41 and NY-41A.

The token's obverse view was taken from this Longworth 1797 directory plate, from a drawing by Elkanah Tisdale, engraved by J. Allen.

Estimated Market Values	Commentary on Value
PF-63 to 65 (choice to gem): $15,000 to $22,000 PF-60 to 62: $10,000 to $15,000	*Commentary:* These were struck for the souvenir and numismatic trade and never circulated.

No. 90

MAINTAINING GOOD RELATIONS
1809 MADISON INDIAN PEACE MEDAL

Julian IP-5 to 7, Prucha Plate 40 • Large size (75.8 mm): 15 to 20 known • Medium size (62.8 mm): 6 to 10 known
• Small size (51.2 mm): 8 to 12 known

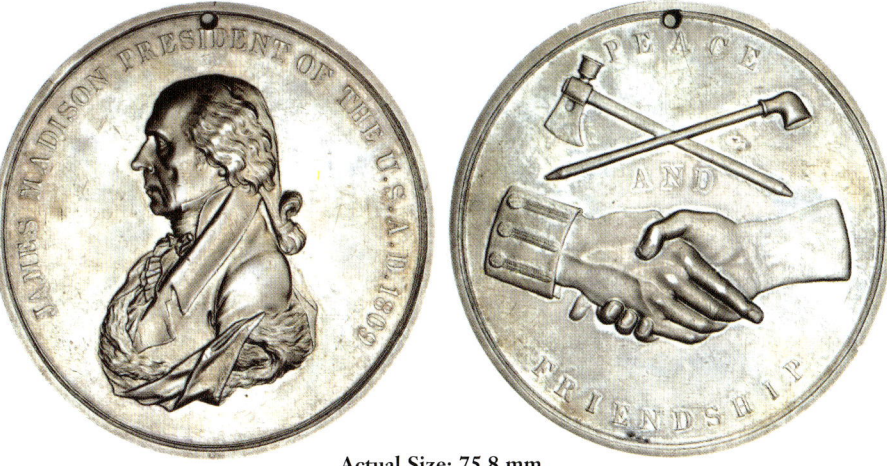

Actual Size: 75.8 mm

The significance of the Madison peace medals to collectors of the series is that they were the first to be struck from solid silver. John Mason, head of the Office of Indian Trade in 1810 when the order for new peace medals came in, stressed the need for the change, noting that the chiefs compared the lightweight, hollow American peace medals of the Jefferson administration unfavorably with the heavy, solid British medals of the era. Like the Jefferson medals (No. 3), the Madison medals would be issued in varying sizes, with the larger pieces being reserved for awarding to the more important chiefs. The 105 mm size, being too large for the Mint's medal presses, was retired in favor of a 76 mm version, and a new middle-sized piece (about 63 mm) was added. According to Tom DeLorey, the fact that lesser chiefs received smaller medals has affected the survival rates of all smaller peace medals in the series, since lesser chiefs died without fanfare and their goods and possessions were less likely to be preserved by their heirs.[109]

The importance of peace medals to the maintenance of good relations with Native Americans increased considerably after the end of the War of 1812. It was a time of great western expansion and settlement through the territories of Michigan, Illinois, and Indiana, and U.S. agents in those regions saw a particular need to replace the George III peace medals that had been handed out so liberally during the war. In order to induce more warriors to lead men into battle on the British side, the king's agents had bestowed medals on hundreds of ordinary braves, along with elaborate paper certificates confirming their authority as chiefs. This was not just a way of mustering troops: it also effectually reduced the authority of the authentic chiefs not interested in fighting alongside the British. At their first opportunity after the war, U.S. agents negotiated the surrender of all British medals, in hopes of creating unanimous tribal loyalty to U.S. interests. They appealed to the Superintendent of Indian Trade, Thomas McKenney, who in 1816 began forwarding large shipments of Madison peace medals to the western territorial governors.

The obverse portrait, by John Reich, was the source of inordinate delay in production. No one experienced in making life masks was available, so Madison had to sit for an Italian sculptor, who modeled a plaster bust and forwarded it to the Mint. Although the obverse of the example shown above reads 1809, the first medals were not delivered until 1813. These medals would retain the handshake reverse design, but with the wrist of the Indian sporting no heavy bracelet.

James Madison

ESTIMATED MARKET VALUES

EF-40 to AU-58 (75.8 mm):	$20,000 to $30,000
EF-40 to AU-58 (62.8 mm):	$20,000 to $30,000
EF-40 to AU-58 (51.2 mm):	$15,000 to $35,000

No. 91

THE FIRST CONGRESSIONAL MEDAL MADE IN AMERICA
1800 THOMAS TRUXTUN NAVAL MEDAL

Julian NA-2, Loubat-21 • Originals: 1 known in gold, 3 known in tin • Restrikes, original dies: 4 to 8 known in copper
• Restrikes, copy obverse die: 30 to 50 known in copper, 1 in silver

Fascination with the Truxtun medal can be ascribed to a number of factors, but three seem to stand out: it is the first congressional medal made in the United States; its "cartwheel" rim design is unique among early American medals; and, until recently, delineating key details of its history frustrated numismatic researchers. Chris Neuzil, Lenny Vaccaro, and Todd Creekman have compiled their research to create the following narrative.

Although medals voted by the Continental Congress for the Revolutionary War preceded the Truxtun medal, they were made in France, as the technology necessary to make them did not then exist in America. It is thus ironic that Thomas Truxtun earned his congressional medal for defeating a French ship. The United States had resumed trade with Britain after gaining independence, prompting French seizure of American vessels. Directed to shepherd American shipping in the Caribbean, Truxtun captured the French frigate *L'Insurgente* late in 1799. In February 1800 he defeated and nearly captured the more heavily armed *La Vengeance*, for which feat Congress voted this medal.

The dies were the handiwork of the Mint's chief engraver, Robert Scot.[110] The encircling legends were punched by hand into the wide rims of each medal after it was struck. Truxtun was presented with the single gold version (illustrated here) but also received (and probably paid for) a number in tin. He detested the jowly portrait, however, calling the medal "badly executed indeed—the prophile shameful."

New research has revealed that Truxtun's medal concealed an odd secret for almost 200 years. In 1808, fully *six years* after receiving his gold medal, Truxtun discovered that it bore incorrect dates for both the battle and the authorizing resolution! After learning of the "anachronisms" from Navy Secretary Robert Smith, President Thomas Jefferson directed the Mint to correct the inscriptions on the gold medal itself, a task that fell to John Reich. A few strikes in tin with the erroneous inscriptions have survived and show what Truxtun's gold medal originally looked like.

Restrikes from the original dies exist in copper; they invariably have blank rims and display a large cud where part of the obverse die broke away. Copies from an obverse replacement die exist in copper and silver; a few have rim lettering, but it is engraved rather than punched.

Actual Size: 57 mm

One of the medals struck in tin at Truxtun's request. It carries incorrect dates, as Truxtun's gold medal once did.

Truxtun's grave. (Benson J. Lossing, *Pictorial Field Book of the Civil War*, 1874)

Illustration of the Truxtun medal by W.L. Ormsby, 1848.

ESTIMATED MARKET VALUES	
COPPER RESTRIKE FROM COPY OBVERSE DIE	
PF-63 to 65 (choice to gem):	$300 to $500
PF-60 to 62:	$225 to $300
PF-50 to 58:	$150 to $225

No. 92

COMPLETE WITH FANCIFUL HISTORY
1792 WASHINGTON "ROMAN HEAD" CENT/TOKEN

Baker-19, Breen-1249 • 18 to 22 known

Actual Size: 30 mm

If we were to write only of *facts* concerning the interesting 1792 Washington Roman Head copper cent/token, a paragraph would do nicely, and it would not be long. First, we would note that the person depicted certainly bears no resemblance to any known likeness of the Father of Our Country. However, as the legend WASHINGTON PRESIDENT surrounds, it might be intended as an idealized tribute to him. The reverse shows the national bird, somewhat resembling a beetle. The word CENT is above. Around the edge appears UNITED STATES OF AMERICA X X X. On the reverse of at least one piece is a more or less horizontal die crack, which might explain why these pieces are so rare.[111]

Seemingly it is a Conder token, as evidenced by a trial impression bearing the name I.G. Hancock (for John Gregory Hancock; it was common to use an I for a J) with the edge inscription PAYABLE AT MACCLESFIELD LIVERPOOL OR CONGLETON—which a student of Numismatics 101 will immediately recognize as Conder token–ish.[112] That's about it, factwise.

Enter Walter Breen, and presto! new "facts" emerge, not substantiated elsewhere. We now have it that Hancock (see No. 72) was angered that the 1791 Large Eagle and Small Eagle cents he had designed had not been accepted for coinage by the American president. The 1791 coins were made in the shop of Obediah Westwood in Birmingham, England:

> When news of Washington's rejection reached Birmingham, John Gregory Hancock (doubtless with Westwood's gleeful consent, possibly even at his instigation) undertook an extraordinary piece of revenge. As Washington's spokesmen had compared the idea of presidential portraits on coins to the practice of Nero, Caligula, and Cromwell, so Hancock's (and/or Westwood's) idea was to portray Washington as a degenerate, effeminate Roman Emperor. . . . Their existence was kept secret for over 40 years lest it become an "international incident."[113]

The reality is that during this time there were *many* depictions of Washington in classical garb and poses, which were intended to honor him (see No. 59). There is no record of Washington's having seen or commented upon these speculative tokens. All we *really* know is what the Washington Roman Head token looks like. Don Taxay's 1966 *U.S. Mint and Coinage* sums up the situation: "From the imperial conception of the bust, it seems likely that the issue was intended for 'collector consumption' in England."

There were many depictions of Washington as an ancient leader, including this laureated head included in an album of Treasury Department vignettes of 1876.

Estimated Market Values	
PF-63 to 65 (choice to gem):	$20,000 to $35,000
PF-60 to 62:	$15,000 to $20,000

No. 93
By Christian Gobrecht
Charles Carroll of Carrollton Medal

Julian PE-6 • Gold: 3 known • Silver: 17 known • Bronzed copper: 6 known

Actual Size: 52 mm

When John Adams and Thomas Jefferson both died on July 4, 1826, fifty years to the day after the colonies first declared their independence from Britain, Charles Carroll became the sole surviving person to have signed the Declaration of Independence. He enjoyed this distinction for the last six years of his life. To mark his 90th birthday in September 1826, a commemorative medal was struck as a keepsake for members of his family. Christian Gobrecht performed the die work, utilizing the facilities of the Mint in Philadelphia. This evidently took some time, because according to an 1828 letter from Carroll to his grandson, three gold and 14 silver medals were still waiting to be made.[114]

Carroll's influence on the movement of the colonies toward independence was far more remarkable than his status as the longest-living signer. When events at Lexington and Concord made it clear that every American must take a position either for or against independence, many businessmen and colonial officeholders struggled to maintain the status quo with England. Carroll, who had studied law for seven years in Europe, oversaw his vast family real estate holdings from his manor at Carrollton in Frederick County, Maryland, and stood to lose much if the colonies failed in their bid for autonomy. Yet his impassioned epistles to the *Maryland Gazette*, as well as his substantial influence as Maryland's wealthiest citizen, helped persuade the colony to reverse its original position against separating from Great Britain. As a Roman Catholic, Carroll was technically barred from political participation by an old act of colonial legislature, and all of his letters were written under the pseudonym "First Citizen." On July 4, 1776, however, Carroll was voted Maryland's representative to the Continental Congress.

His signature on the Declaration, repeated on the medal, indicates one further act of courage. Every signer knew that placing his name on the document would automatically make him a criminal, guilty of sedition against King George. One of the men present on that day gibed that Carroll took no risk in placing his name on the parchment, because it was such a common name that the King's men would never be able to press a sedition charge upon him. Carroll immediately returned to the table, took up the quill, and added "of Carrollton" beside his name.[115] The manor he financed for his son Charles, known as Homewood House, has been carefully restored and is preserved today by Johns Hopkins University in Baltimore.

Charles B. Carroll

Estimated Market Values	
Silver Strikings	
PF-63 to 65 (choice to gem):	$6,000 to $8,000
PF-60 to 62:	$4,500 to $6,000
PF-50 to 58:	$3,000 to $4,500

Commentary on Value

Commentary: Copies made in electrotype form by Dr. Frank Smith Edwards of New York City, prior to the sale of his collection by Edward Cogan in October 1865, can be identified by wider spacing between the letters in TO. One is known in silver, with COUNTERFEIT BY EDWARDS scratched into the obverse field. Another is known in copper.[116]

No. 94
ENTER THE "FLATTY"
ELONGATED NICKEL OF THE COLUMBIAN EXPOSITION
Varieties range from scarce to rare

The Elongated Collectors Club has an official definition for the exonumia they pursue: "coins rolled through hand-cranked mill-type machines consisting of reverse-engraved dies cut in steel rollers, similar in concept to wringers on old-fashioned washing machines."

We've all seen them, and most of us have made them, by feeding a cent into a slot, turning the handle, and retrieving our flattened, elongated prize. Penny-rolling machines may be found everywhere on earth, from amusement parks to museums, from national monuments to famous tourist sites. Designs on their dies can be updated at any time, to create a staggering total of available varieties. Machines that press pennies are the most common, but models exist for pressing dimes, nickels, and quarters as well. A timeworn numismatic rule dictates that the earlier the piece and the more historically interesting its place of origin, the greater its desirability (assuming good condition). Elongated specimens that reveal the date and mintmark of the underlying coin, of course, have added value.

By the foregoing criteria, the world's first elongated coins—made at the 1893 Columbian Exposition in Chicago—are the crème de la crème. It cost 5¢ to flatten a coin at the fair, and there were six machines stationed around the grounds from which to choose. Unlike modern devices, which will jam if the wrong denomination coin is fed into the slot, the machines at the expo could flatten coins of any size below a half dollar. Impressions on Canadian and European coins are also known. Coins bearing the Cairo Street design are the hardest to find, but our voters deemed an elongated Liberty Head nickel, considered the key to the series for collectors of undamaged coins, to be king of the mountain. Illustrated here is a "flatty" made from a nickel of the prized 1885 date.

Penny presses appeared again at the Louisiana Purchase Centennial Exposition of St. Louis in 1904, and this time the host coin of choice was the Indian Head cent. The expo's mile-long amusement thoroughfare was known as "the pike," and, appropriately, the roller dies on two machines featured a fish, the northern pike (see No. 172 in the appendix).

Illustrated on this page are various unusual host coins rolled out at the Columbian Exposition.

Actual Size: Depends on host coin

As with our No. 77, the Columbian Exposition counterstamp was always the same size, regardless of the original (or final!) size of the host coin. From the top of the page to the bottom: The 1885 nickel was originally 21.2 mm; the 1876-CC quarter dollar, 24.3 mm; and the 1847 copper cent, 27.5 mm.

ESTIMATED MARKET VALUES	COMMENTARY ON VALUE
ON LIBERTY HEAD NICKEL EF-40 to AU-58: .... $30 to $50 **ON INDIAN HEAD CENT** EF-40 to AU-58: .... $10 to $20	*Commentary:* Many other coins were used in addition to Liberty Head nickels. In all instances these are more valuable, as are any from scarce or rare dies.

No. 95

THE "MICMAC MEDAL"
WASHINGTON / COLUMN INDIAN PEACE MEDAL

Baker-174Y • 2 known

Actual Size: 58 mm

While examining medals at the British Museum in 1960, George Fuld made an exciting discovery. It was a silver medal bearing a front-facing portrait of George Washington in a tricorne hat. On the reverse was the scene of an Indian sitting beneath a strange column outlined in hands. Since it combined a Washington portrait with an Indian motif, it must be a peace medal, and since Washington was dressed in military attire, it was likely presented during the Revolutionary War. What Fuld had found was conceivably the earliest medal issued by an independent American authority, and possibly the first medal of the Washington portrait series, as well as of the U.S. peace-medal series.

In 1975, Dutch historian Harald Prins published news of a second medal of the same design. This piece belonged, and still belongs, to members of the Micmac Indian tribe. Now headquartered in Nova Scotia, during the Revolution the tribe had occupied a territory stretching from Massachusetts to Newfoundland.[117] On July 19, 1776, acting on behalf of the 13 newly united colonies, the Commonwealth of Massachusetts signed the Treaty of Watertown with Micmac chiefs. Peace medals were duly awarded, and the document secured the Indians' support and their willingness to "supply 600 strong men . . . who shall march to join the Army of the United States of America, now at New York, under the immediate command of his Excellency, General George Washington, there to take his orders."[118] Since the Micmac signed no other treaties during the Revolution, and since this medal today resides in Micmac hands, it is clearly associated with this treaty.

A British Indian agent received the specimen shown here from a chief who had been party to the treaty and presented it to George III for the royal cabinet, from which the British Museum accessioned it in 1802. By 1776, British medallic art had evolved to a very high standard; the king must have been amused by the awkward, childlike execution on the first official medal of his fractious colonies.

The evidence proving that this medal was issued by the revolutionary government and not the Commonwealth of Massachusetts is the column-and-hands motif on the reverse. The original seal of the first Continental Congress of September 1774, which appeared on the cover of its proceedings, employed the same design. In the seal, a free-standing column representing independence, topped by a liberty cap, rested on the Magna Carta. Twelve strong arms (representing the original colonies, before Georgia joined in 1775) supported this column. The Latin inscription, HANC TUEMER, HAC NITIMUR, translates to "Supporting this, we protect this." Of course, "this" refers to both liberty and the Magna Carta, long considered the legal guarantee of individual rights.

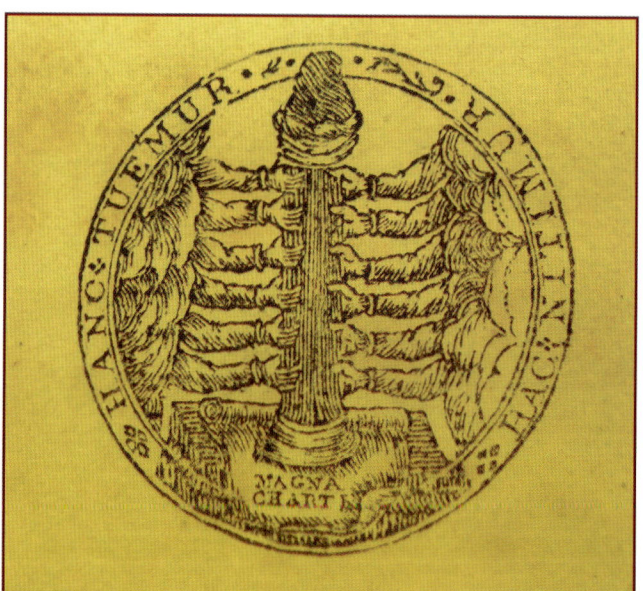

The 1774 seal of the Continental Congress. The seal's cap-atop-pole image was deemed uncomfortably phallic, and in 1776, Congress appointed John Adams, Thomas Jefferson, and others to a committee for its redesign.

Commentary on Value

Commentary: None have ever been offered for sale.

No. 96
MINTED IN TEXAS
1818 NEW SPAIN JOLA

Breen-1081 (19 mm large planchet), 1082 (17 mm small planchet) • Fewer than 100 known of both large and small planchets

In late 1958, the San Antonio River Authority was widening the channel next to the municipal golf course for a flood-control project. As the construction equipment sat idle one weekend, 18-year-old James J. Zotz Jr., in company with his father and brother, decided to explore the area. One of them noticed a copper coin in the freshly excavated earth. Mr. Zotz Sr., a part-time coin dealer, didn't recognize the specimen but, seeing the 1818 date, knew enough to tell the boys to look for more. They returned to the site on weekends until they had gathered 60 or so pieces from an area that in the 19th century had been the site of a campground for cowboys.

Actual Size: 19 mm

It turned out that the existence of this long-forgotten Spanish colonial issue of Texas *had* been known to collectors in 1903, when a specimen from a private collection was reported in *The Numismatist*. Mr. Zotz, however, researched their story from primary sources in San Antonio.

In 1818, the entire southwestern United States was part of the viceroyalty of New Spain. Starting in the late 17th century, Franciscan Catholic missionaries began to colonize the territory, beginning with a chain of missions in the San Antonio River valley. The Alamo, erected in 1718, was the first built. Over the next century, the area's population of missionaries, Native Americans, Spanish soldiers, ranch workers, and other newcomers grew to such an extent that a local coinage became necessary. Military governor Lieutenant Colonel Manuel Prado authorized a member of the *ayuntamiento* (city council) to arrange for the striking of copper tokens worth one-half real. Over an 18-month period in a building on the corner of what are now Houston and Soledad streets, this individual minted 8,000 jolas bearing his own initials, JAG, on the obverse. The reverse was blank except for a small five-pointed star at the center, which some say constitutes the earliest use of the Lone Star of Texas.

"JAG" was José Antonio de la Garza, a San Antonian by birth and a widely respected gentleman who in 1823, during the government-mandated secularization of mission estates, obtained for himself the Mission San Francisco de la Espada with its two-league tract of ranchland.[119] It is quite likely that Don José paid his workers with jolas. Certainly he retained his high status in the region until his death in 1851, because eventually a Texas county was named after him.

An early 20th century view of the Mission San Francisco de la Espada. (Historic American Buildings Survey, Library of Congress, HABS TEX,15-SANT.V,2-A-1)

ESTIMATED MARKET VALUES
1818 COPPER ONE-HALF REAL

VF-20 to 35:	$9,000 to $14,000
F-12:	$6,000 to $9,000
VG-8:	$4,000 to $6,000

COMMENTARY ON VALUE

Commentary: Most examples exhibit corrosion damage from long burial. The market for these pieces is untested, as they were not widely known until recent years. Values listed are speculative. One specimen each of large and small planchets sold through Heritage Galleries in 2006 for $19,550 and $14,950, respectively. These were of higher grades than those listed here.

No. 97
"PARVA NE PEREANT"
1919 TO DATE, THE J. SANFORD SALTUS MEDAL
Baxter 182 • More than 50 have been awarded

"Let not the little things perish"—in Latin, *parva ne pereant*—is the motto of the American Numismatic Society (ANS), a national institution for advancing the study and appreciation of coins, medals, tokens, seals, and related objects. At first, medals played a minor role in the business of the society, which was formed in 1858 by Augustus B. Sage and 11 other New York City collectors. Early members collected, displayed, and discussed medals, but commissioned few of them, and devoted only a tiny proportion of the society's funds to acquiring them. A key figure in shaping a much stronger emphasis on medals between 1892 and 1922 was longtime patron of the arts, numismatist, and ANS officer J. Sanford Saltus (1853–1922). Saltus encouraged the ANS to commission the striking of medals on many occasions, and usually sat on the committees that oversaw their design and production.

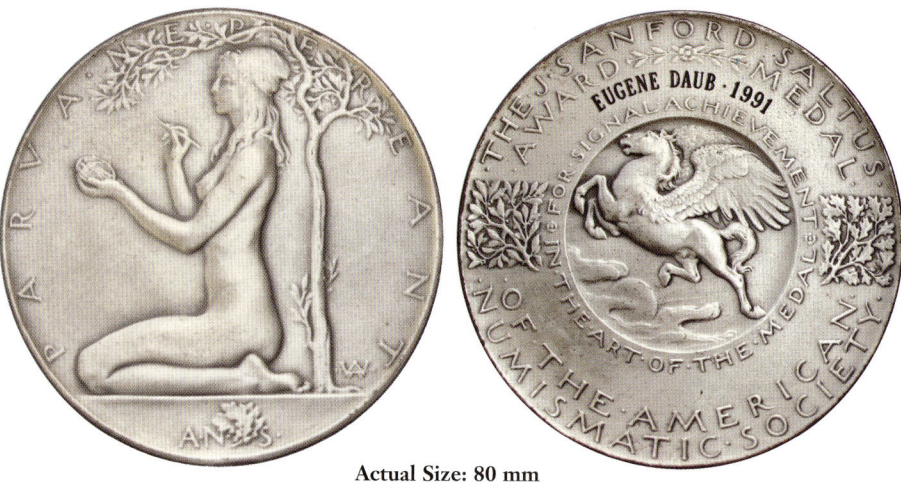
Actual Size: 80 mm

He was especially drawn to the sculpted medal in an improved format, enabled by pantographic reducing machinery, that allowed bas-relief modeling methods (rather than diesinking) to be used in the creation of medals. With his own funds, he established an ANS program to promote the art form. Beginning in 1913, he endowed the J. Sanford Saltus Award for Signal Achievement in the Art of the Medal, a prize that has brought honor and recognition to 52 recipients to date. The criteria for consideration for a Saltus award have evolved over the years. Until 1983, only American sculptors were evaluated, but today the award is available internationally, for lifetime achievement in medallic art.

As reported under No. 38, the first winner was James Earle Fraser in 1919. The following year, the prize went to the award's designer himself, Beaux Arts master sculptor Adolph Alexander Weinman. His design, executed in solid silver at a hefty 80 mm, won a competition open to any sculptor who was an ANS member. Fifteen of the era's leading medalists submitted models, but the review panel chose Weinman's elegant statement as the one that best conveyed the society's esteem. The medals, also issued in bronze in limited numbers, were struck by elite jeweler Tiffany & Company, which had been making important commemorative medals for New York City and national institutions for more than six decades.

Architect's rendering of the new American Numismatic Society building, which opened in 1908. This facility was used until the early 21st century.

Seal of the American Numismatic Society.

COMMENTARY ON VALUE

Commentary: There are no modern sales records for awarded medals, all of which seem to still be in the hands of the recipients or their families. Trial strikes are known.

No. 98
ISSUES OF 1860
STORE CARDS OF AUGUSTUS B. SAGE

Rulau/Miller-749 to 756 • 80 to 100 known of each

In 1859, Augustus B. Sage was the most active rare coin dealer in New York City. During the year he produced four auction catalogs, more than all other dealers combined. From his store at 24 Division Street he offered coins, tokens, medals, paper money, and numismatic books, the last a particular specialty. In 1860 his activity continued, expanding to include the issuing of the two store cards showcased here.

Beginning in 1858, in cooperation with diesinker George H. Lovett, Sage issued several series of medalets, typically struck in copper, often with additional impressions in brass, white metal, and, for a few, silver. The first, Aug. B. Sage's Odds and Ends, was brief and featured just three subjects: the burning of the Crystal Palace, the Old Sugar House (a prison during the Revolutionary War), and chess champion Paul Morphy. Aug. B. Sage's Numismatic Gallery (see No. 58) featured the portraits of nine prominent numismatists. The most extensive, Sage's Historical Series, mostly featured buildings associated with the Revolutionary War or the life of George Washington, 14 subjects in all.

Among Sage's other tokens and medals were store cards advertising his business, of which several varieties were made to his order by Lovett. These are especially popular today (see also No. 100, another Sage medal). Voted into the 100 Greatest in the No. 98 position were the store cards combining two obverse dies of his Historical Series medalets, each measuring about 31 mm and illustrating a Revolutionary-era building in New York City: City Hall on Wall Street (Miller-749 to 752) and Sir Henry Clinton's House (Miller NY-753 to 756). A single die was used for the reverse of each, lettered A.B. SAGE & CO. / DEALERS IN / COINS / MEDALS & TOKENS / BOOKS, STATIONERY, / ENGRAVINGS & PAINTINGS / AUTOGRAPHS / & / CURIOSITIES. / CIRCULATING LIBRARY. / 24 DIVISION ST. / NEW YORK. / 1860.

Of the City Hall variety, an estimated 30 to 50 are known in brass and a lesser number in copper and white metal. The Clinton's House issue is usually seen in white metal, of which an estimated 30 to 50 are known; copper impressions are slightly scarcer, and brass store cards scarcer still. In total, perhaps 80 to 100 are known of each.

Several other varieties of store cards were issued by Sage, each of a smaller size. These are described in Russell Rulau's *Standard Catalog of United States Tokens 1700–1900*.

Actual Size: 32 mm

An 1861 view of lower Broadway, a district not far from Augustus B. Sage's office. ("Broadway in 1861," *Harper's Weekly*, December 5, 1885)

Sage's first store card, a tiny 16 mm token that must have been given out casually, as business cards are today, for most examples show extensive wear.

ESTIMATED MARKET VALUES	
TYPICAL VARIETY	
MS-63 to 65:	$50 to $100
MS-60 to 62:	$30 to $50
PF-50 to 58:	$20 to $30

No. 99

A CARTOGRAPHER'S DREAM
SIR FRANCIS DRAKE'S GLOBE CIRCUMNAVIGATION MEDAL

Betts-9, Rulau E-8 • 9 known in silver

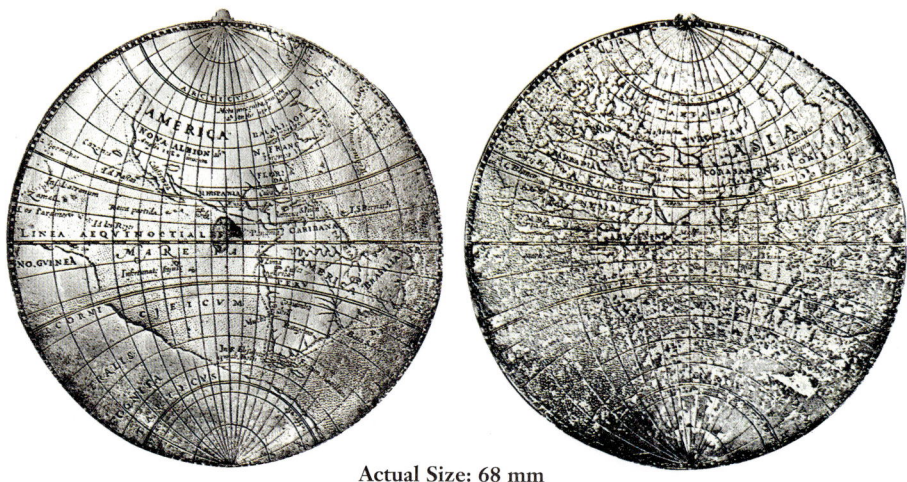

Actual Size: 68 mm

The major advantage of the commemorative medal over two-dimensional art forms, such as painting, is the unique relationship between obverse and reverse in the presentation of a theme. A brilliant example of how two sides combine to form a unified statement is the piece Sir Francis Drake ordered around 1586 to commemorate his circumnavigation of the globe (1577–1580). The design consists of a precise rendering of the 16th-century world map, with the western hemisphere on one side and the eastern on the other. The route taken by *The Golden Hind* is seen as a dotted line.

Upon his return to England, Drake presented his queen not only the fabulous gold and silver treasure he had captured from the Spanish off the coasts of Peru and Mexico, but an even better prize from the standpoint of history: a completely updated world map. To every European nation vying for territory across the oceans, accurate maps were critical to superiority. Drake's greatest coup for England may have been his March 1579 capture of a tiny Spanish vessel off Costa Rica that yielded a collection of navigator maps and charts of the Pacific detailing a trade route to China. Historians contend that Drake had not originally planned to circle the world but that, once laden with Spanish treasure and pursued by Spanish ships along the Pacific coast, he could not very well return home by way of the Straits of Magellan. The captured Pacific-route information gave him the means to go home the other way.

Although the original map given to Elizabeth I has been lost, five copies survive, one of which was drawn by Michael Mercator, a grandson of cartographic innovator Gerardus Mercator. In his 1923 *Biographical Dictionary of Medallists*, Leonard Forrer attributed our subject medal to Dutch mapmaker Jodocus Hondius. Of the nine known examples, however, one that belonged to the Earl of Caledon bears a cartouche identifying Michael Mercator as the maker. Its documentation shows that the earl bought his medal in London in 1589.[120]

Drake's medal belongs among the 100 greatest *American* medals because it bears the first known use of the term "America" in struck form, and because it specifically names places that later became part of U.S. territory, such as Florida and California. Its association with the shrinking of the globe through cartography and ocean travel, however, makes it equally important to world history.

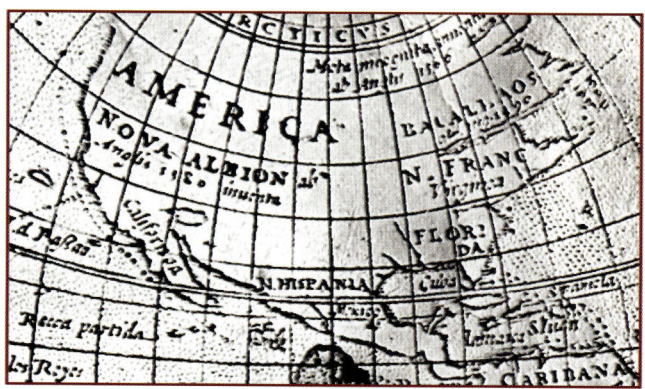

Detail from the obverse of the medal showing North America. The route of Drake's ship, shown as a dotted line, is visible off the coast of California.

COMMENTARY ON VALUE

Commentary: Most if not all specimens are believed to be in museums. No relevant sales records have been found.

No. 100

FIRST MEDAL OF THE CIVIL WAR
1861 FORT SUMTER MEDAL

Bronze: 10 to 20 known • Silver: 2 known • Silvered white metal: 2 or 3 known • Brass: 1 known

By 1861 Augustus B. Sage was one of America's best-known numismatists. His medalets of 1858 and 1859, including the Odds and Ends, Numismatic Gallery, and Historical Tokens series, were foundation stones on the collecting scene. Listings in auction catalogs were frequent.

Not much is known today of his rare-coin business in that year, as little notice of him appeared in print. His interest remained undiminished, though, as evidenced by the impressive (80 mm) Fort Sumter medal he published soon after the beginning of the Civil War—the earliest such production in the War between the States. This medal is not widely known today because of its rarity, so those who voted for its inclusion in the 100 Greatest were part of a very sophisticated group.

During the months following South Carolina's secession on December 20, 1860, ten other states seceded from the Union to form the Confederate States of America. By early 1861, southern militia had been armed and a commission had been named to explore future relations with that *other* country, the United States. Inaugurated on March 4, President Abraham Lincoln tried to resolve the problem by negotiation. The situation worsened—and then, Fort Sumter.

On the morning of April 12, shore batteries began bombarding the stone fort in the harbor of Charleston, South Carolina. Housed in the fort were nearly 100 men under Major Robert Anderson. After 34 hours of shelling, the fort was reduced to rubble, although no lives were lost. Anderson accepted terms that allowed him and his men to vacate the fort with dignity. He then departed for New York City, where he was given a hero's welcome on the 18th. In the meantime, President Lincoln addressed a special session of Congress. The Civil War had begun.

On April 28 the *New York Herald* reported that a special gold medal was to be presented to Major Anderson, and bronze specimens could be subscribed for at $5 each at 64 Division Street, the coin store of Augustus B. Sage. At that time, 84 had been spoken for. A few impressions were made in silver and white metal as well.

Actual Size: 80.1 mm

One can envision a scenario in which George H. Lovett, hearing of the fall of Fort Sumter and the impending arrival of Anderson in New York, quickly prepared dies for this medal. Enlisted to help sell them was his old and reliable customer, Augustus B. Sage.

Within a year the Fort Sumter medal was recognized as being important and rare.

Shore batteries in Charleston bombarding Fort Sumter, April 12, 1861. (John Gilmary Shea, *History of the United States*, 1872)

Estimated Market Values	
White Metal, Silvered	
PF-60 to 62:	$500 to $750
PF-50 to 58:	$250 to $500

Commentary on Value

Commentary: A bronze example brought $4,600 at a 2001 Bowers and Merena sale.

APPENDIX

WHAT MIGHT HAVE BEEN

"Always a bridesmaid, never a bride," as they say. Here are the 100 *next* most popular tokens and medals—faces on the numismatic cutting-room floor, entries that came close but did not enter the winners' circle. And yet, the "Second 100 Greatest" listings include many wonderful pieces, most of which are highly affordable.

NO. 101: 1829 WRIGHT & BALE STORE CARD (RULAU HT-340). The partnership of the talented C.C. Wright and James Bale in New York City lasted until 1833. The duo engraved token, medal, and seal dies as well as plates for paper business cards.

NO. 102: 1789-DATED MOTT TOKEN (RULAU NY-610 TO 613). Research by Bowers and Rulau and die-evidence studies by Wesley Cox suggest this store card was issued around 1833 by Robert Lovett Sr. The eagle design on the reverse is a copy of that used on gold coins of 1807. The date 1789 refers to the inaugural year of Mott's business.

NO. 103: 1867 TO 1876 SHELL STORE CARDS AS A CLASS. Most bear advertisements—for everything from circus troupes to wines—and usually boast colorful reverses. These certainly are interesting, but not enough to land in the top 100.

NO. 104: 1763 CHARLES TOWN SOCIAL CLUB MEDAL (BETTS-508, RULAU SC-1). A rare bird with only three pieces known, this European-made membership medal recalls the days when Charleston, South Carolina, was a southern seat of high society and culture. Is it still?

NO. 105: 1965 HARRAH'S $1 TOKEN OF RENO, NEVADA, AND RELATED ISSUES. This is an early entry in what became the vast field of dollar-sized casino tokens, used after silver dollars disappeared from circulation. The Franklin Mint was a prominent maker of these.

NO. 106: 1904 LOUISIANA PURCHASE AWARD MEDAL BY ADOLPH WEINMAN. An unusual circle-within-triangle shape distinguishes this high point in U.S. medallic art, one of a quartet of gorgeous off-round awards for this exposition by the American Beaux Arts master sculptor.

NO. 107: 1917 PULITZER PRIZE MEDAL. Renowned sculptors Daniel Chester French and Augustus Lukeman designed this award, which was struck by Medallic Art Company. The biographies of Pulitzer and the sculptors, and the histories of the Pulitzer organization and all the winners, are facets of this object's story. Wonder if *this* book will get a Pulitzer prize? If not, blame the voters for not placing this item higher.

NO. 108: 1927 CONGRESSIONAL MEDAL AWARDED TO CHARLES LINDBERGH. Sculptor Laura Gardin Fraser provided the soaring design. Although "Lucky Lindy" was a latecomer in transatlantic flying, he was the first to do it *solo*. America gained a hero.

NO. 109: 1856 COMMITTEE OF VIGILANCE MEMBERSHIP MEDAL. A souvenir from the wild and woolly West when citizens of San Francisco, dissatisfied with local law enforcement, took matters into their own hands.

NO. 110: 1834 PUECH, BEIN & CO. TOKEN (RULAU HT-123). Issued way down yonder in New Orleans, this store card of the gun and pistol importers is one of the rarest tokens in the Hard Times series, with just two recorded.

NO. 111: 1803 HENRY KETTLE GAME COUNTERS. These brass tokens imitate U.S. $2.50 and $5 gold coins; years ago some unknowing numismatists considered them to be *patterns*.

NO. 112: 1829 C. WOLFE, CLARK & SPIES TOKENS. Store card issues of a prominent New York military and nautical supplier, these are popular with Washington and Jackson series collectors, since three types feature portraits of both presidents. There are five types in all.

NO. 113: 1850 PALMETTO REGIMENT MEDAL. Authorized by the South Carolina legislature in 1848, Colonel Butler's regimental medals were struck by Charleston silversmiths Gregg, Hayden & Co. in early 1850 from dies cut by William J. Keenan.

NO. 114: 1848 ZACHARY TAYLOR BUENA VISTA MEDAL (JULIAN MI-24). Stunning design by Frederick A. Smith and execution by Charles Cushing Wright distinguish this U.S. Mint congressional medal recording Taylor's Mexican War success. (See the illustration of the unique gold medal in the volume introduction.)

NO. 115: 1975 TO PRESENT, MILITARY CHALLENGE COINS. Although these modern issues are not well enough known or appreciated to land them in the top 100, perhaps in some future day they will be popular with numismatists.

NO. 116: 1837 AMERICAN SILVER 25 CENT TOKEN. Made of an alloy designated as "American silver," this seems to be an issue by Lewis Feuchtwanger.

NO. 117: 1900S TO DATE, AMERICAN NUMISMATIC ASSOCIATION MEDALS AS A CLASS. These annual medals, some of which were used on badges, were commissioned by numismatists, for numismatists, about numismatic gatherings—irresistible.

NO. 118: 1860 EDWARD COGAN STORE CARD. Cogan, an English immigrant who became a part-time coin dealer in autumn 1858, then a full-time one in the 1860s, started in Philadelphia, then moved to New York City.

NO. 119: 1863 "OUR LITTLE MONITOR" CIVIL WAR TOKEN. Struck in several different versions, this token depicts the fearless little ironclad ship that dueled with the CSS *Merrimac* off the coast of Virginia, changing the course of naval history—never mind that the engagement was a draw with no clear winner.

NO. 120: 1799 NEW YORK ASSOCIATE CHURCH COMMUNION TOKEN. This white-metal issue has been called the earliest dated American communion token, a Presbyterian tradition popularized in Scotland. The only way to get one to pay for the privilege of taking communion was to be deemed devout enough by the church elders.

NO. 121: 1849 CALIFORNIA GAME COUNTER. A brass half eagle–size token depicting a gold miner, this is said by some to have been used in gold rush times, although documentation is scarce.

NO. 122: DR. G.G. WILKINS COUNTERSTAMP. This clever dentist from Pittsfield, New Hampshire, seems to have counterstamped thousands of coins of various denominations, mostly cents, dating back to the early 19th century, for so many exist today. He also ran a restaurant and store, and kept a caged bear out front.

NO. 123: 1837 ROXBURY COACHES TOKEN. These elegant horse-drawn coaches ran out of East Boston, Massachusetts. According to Lyman Low, "These coaches were long omnibuses carrying 16 to 20 persons inside and were drawn by four horses. . . . They were handsomely painted, and on their sides bore a distinguishing name—*Regulator*, *Conqueror*, and one, the *Aurora*, with the goddess in her cloud-borne chariot on its yellow sides." The tokens are in Feuchtwanger's Composition.

NO. 124: 1840 WILLIAM HENRY HARRISON CAMPAIGN TOKEN. Harrison's supporters produced an avalanche of different campaign tokens, awakening the American concept of "campaign science." Tippecanoe and Tyler too! Wherever old Tippecanoe stopped to speechify, hard cider flowed by the barrel.

NO. 125: 1871 RITTENHOUSE MEDAL (JULIAN MT-1). William Barber created this tribute to the Mint's first director, who was also an astronomer, mathematician, surveyor, and maker of scientific instruments and clocks.

NO. 126: 1835 I. GIBBS STAGE TOKEN. An overland trip on a bouncing horse-drawn stage took you from a Hudson River landing at New York City to Newark, New Jersey, in an hour, if you had the token fare.

NO. 127: 1859 AND 1860 JOHN K. CURTIS STORE CARDS. Curtis, a young rare-coin dealer in New York City, was active in the cradle days of the numismatic hobby.

NO. 128: 1830S ONWARD, AMERICAN INSTITUTE AWARD MEDALS. Moritz Fürst designed the award medals for the association, which hosted national exhibitions of art, invention, and technology in New York City through 1897. Later dies were made by others.

NO. 129: CIRCA 1878 BOYD'S BATTERY. A token of sorts, this hokey combination of metals enclosed in a frame was supposed to generate electricity when worn in contact with the skin, and thus promote good health.

NO. 130: 1826 INAUGURAL MEDAL FOR JOHN QUINCY ADAMS (JULIAN PR-5). Moritz Fürst offered these by public subscription. He sold some silver strikes directly to Adams, and at least 100 copper medals went to the War Department. The reverse motif seems suitable for an Indian peace medal.

NO. 131: 1860 WILLIAM IDLER STORE CARD. Idler entered the coin business in Philadelphia in 1859 and soon profited handsomely as an unofficial outlet for restrikes, patterns, and other rarities made secretly at the Mint.

APPENDIX

No. 132: 1846 W.W. Wilbur Store Card. This South Carolina businessman advertised his services as an auctioneer, but doesn't mention on his token that his commodity was slaves.

No. 133: 1867 Joseph J. Mickley Medal. Struck from dies by Lea Alborn, this medal commemorates the life of numismatist Joseph Mickley (1799–1878).

No. 134: Early 20th-Century Mining Company Store Tokens. These tokens were good for merchandise at the company store in an era that inspired the song "Sixteen Tons."

No. 135: 1837 R.L. Baker Token. Made of Feuchtwanger's Composition, this piece was issued in Charleston, South Carolina, by a seller of soda water.

No. 136: 1804 Edward Preble Medal (Julian NA-3). Awarded by Congress for Preble's gallantry as "the avenger of American commerce" against the ravages of pirates, it shows his fleet's triumph before Tripoli.

No. 137: 1829 John Stevens Hoboken Ferry Token. This was good for $1 (when a dollar went a long way!), payable in specie at the ferry master's office.

No. 138: 1789 Zespedes Florida Proclamation Medal. Issued by the Spanish governor of Florida at the assumption of the throne of King Charles IV, the medal was meant to denote just who was in charge of the important peninsula.

No. 139: 1863 "The Flag of Our Union" Civil War Token. The flag "must and shall be preserved," the token proclaims. One with an error inscription (Fuld-209 to 414a) reads, "Shoot him on the *spoot*" instead of "spot."

No. 140: 1933 Huey Long Toilet Seat Medal. This issue by the Medallic Art Co., no less, is one of the most improbable subjects ever rendered on a medal. But then, Huey Long (the "Kingfish"), with his one-man rule of Louisiana politics, was a rather improbable politician. This satirical medal commemorates a set-to on August 28, 1933, when Long left a restroom in Sands Point, Long Island, and was set upon by a concerned citizen. Accounts of what happened varied widely; *Time* magazine reported that a drunken Long had urinated on the trousers of the citizen. The shape of a convenient restroom facility defines the outline of this medal.

No. 141: 1859 James Ross Snowden Medal (Julian MT-3). Anthony C. Paquet, an assistant engraver at the Mint, turned out this splendid medal honoring the director.

No. 142: 1850s State Department Lifesaving Medals (Julian LS-1 [eagle obverse] and LS-2 [man in sea]). Elegant medals by Emmanuel Leutze and Francis Koehler were awarded to heroes of sea emergencies. Both depict vivid scenes of shipwreck and disaster.

No. 143: 1860s to 1870s Bolen Medals as a Class. Bolen was the Massachusetts diesinker of No. 84, the Pioneer Base Ball Club Medal. Bolen's other medals and copies of colonial coins are superbly done and are widely collected today.

No. 144: 1863 Grant Congressional Medal. This medal shows just how important Grant's 1863 victories were to the Union, particularly in terms of national morale. The medal was awarded before Grant took command of the Army of the Potomac.

No. 145: 1846 USS *Somers* Rescue Medal (Julian NA-24). This commemorates the rescue of American sailors from the sinking brig *Somers* off Santa Cruz, Mexico, by French and Spanish vessels. C.C. Wright's accuracy at depicting sailing ships (even sinking ones) came from living with his uncle, Maine shipbuilder Nathan Bryant.

No. 146: 1849 Lifesaving Benevolent Association Medal. This issue from an important commercial marine insurance association depicts another sinking ship, with a Francis Lifecar coming to the rescue. The dies are by George H. Lovett.

No. 147: 16th-Century One World Is Not Enough or "Le Concordat" Medal. Francois I of France and two globes on pedestals are featured on this Paris Mint production. It is not certain whether the imagery relates to the New World versus the Old, or earthly versus heavenly existence. It shows the earth as round, establishing the impact of Columbus's discovery.

No. 148: 1837 Half Cent Token. Popular as the only Hard Times token of this denomination, this piece was struck in a year in which no federal half cents were made.

No. 149: 1824 Andrew Jackson Campaign Token. The Hero of New Orleans did not make the ballot on this try, but succeed he did the next time around, in 1828, and again in 1832, ending up in the White House. There are several different varieties of Jackson tokens similar to this one, differing mainly in their reverse inscriptions.

No. 150: 1784 Washington Ugly Head Token. The obverse of this apparently satirical token bears an unrealistic portrait of Washington, bald (without his wig), and without his teeth. Surrounding is the legend WASHINGTON THE GREAT D.G. "D.G." was a common inscription on British coins at the time and stood for *Dei Gratia* ("by the grace of God"). But it has been theorized that in this instance the D.G. may refer to "Dictator General."

No. 151: 1790s Franklin Press Token. This store card, one of the Conder token series, is for an English printer that took Ben Franklin's hand press for its name; it depicts the device on its obverse.

No. 152: 1806 to 1820 C & H Turnpike Token. They had to pay turnpike tolls even in 1806, around Lancaster, Pennsylvania, the birthplace of this evil American tradition.

No. 153: 1826 New England Society for the Promotion of Manufactures and Mechanic Arts Medal (Julian AM-55). Christian Gobrecht produced the medals for the society with the long name, one of the earliest societies to encourage domestic invention and stimulate American manufacture.

No. 154: 1860 Hawaiian Waterhouse Plantation Token. This first token of Hawaii, a pewter token circa 1855–1860, was a work check issued by John T. Waterhouse, a plantation farmer of Honolulu.

No. 155: 1933 Pedley-Ryan "Dollars." In the depths of the Depression this Denver company sought to promote the use of silver, mined extensively in the state, by issuing its own "dollars."

No. 156: 1863 Gustavus Lindenmueller Civil War Token. The tokens of this beer hall owner were passed out in profusion to use as "cents" when real cents were scarce, but Lindenmueller caused a ruckus when he refused to redeem them.

No. 157: 1860s C. Wyllys Betts Tokens as a Class. The Novum Belgium token was the sensation of its era, and the others are fascinating as well. All are fantasies. Betts also produced a set of tokens honoring himself, just for fun.

No. 158: 1907 to 1917 Valdez, Alaska, Copper Block Buffet Token. Good for $1.00 in trade, this nickel-alloy token has a small piece of native gold affixed to it.

No. 159: 1858 Crystal Palace "Odds and Ends" Medal. Augustus B. Sage's first medal, from dies by George H. Lovett, described the fiery destruction of this elegant building with a mournful line from Ecclesiastes.

No. 160: 1980s to 2005 New Hampshire Turnpike Token. This Public Works and Highways brass token, 25¢ in toll value, was used from the 1980s to 2005. The Old Man of the Mountain may be gone and his tokens discontinued, but his statehood quarters, dated 2000, live on.

No. 161: 1823 Richard Trested Store Card. This is the rare store card of an important early New York City engraver/diesinker who also called himself a "stamper" and "piercer."

No. 162: 1914 Circle of Friends of the Medallion Issue Number 11. A favorite from an illustrious 12-medal multi-artist series, Paul Manship's homage to the New Netherlands Tercentenary features bold figures that burst from their background and exude power.

No. 163: 1980s Onward, Arcade Tokens. Remember Pac-Man, Donkey Kong, Space Invaders, and Missile Command? To play these arcade games tokens were ideal.

No. 164: 1848 Gilbert Stuart and Other Art Union Medals. These medals are from the hand of Charles Cushing Wright. Important in its time, the American Art Union was a lottery where fine art was the prize. It is little remembered today.

No. 165: 1850s "Use G.G.G. and G.G.G.G." Counterstamps. Charles Goodwin of Exeter, New Hampshire, used large copper cents and other coins to promote Goodwin's Grand Greasejuice and Goodwin's Grand Glittering Globules. For many years numismatists did not know what the mysterious G's stood for, until an advertisement for them was found in an obscure 1856 directory.

No. 166: 1950s Frederick Earl Fankhauser Encased Coin. Fankhauser ("Your Penny Man") was a coin dealer of Fort Wayne, Indiana, and a major promoter of encased cents. He arranged the manufacture of over 700 varieties, and is probably the reason they are still so collectible today.

APPENDIX

No. 167: 1864 Lincoln Campaign Ferrotype. Made under the same patent as encased postage stamps, these brass encasements depicted the candidates for president and vice president. Especially important are those bearing beardless tintypes of the 16th president.

No. 168: 1826 National Jubilee Medal (HK-2). This artistic but little-known medal observes the 50th anniversary of American independence, and its reverse bears a pledge to support the principles of the Declaration of Independence.

No. 169: 1890 Benjamin Harrison Indian Peace Medal (Julian IP-48). This is the last official peace medal struck at the Mint.

No. 170: 1970s Onward, Patrick Mint Tokens. Jesse Patrick has turned out over a thousand different tokens, creating a popular collectible series. Many have been made to the order of numismatists, others are for honors or anniversaries, and still others advertise businesses and professions.

No. 171: Massachusetts Charitable Mechanic Association Medals (Julian AM-33). These popular early medals by Christian Gobrecht were awarded enough times that examples turn up with regularity today. Paul Revere was the first president of the group, which was founded in 1795.

No. 172: 1904 "Pike" Elongated Cent from the St. Louis World's Fair. "Meet me in St. Louis, Louis; meet me at the fair," the popular song went. While there, some visitors had their "pennies" rolled out with special inscriptions. The "Pike" was a cluster of arcades and amusement parlors.

No. 173: Early 20th-Century Dude Saloon Token. This "one drink" piece from an Alabama saloon, restaurant, and brothel features a compelling design, which is, of course, a dude. Two die varieties are known.

No. 174: 1825 Castle Garden Admission Token. From dies by Richard Trested, this elliptical token was issued by proprietors Rathbone and Fitch. In 1824 Lafayette disembarked at Castle Garden for his return trip to America. In 1850 P.T. Barnum presented Jenny Lind in this large hall.

No. 175: 1845 Johnson, Himrod & Co. Token. This very early dollar-sized $1 trade token from Erie, Pennsylvania, was good for castings and other merchandise at a foundry.

No. 176: Circa 1820 Washington Double Head Cent. Not a real cent, but a token, this depicts the Father of Our Country on both sides.

No. 177: 1862 Siege of Vicksburg Counterstamped Cent/Dime. During this famous standoff, Vicksburg merchant Jacob Schiller counterstamped many 1860-dated cents with his name and an X, for 10, after which they did service as dimes.

No. 178: 1833 Tisdale & Richmond Merchant Token (Rulau HT-A335). This item was probably included in our ballot because it is unique. Tisdale & Richmond sold hardware in New York City.

No. 179: 1834 Gulian C. Verplanck, "Our Next Govnr" (Low-16). Although undated, this piece is known to be a Whig issue of 1834; the portrait of Verplanck on its obverse is almost identical to that of his Democratic opponent, William H. Seward, on a companion piece.

No. 180: 1857 Aaron White Satirical Token. White, a lawyer and coin hoarder from Connecticut, must have had an unfortunate experience with paper money. Part of the inscription reads, "Never keep a paper dollar in your pocket til tomorrow." The dates 1837 and 1857 relate to financial panics, and the hanging hog is an allusion to the suspension of specie payments.

No. 181: 1860s Merriam Medals. This whole class of issues made our ballot because, without a doubt, Joseph Merriam was one of America's most talented diecutters (see No. 83). Merriam issued a wide series including political figures, people in the news, and store cards.

No. 182: 1751 Franco-American Jetons (Betts-385 to 395). These Paris Mint pieces depict a French view of North America, probably struck to stimulate interest in the New World. You can still order restrikes from the Paris Mint today.

No. 183: 1849 Zachary Taylor Medal. Taylor, from Louisiana, is front and center on this scarce medal designed by P.P. Duggan, engraved by C.C. Wright, and published by H.F. Baldwin & Co. of New Orleans. Its distinguishing feature: a pelican.

No. 184: 1905 Las Cruces Majestic Saloon. Issued in New Mexico, this token, actually an encased cent, bespeaks an era of booze, gambling, and—who knows?—perhaps outlaws too. Judge Roy Bean, "the law west of the Pecos," had a connection with this establishment, which burned in 1905.

No. 185: 1860 "Abra-Ham Lin-Coln, the Hannibal of America" Token. This punny token, created by William Leggett Bramhall, gives semi-cryptographically the name of Lincoln's running mate, Hannibal Hamlin. The center of the reverse die at first read THE HANNIBAL OF AMERICA. Perhaps the comparison ruffled some feathers; for whatever reason, the inscription was blanked out by the heavy engraving of WIDEAWAKES over it. The Wideawakes were mostly young men who supported Lincoln.

No. 186: 1892 Landing of Columbus Medal. Sculptor Bartolome Maura shows Columbus pointing to land from the deck of his ship on the obverse, and kneeling before Queen Isabella on the reverse. The medal commemorates the 400th anniversary of the discovery of the New World (never mind that the Vikings discovered it earlier!).

No. 187: 1844 J. Cochran Bellfounder Token. J. Cochran made bells in Batavia, New York. His cent-sized token, with the rather late date of 1844, is often included as part of the Hard Times series. For this token you take what you can get, no matter the condition, for only four are known.

No. 188: 1910s to 1920s Mills and Caille Slot Machine Tokens. The Mills Novelty Co. of Chicago and Caille Brothers of Detroit produced a dazzling array of gambling machines. Nickel-sized tokens, usually of brass, were sold to be used in them.

No. 189: 1870s Alcatraz Island Post Exchange Token. This scarce and desirable trading-post token was issued for trade at Fort Alcatraz, a U.S. army garrison from 1859 to 1906, which became the site of the world-famous prison.

No. 190: 1783 Peace of Versailles Medal (Betts-610). Britain recognized American independence with a medal in silver and white-metal versions.

No. 191: 1893 Ferris Wheel Medal. Struck in aluminum and issued at the World's Columbian Exposition, this medal showcased the entertainment wonder of the age. In 1904 the ride was used at the St. Louis World's Fair, after which it met an ignominious end as scrap metal.

No. 192: 1834 Howell Works Garden Token. Issued in New Jersey, this payroll token is collected with the Hard Times series. There are two tokens from this issuer, one sporting a rose, the other illustrating a bunch of grapes.

No. 193: 1840 Astor Fur Trade Indian Peace Medal. The writers would not have been surprised to see this historical medal enter the charmed inner circle of 100, but it didn't.

No. 194: 1779 DeFleury at Stony Point Medal (Julian MI-4). This first Comitia Americana Revolutionary War issue depicts a detailed scene of the fort at Stony Point on the Hudson River.

No. 195: 1873 Elgin National Watch Co. Token. The Elgin watch, made in the Illinois town of the same name, was durable, inexpensive, and widely sold in the late 19th and early 20th centuries.

No. 196: Circa 1828 Goodyear & Sons Merchant Token. This Philadelphia merchant issue is probably here because it is so rare: only two or three are known.

No. 197: 1863 A. Cohen's Civil War Token. These Leavenworth tokens are rare and in demand, as Cohen was the only Kansas issuer of these tokens. Only 20 to 30 are known.

No. 198: 1876 J.W. Scott & Co. Centennial Medalets (Rulau NY NY-835). This series of white-metal tokens, depicting Independence Hall, commemorates the centennial of American independence.

No. 199: 1933 Crescent City, California, Clamshell Money. Issued during the bank holiday proclaimed by Governor James Rolph Jr., this is one of the many tokens (such as wooden nickels) issued in odd materials during the Great Depression.

No. 200: 1850 to 1857 Royal Hawaiian Agricultural Society Medals (Julian AM-24). These showy silver and bronze award medals by Francis N. Mitchell were struck after hours at the Mint. The center of the reverse was hand engraved before presentation.

NOTES

1. Betts acknowledged a debt to Joseph Addison's *Dialogues Upon the Usefulness of Ancient Medals*.
2. His biography is detailed in *The Eagle That Is Forgotten: Pierre Eugène du Simitière, Founding Father of American Numismatics*, by Joel J. Orosz (1988).
3. Illustrated in Orosz, p. 40; the sketch is now owned by the Library Company of Philadelphia.
4. Newspaper name and location not given. Quoted in the *American Journal of Numismatics*, July 1886, p. 22. *The Journals of Congress*, November 29, 1776, p. 485, recorded the $32 payment.
5. *American Journal of Numismatics* (April 1874).
6. Ibid.
7. Bentley's diary entries were quoted in *The Numismatist* in January 1907 and June 1945.
8. Judge James Winthrop (1752–1821).
9. Sources include "Robert Gilmor, Jr., and the Cradle Age of American Numismatics," by Joel J. Orosz, *Rare Coin Review*, no. 58 (1985); Orosz's similarly titled article in *The Numismatist* (May 1990); and the same writer's "New Research Illuminates Robert Gilmor, Jr.," coauthored with Lance Humphries, *The Numismatist* (November and December 1996).
10. Equivalent to slightly over $7,500 in U.S. funds at the time.
11. *American Journal of Numismatics* (April 1872).
12. Jackson's gold specimen of the Erie Canal medal later appeared and was illustrated as Lot 823 in Wayte Raymond's sale of the W.W.C. Wilson Collection, November 1925, with a commentary concerning its presentation to Jackson at a ceremony in 1828.
13. *American Journal of Numismatics* (October 1892), commentary by G.P. Thruston.
14. Winslow Lewis in the *American Journal of Numismatics* (June 1866).
15. E.J. Attinelli, *Numisgraphics* (1876), p. 75.
16. *American Journal of Numismatics* (January 1868).
17. Attinelli, *Numisgraphics* (1876), p. 82.
18. *The Proceedings of the Numismatic and Antiquarian Society of Philadelphia*, January 4, 1866.
19. On July 1, 1907, the American Numismatic Society title was resumed; this style has been continued to the present time.
20. Bushnell's book was favorably reviewed in *Historical Magazine*, December 1858, pp. 368–369. The title may vary slightly among examples, and versions of this scarce work are known with and without plates.
21. *American Journal of Numismatics* (September 1867).
22. Letters from Jared Sparks, *Franklin's Works*, as quoted by William Sumner Appleton, *American Journal of Numismatics* (November 1867), pp. 63–64.
23. J.F. Loubat, *The Medallic History of the United States of America, 1776–1876*, Flayderman reprint (1967), p. xxiii.
24. As cited by Eric P. Newman in "The Promotion and Suppression of Hard Times Tokens," *The Token: America's Other Money*, ANS COAC Proceedings No. 10 (New York, 1995).
25. Joseph C. Mitchelson, "Granby Tokens," *Mehl's Numismatic Monthly* (June 1910), pp. 54–55. The most comprehensive study is that of Daniel Freidus, "The History and Die Varieties of the Higley Coppers," *The Token: America's Other Money*, ANS COAC Proceedings No. 10 (New York, 1995).
26. Duffield was the author of another American first, a watch made entirely from American raw materials. His standing case clocks rank among the finest produced in this country.
27. "Description of some of the Medals struck in relation to Important Events in North America," in *The Saturday Magazine* (January 5, 1822), from an 1821 paper read before the New-York Historical Society.
28. Franklin cited on the Web site of the Wedgwood Museum, www.wedgewoodmuseum.org.uk.
29. Newman, "Promotion and Suppression of Hard Times Tokens."
30. Citation furnished by Anne Bentley, curator, Massachusetts Historical Society.
31. Commentary as part of W. Elliot Woodward's catalog of the Francis S. Hoffman Collection, April 1866, Lot 944. It is not known whether this was conjecture or fact.
32. *American Journal of Numismatics* (October 1892).
33. "Sturgis Lectures on the Fur Trade," *Hunt's Merchants' Magazine and Commercial Review* (1846), cited by Bowers, *More Adventures With Rare Coins*.
34. Minutes of the Friendly Association for Regaining and Preserving Peace with the Indians by Pacific Measures, 1755–1757, at Friends Historical Library, Swarthmore College, Swarthmore, PA.
35. Discourse before the Historical Society of Pennsylvania, January 1, 1827, cited in "Indian Medal," *Casket*, no. 10 (October 1827).
36. Useful references include a brief listing in *A Guide Book of United States Paper Money* (Friedberg EP numbers); Michael Hodder and Q. David Bowers, *The Standard Catalogue of Encased Postage Stamps* (1989; HB numbers); and Fred Reed III's *Civil War Encased Stamps* (1995; S numbers).
37. In 1887 the bridge was torn down and replaced by an iron one, at which time these were found along with coins, old newspapers, and other items.
38. For additional reference, see Farran Zerbe, "The Lesher or Referendum Pieces," *Mehl's Numismatic Monthly* (May 1919).
39. For a history see David T. Alexander, *The Society of Medalists* (Medal Collectors of America, 2005).
40. A comprehensive reference book is in preparation by numismatist Donald Scarinci. It will contain in-depth historical and mint information, biographical information, and interviews with sculptors. For the present, refer to the fine Web site of the Medal Collectors of America, www.medalcollectors.org, for images of the medals in this series.
41. Per author's telephone conversation with chief executive Robert Hoff, March 23, 2006.
42. Historical references taken from Carrie Rebora Barratt and Ellen G. Miles, *Gilbert Stuart*, the catalog of an exhibition by the Metropolitan Museum of Art, March 27–July 31, 2005. Major research for their entry number 55, "John Bill Ricketts," was done by Christopher H. Jones. William L. Slout, in "From Rags to Ricketts: The Roots of Circus in Early Gotham," *Bandwagon: The Journal of the Circus Historical Society* 48, no. 5 (September–October 2004), gives details of the acts performed in New York City in the 1790s.
43. May 1807 and January 1810 citations furnished by John J. Kraljevich.
44. Henry Adams, *The Education of Henry Adams* (New York: Modern Library, 1999), pp. 391 and 465.
45. Letter cited in Neil MacNeil, *The President's Medal, 1789–1977* (New York: Clarkson Potter, 1977), p. 61.
46. Information from the Web site of the Franklin Institute, www.fi.edu.
47. R. Neil Fulghum, "The Hunt for Carolina Elephants: Questions Regarding Genuine Specimens and Reproductions of the 1694 Token," *Colonial Newsletter* 43, no. 1 (April 2003).
48. J. Doyle DeWitt, *Alfred S. Robinson, Hartford Numismatist* (Hartford: Connecticut Historical Society, 1968).
49. Edwin L. Johnson, *J.A. Bolen's Medals, Cards, and Fac-Similes: An Accurate and Comprehensive Descriptive Catalogue of Bolen's Works, With Number Struck in Each Metal, Disposition of Dies, and Other Detail* (1882).
50. Also see Anne Bentley, "The Columbia-Washington Medal," *Proceedings of the Massachusetts Historical Society* 101 (1989).
51. The standard reference on the voyage is Frederic W. Howay, ed., *Voyages of the "Columbia" to the Northwest Coast 1787–1790 and 1790–1793* (Massachusetts Historical Society, 1941). Other sources include Edward G. Porter, "The Ship *Columbia* and the Discovery of Oregon," *New England Magazine* 6 (1892): 272–278, and Malcolm Storer, *Numismatics of Massachusetts*, volume 76 in the Collections of the Massachusetts Historical Society (Boston: Quarterman Publications, 1981).
52. The authors found no primary-source data confirming this, but note that Laurence Brown listed the piece in *A Catalogue of British Historical Medals 1760–1960* as having an English origin. See "The William Pitt Tokens of 1766," http://www.coins.nd.edu/ColCoin/ColCoinIntros/Pitt.intro.html.
53. In the 1980s the second specimen, ex W.S. Appleton Collection, was identified as a cast copy. However, another genuine piece was found and sold in the Gerry Nelson Collection sale in 1982. The discovery of a smaller but possibly related piece, dated 1715, was reported in 1982, but this piece has not been seen by the authors.
54. This theory was suggested by one of the authors (Bowers) in his description of the Garrett Collection coin in 1980.
55. In "Home Is the Sailor," an April 2006 *Smithsonian* article, Adam Goodheart summarized a detailed investigation into whether the remains brought home a century ago were in fact those of Jones. Although the U.S. Navy has not as yet authorized DNA testing for incontrovertible proof, Goodheart concluded that General Porter was probably correct in his identification.
56. Quoted in W. Elliot Woodward's sale of April 28, 1863, Lot 2079.
57. "History of the City of Troy," http://www.rootsweb.com/~nyrensse/troy.htm.
58. "The Ever-Present Church Penny," *The Ladies' Home Journal*, February 1898, p. 14.
59. Cited in *Walter Breen's Complete Encyclopedia of United States and Colonial Coins* (1988).
60. William L. Calver, "Researches Into the American Army Button of the Revolutionary War," *Journal of the American Military History Foundation* 1, no. 4 (Winter 1937): 151–164.
61. Stanley J. Olsen, "A Colonial Button Mold," *American Antiquity* 29, no. 3 (January 1964): 389.
62. Russell Rulau, "Token Researchers Uncover New Information," *Numismatic News*, July 20, 2004.
63. Gregory G. Brunk, *Merchant and Privately Countermarked Coins*, manuscript for revised edition, June 2006, crediting the research of Robert D. Leonard. Earlier, many numismatists thought that PB stood for Puech, Bein & Co., a New Orleans firm that issued tokens dated 1834.
64. R.W. Julian, "The Philadelphia Mint and Coinage of 1814–1816," *American Numismatic Association Centennial Anthology* (1991).
65. Daniel Jackson had no family relation to the president.
66. William Cowper Prime, *Coins, Medals, and Seals, Ancient and Modern...* (New York: Harper Bros., 1861), p. 268.

NOTES

67. Items, *Workingman's Advocate*, February 5, 1831, p. 4.

68. *The Round Table: A Saturday Review of Politics, Finance, Literature, Society and Art*, January 26, 1867, p. 58. The writer was actually talking about fishing.

69. Gustav Kobbé, "Presidential Campaign Medals," *Scribner's Magazine*, September 1888.

70. In November 1999, John Kleeberg, at the Coinage of the Americas Conference of the American Numismatic Society, identified the maker as Joseph Lewis, citing contemporary notices and advertisements. For a long time it had been thought that C.C. Wright or another early engraver was responsible. The name of Lewis had not been mentioned.

71. James Hardie, *The Description of the City of New York* (New York: Samuel Marks, 1827).

72. Q. David Bowers's award-winning book, *A California Gold Rush History Featuring the Treasure From the SS Central America* (2002), is an invaluable resource.

73. The original purchase was to have been 650,000 acres, for division into 6,000 farms of 100 acres each, but when the final deal was struck, much of the land was discovered to have been sold to others.

74. Sources are many, with the best being Thayer Tolles's "A Bit of Artistic Endeavor," in *The Medal in America: Vol. 2*, ed. Alan M. Stahl, Coinage of the Americas Conference Series no. 13 (New York: American Numismatic Society, 1997).

75. The pheasants are now owned by Harvard University.

76. This fact, pointed out in a letter of June 27, 2006, from John W. Adams to the authors, is reiterated by all respected Revolutionary War historians.

77. Mark Jones, *The Art of the Medal* (London: British Museum Publications, 1979), p. 93.

78. Klaus Lubbers, "Strategies of Appropriating the West: The Evidence of Indian Peace Medals," *American Art* 8 (Summer/Fall 1994): 78–95.

79. Julian cited in Rita Laws, *Indian Peace Medals and Related Items: Collecting the Symbols of Peace and Friendship*, 2nd ed. (Harrah, OK, 2005), p. 136.

80. *The Historical Magazine, and Notes and Queries Concerning the Antiquities, History and Biography of America*, March 1861. The queries editor may have been Jeremiah Colburn, Boston numismatist.

81. "Early Washington Medals," *American Journal of Numismatics* 14 (2002): 108.

82. The full-text army case files from 1861 to 1973, arranged chronologically by war, are accessible at http://www.army.mil/cmh-pg/Moh1.htm, along with a short history of the award and statistics of its distribution. A full history of the medal, its design, and its recipients is given on the Web site of the Congressional Medal of Honor Society, www.cmohs.org.

83. In a November 2, 1848, letter to his son, who was recovering from dengue fever in Bayou Sara, Louisiana, C.C. Wright stated, "I have furnished the city's corporation with their medals for the New York Regiment of Volunteers, I suppose that you would be entitled to one if you were here to look for it" (Manuscript Collections of the New-York Historical Society).

84. J.N.T. Levick, "Reminiscences of Coin Collecting," *American Journal of Numismatics* (November 1868): 55–56. "Thick die" refers to what today is called *thick planchet*, that is, the early-style planchet of 1795 with lettered edge.

85. From the American Numismatic Association Web site: http://www.numismatics.org/archives/levickbio.htm.

86. As quoted by Robert Sobel, *Machines and Morality: The 1850s* (New York: Crowell, 1973), p. 249; original text not seen.

87. This can be seen as plate 2 in James Ross Snowden's *Description of the Medals of Washington; of National and Miscellaneous Medals; and of Other Objects of Interest in the Museum of the Mint* (1861). Medals expert Joseph Levine reports owning a lightly silvered copper electrotype of this medal, but a solid-silver struck version is known from S.H. and H. Chapman's 1882 Bushnell sale.

88. Quotations from Francis P. Prucha, *Indian Peace Medals in American History* (Norman: University of Oklahoma Press, 1994).

89. Chris Neuzil, "A Reckoning of Moritz Fürst's American Medals," in *The Medal in America: Vol. 2*, ed. Alan M. Stahl, Coinage of the Americas Conference Series no. 13 (New York: American Numismatic Society, 1997).

90. Precocious teenager (life dates 1775–1815): *Walter Breen's Complete Encyclopedia of U.S. and Colonial Coins* (1988), p. 137, citing C. Wilson Peck, *English Copper, Tin, and Bronze Coins in the British Museum, 1558–1958* (1964), p. 239. Dissipated man: letter from Thomas Digges to Thomas Jefferson, March 10, 1793, Don Taxay, *The U.S. Mint and Coinage* (1966), p. 53, drawing on research by R.W. Julian.

91. *Walter Breen's Complete Encyclopedia of U.S. and Colonial Coins* (1988), p. 139.

92. David Hackett Fisher, *Liberty and Freedom: A Visual History of America's Founding Ideas* (New York: Oxford University Press, 2005), p. 140.

93. Donald Jackson and Dorothy Twohig, eds., *The Diaries of George Washington*, vol. 6 (Charlottesville: University Press of Virginia, 1979). Full text online at www.loc.gov.

94. He held directorships of the Savannah Bank of Commerce, the Albany and Gulf Railroad, and the Plank Road Company, and owned Savannah's largest cotton warehouse.

95. Company H, Georgia 1st Cavalry Battalion, later merged with Georgia 2nd Cavalry and was redesignated the 5th Cavalry Regiment.

96. *New York Herald*, February 1, 1849.

97. Gregory G. Brunk, *Merchant and Privately Countermarked Coins*, manuscript for revised edition, June 2006.

98. Q. David Bowers, *Thanhouser Films: An Encyclopedia and History* (Greenwood Press, 2004).

99. F.B. Mayer, "The Western Shore of Maryland," *Frank Leslie's Popular Monthly*, April 1886, p. 407.

100. Grantland S. Rice, review of *Records of the Tuesday Club of Annapolis, 1745–1756*, by Elaine Breslaw, *The William and Mary Quarterly* 53, no. 1 (January 1996), pp. 219–221.

101. For general information also see A.R. Frey, "Tokens and Medals Relating to Numismatists and Coin Dealers," *The Numismatist* (February 1905), and David E. Schenkman, "Joseph H. Merriam, Die Sinker," *The Numismatist* (April 1980). Q. David Bowers is preparing a text on Merriam and John A. Bolen medals, which in some instances combine dies from both makers.

102. Reported in a special article submitted to *Coin World* on August 10, 2006, from findings made but not published in 2000.

103. Moses King, *King's Handbook of Springfield, Massachusetts* (1884); Farran Zerbe, "Fifty Years of Base Ball," *The Numismatist*, October 1908; David Schenkman, "Token Mementos of Our National Pastime," *TAMS Journal* (December 1998); Neil Musante, *The Medallic Work of John Adams Bolen* (2002); and Bowers archives of Bolen material.

104. *Proceedings*, 1887.

105. Russell Rulau, *Standard Catalog of United States Tokens 1700–1900*, 4th ed., p. 203.

106. Robert J. Lindesmith, "Edward Hulseman, Hard Times Token Engraver," *TAMS Journal* (June–July 1967): 71–82. The name of the English diesinker was not given.

107. For other early numismatic discussions see Lyman H. Low, "Hard Times Tokens," *American Journal of Numismatics* (July 1899), and Edgar H. Adams, "J.M.L. & W.H. Scovill," *The Numismatist* (July 1912).

108. An article by John Kleeburg in *The Token: America's Other Money*, ed. Richard Doty, Coinage of the Americas Conference Proceedings no. 10 (1994), gives a detailed account of the tokens and the theater. Kleeburg identifies the architect as Marc Brunel, who apparently won a design competition for the privilege, but recent research has proven that Mangin was the lead architect. See *Encyclopedia of New York City*, ed. Kenneth T. Jackson (Yale University Press, 1995), entries for "Park Theatre" and "Theater."

109. "Counterfeit Indian Peace Medals," *COINAge*, March 1996, available on the Web site www.harlanjberk.com.

110. Although some believe John Reich engraved the Truxtun dies, comparison of their style with dies known to be by Reich (such as the congressional medal to Isaac Hull) leaves little doubt that they were engraved by Scot. Details of the Truxtun medal's history are in Chris Neuzil, Lenny Vaccaro, and Todd Creekman, "Captain Truxtun's Congressional Medal," *Numismatist* (February 2007), pp. 32–43.

111. Louis Jordan of Notre Dame University reports an *electrotype* with this crack, leading to the assumption that it was made from a coin with this feature.

112. This trial piece was stolen from Richard Picker while under security at the ANA convention in Washington, DC, in 1971 (the security service in question was not later employed).

113. *Breen's Complete Encyclopedia of United States and Colonial Coins* (1988), p. 140.

114. Stack's *Catalog of The John J. Ford Jr. Collection of Coins, Medals and Currency, Part V*, October 12, 2004, citing the research of David Tripp, p. 134.

115. Wikipedia entry for Charles Carroll, citing 1940 newspaper research by John Hix.

116. Robert Lindesmith, "The Charles Carroll of Carrollton Medal and the Dr. Edwards Copy," *TAMS Journal* (December 1971).

117. George Fuld, "Early Washington Medals," *American Journal of Numismatics* 14 (2002): 105–107; John W. Adams, *The Indian Peace Medals of George III* (1999); and Harald Prins, "Two George Washington Medals: Missing Links in the Chain of Friendship Between the United States and the Wabanaki Confederacy," *Maine Historical Society Quarterly* 28, no. 4: 225–234.

118. *A Treaty of Alliance and Friendship entered into and concluded between the Governors of the State of Massachusetts Bay, and the Delegates of the St. John's & Mickmac Tribes of Indians*, July 19, 1776.

119. Felix D. Almaraz Jr., "San Antonio's Old Franciscan Missions: Material Decline and Secular Avarice in the Transition From Hispanic to Mexican Control," *The Americas* 44, no. 1 (July 1987): 16.

120. Online collection catalog of the National Maritime Museum, London: http://www.nmm.ac.uk/collections.

AUTHORS AND ACKNOWLEDGMENTS

ABOUT THE AUTHORS

Katherine Jaeger earned a B.A. from Allegheny College in 1979, and spent each of her college summers working at archaeological digs in Israel. There she first heard the peculiar term *numismatics*, and began to view coins as archaeological dating tools and as pieces of the historical record. From 1979 to 1986, she worked in New York City as a copy editor and then managing copy editor; later, while raising a family with her husband, Tom, she switched to freelance editing. In 1999 she began writing history features for magazines such as *American History* and *American Heritage*. The "hook" into exonumia came when she found a clipping of an 1885 newspaper interview with diesinker George H. Lovett, her great-great-grandfather. Immersed in the study of medals and tokens since then, she has authored several features for *Numismatist* and is the author of Whitman's *Guide Book of United States Tokens and Medals*. In 2006 she received the American Numismatic Association's Heath Literary Award, and, in 2007, the ANA's Wayte and Olga Raymond Literary Award.

Q. David Bowers became a professional numismatist as a teenager in 1953, later earning a B.A. in finance from the Pennsylvania State University (1960), which in 1976 bestowed its Distinguished Alumnus Award on him. He served as president of the Professional Numismatists Guild (PNG) from 1977 to 1979 and president of the ANA from 1983 to 1985. He is a recipient of the Founder's Award and Farran Zerbe Award, the highest honors of the PNG and the ANA. He is the author of over 50 books and has received more honors from the Numismatic Literary Guild than has any other person. His column, "The Joys of Collecting," has been a feature of *Coin World* for over 40 years and is the longest-running column by any author in the history of numismatics. He is coauthor, with David Sundman, of the *100 Greatest American Currency Notes*, and is also an award-winning columnist for *Paper Money* magazine. As cochairman of Stack's in New York and New Hampshire, and as numismatic director for Whitman Publishing, he is also in the forefront of current events in the hobby.

FOREWORD AUTHORS

David T. Alexander, who has served on the staff of Stack's since 1990, has been prominent in the field of medals for a long time. Earlier he served in academic positions, then on the staff of *Coin World* and as editor of the *Numismatic Scrapbook Magazine*, among other posts. The recipient of many honors given by the American Numismatic Association and the Numismatic Literary Guild, he is best known for his articles on medals, although he has covered many other topics. He was a founding board member of the American Medallic Sculpture Association (AMSA) and with John W. Adams was a cofounder of the Medal Collectors of America (MCA).

Russell Rulau was born in 1926 and acquired his first Civil War token in 1939, while residing on a turkey ranch in what is now El Cajon, California. His first article, again about Civil War tokens, was published in 1958. Later, he enjoyed a career with *Coin World* in Sidney, Ohio, and Krause Publications in Iola, Wisconsin. For Krause he produced many important works, including a revision (with George Fuld) of *The Medallic Portraits of Washington*, studies on Hard Times tokens and other specialties, and his magnum opus, the essential *Standard Catalog of United States Tokens 1700–1900*. The recipient of many awards, he was inducted into the ANA Hall of Fame in 2000.

CREDITS AND ACKNOWLEDGMENTS

The authors express appreciation to the many collectors, dealers, and scholars in the field of American tokens and medals who completed our survey and cast their votes for their favorite 100 Greatest, ranking them in order. Thousands of votes were tallied by Whitman Publishing, to yield the results given here.

Steve Hayden, Joseph Levine, and Steve Tanenbaum provided valuations and market history information. John Kraljevich served as research consultant. We also thank the following for help in the ways indicated:

John W. Adams reviewed portions of the manuscript, made suggestions, and contributed the essay for No. 21. **American Numismatic Rarities**, Wolfeboro, NH, and the firm into which it merged in 2006, **Stack's**, provided many illustrations. The **American Philosophical Society** provided a William Cole engraving. **Georgia Barnhill**, curator at the American Antiquarian Society, assisted with research. **Anne Bentley**, curator at the Massachusetts Historical Society, was helpful in multiple ways, including making the society's holdings available for photography, reviewing the manuscript, and suggesting sources for information. **Remy Bourne** provided items for photography. **Wynn Bowers** reviewed the book and made suggestions. The **Buffalo and Erie County Historical Society** provided information on the Red Jacket Washington peace medal. **Jessica Coil** of the Armstrong County Tourist Bureau arranged photography of the Battle of Kittanning reenactment. **Todd Creekman** provided information regarding the Truxtun medal. **Eugene Daub** sent photos of his Saltus medal. **Ray Dillard** provided elongated coins for illustration and made suggestions. **Dr. Richard Doty**, curator of the American Numismatic Collection, Museum of American History, Smithsonian Institution, helped in several ways. **Hal V. Dunn** provided elongated coins for photography. **Lloyd Engeran** provided the unique gold medal presented to President Zachary Taylor (Julian MI-24). **Clark W. Fogg** provided photographs of items from the Weinberg Collection. **Dr. Carl Francis** of Harvard University helped with a request. **Kay O. Freeman** furnished research on John Bill Ricketts, C.C. Wright, and Henry C. Atwood. **Dr. George J. Fuld** reviewed the manuscript, made suggestions, reviewed and revised certain rarity estimates, and helped in other ways. **Catherine Fuller** of University College London helped with research on the 1778 Voltaire medal of Washington. **Hugo Greco** offered a medal for photography. **Richard Gross** provided a token for photography. **Earle Havens** of the Boston Public Library provided images of the unique Washington Before Boston medal in gold. **Steve Hayden** helped in many ways, including with research information, pricing, and specimens for illustration. **Tom Hoffman** provided elongated coins for photography. **Robert Hoge**, curator of the American Numismatic Society, reviewed the manuscript and made suggestions. **Dick Johnson** furnished a medal for photography. **Patrick Kavanaugh** provided information on the Red Jacket monument and the disposition of the chief's remains. **Bob Kozlowski** provided the photo of Monticello for our No. 26. **John Kraljevich** created the text for Nos. 69, 70, 71, and 76 and helped in many other ways. **Robert Leonard** provided items for photography. **Joseph Levine** helped in many ways, including with research information and pricing. **Christopher Linnane** of the Harvard University Art Museums provided an image of Edward Savage's portrait of George Washington. The **Metropolitan Museum of Art**, New York City, provided an engraving. **Thomas Mulvaney** provided several photographs. The **National Portrait Gallery** provided an image of Gilbert Stuart's portrait of John Bill Ricketts. **Christopher Neuzil** provided information on and images of the Truxtun medal. **David Perkins** provided items for photography. **Douglas Plasencia** of Stack's Rare Coins photographed certain items. **Harald Prins** helped with research on an Indian peace medal. **Randy Quinn** supplied photographs of the Battle of Kittanning reenactment. **Robert Schuman, M.D.**, provided a citation. **Rachel Seligman** of Union College provided Henry Inman's portrait of Eliphalet Nott. **Pete Smith** provided items for photography. **Stack's**, New York City (incorporating the former American Numismatic Rarities of Wolfeboro, NH), provided images, including items from the John Jay Ford Jr. collection. **Elena Stolyarik** of the American Numismatic Society provided images. **Steve Tanenbaum** helped in many ways, including with research information, pricing, and specimens for illustration. **Judith Townsend** of the State Library of Pennsylvania arranged for photography of the Continental Congress seal. **Lenny Vaccaro** provided information regarding the Truxtun medal. **Frank Van Valen** read the manuscript and made suggestions. **The Lewis Walpole**

Library at Yale University provided the illustration of "The Female Combatants." **Alan V. Weinberg** provided tokens and medals for illustration, including rarities, and helped in other ways. **Dr. Benjamin Weiss** provided images of the C.C. Wright "Declaration of Independence" medal. **Vicken Yegparian** of Stack's helped with requests for images. **James J. Zotz Jr.** gave an interview about finding the San Antonio River jola hoard.

The sources providing the most items for illustration were, alphabetically, the American Numismatic Society, Q. David Bowers, the Massachusetts Historical Society, Stack's (incorporating the American Numismatic Rarities archives), and Alan V. Weinberg.

Prominent collectors, dealers, and scholars who participated in the nominating and voting process for the *100 Greatest American Medals and Tokens*, and who helped in other ways, include the following:

John Adams, David T. Alexander, Stephen P. Alpert, Anne Bentley, Harlan J. Berk, Allen G. Berman, David Boitnott, M. Remy Bourne, Andrew Bowers, Ken Bressett, John Burnham, Francis Campbell, Paul Cunningham, Beth Deisher, Tom DeLorey, Richard Doty, Brian E. Fanton, Michael S. Fey, Prue Morgan Fitts, Robert F. Fritsch, George Fuld, David M. Gale, David Ganz, Paul Gilkes, David Gladfelter, Barbara Gregory, Dick Grinolds, Thomas Hallenbeck, Andrew Harkness, David Harper, Rich Hartzog, Steve Hayden, Alan Herbert, Michael Hodder, Robert Hoge, Wayne Homren, William H. Horton Jr., Gene Hynds, Peter Irion, Rachel Irish, Patricia Jagger-Finner, Dick Johnson, Louis Jordan, R.W. Julian, Ute Wartenberg Kagan, Donald H. Kagin, John K. Kallman, Chris Karstedt, John Kraljevich, Chester Krause, Rita Laws, Robert Leonard, Joe Levine, Stuart Levine, Mark Lighterman, Dana Linett, Thomas A. Logan, David McCarthy, Charles McSorley, Bill Michal, Cliff Mishler, Richard D. Mitchell, Doug Mudd, John Mutch, Chris Neuzil, Eric P. Newman, Joel Orosz, John Pack, Donald Partrick, W. David Perkins, Gary Pipher, Frederick Reed III, Joel Reznick, P. Scott Rubin, Russell Rulau, Dr. Harry Salyards, Donald Scarinci, David Schenkman, Bill Shamhart, David Sklow, Arlie Slabaugh, Pete Smith, Larry Stack, Alan Stahl, Barry S. Stuppler, David Sundman, Stephen L. Tanenbaum, Barry Tayman, Anthony Terranova, Frank Van Valen, Eric von Klinger, Alan Weinberg, Cindy Wibker, Vicken Yegparian, and Donald Young.

SELECTED BIBLIOGRAPHY

Listed are the more important works used or cited in the text. The field of tokens and medals is sufficiently extensive that an entire library could be formed of useful volumes. For additional titles see the Token and Medal Society publication list as well as the library lists of the American Numismatic Association and the American Numismatic Society. Also consult auction catalogs, past and present, which include hundreds of prominent collections of tokens and medals.

Adams, Edgar H. *United States Store Cards*. New York, 1920.

Adams, John. *The Indian Peace Medals of George III*. Crestline, CA: George Frederick Kolbe, 1999.

American Heritage Illustrated History of the United States. Vols. 1–18. New York: Choice Publishing, 1988.

American Journal of Numismatics. Various issues 1866 to 1912 plus later monographs.

Annaloro, Victor. "Official Medals of the 1876 U.S. Centennial." *Numismatist* (July 2006): 55.

Baker, W.S. *Medallic Portraits of Washington*. Philadelphia, 1885.

Baldwin, Agnes. *Catalogue of the International Exhibition of Contemporary Medals*. New York: American Numismatic Society, 1910.

Barratt, Carrie Rebora, and Ellen G. Miles. *Gilbert Stuart*. New Haven, CT: Yale University Press, 2004. An exhibition catalog.

Baxter, Barbara. *The Beaux-Arts Medal in America*. New York: American Numismatic Society, 1988.

Becker, Carl. "Growth of Revolutionary Parties and Methods in New York Province, 1765–1774." *The American Historical Review* 7, no. 1 (October 1901): 56–76.

Bentley, Anne. "The Columbia-Washington Medal." *Proceedings of the Massachusetts Historical Society* 101 (1989): 120–127.

Betts, C. Wyllys. *American Colonial History Illustrated by Contemporary Medals*. Edited by William T.R. Marvin and Lyman H. Low. New York, 1894.

Bigelow, John. "Franklin's Home and Host in France." *Century Illustrated Magazine*, March 1888.

Bowers, Q. David. *American Numismatics Before the Civil War*. Wolfeboro, NH, 1998.

———. *The History of United States Coinage*. Los Angeles, CA, 1979.

———. *More Adventures With Rare Coins*. Wolfeboro, NH, 2002.

Breen, Walter H. *Walter Breen's Complete Encyclopedia of United States and Colonial Coins*. New York: Doubleday, 1988.

Brunk, Gregory. *Merchant and Privately Countermarked Coins: Advertising on the World's Smallest Billboards*. Rockford, IL: World Exonumia, 2003.

Buffalo Express. "Red Jacket in Bronze: A Great Historical Figure at Forest Lawn; After Years of Effort, the Monument to the Great Orator Is in Place." December 27, 1891.

Bushnell, Charles I. *An Arrangement of Tradesmens' Cards, Political Tokens, Also Election Medals, Medalets, &c. Current in the United States of America for the Last Sixty Years, Described From the Originals, Chiefly in the Collection of the Author*. New York, 1858.

———. *An Historical Account of the First Three Business Tokens Issued in the City of New York*. New York, 1858. Also exists with 1859 imprint.

Carnegie Hero Fund Commission. *A Century of Heroes*. Pittsburgh, PA: University of Pittsburgh Press, 2004.

Cavendish Philatelic Auctions, Ltd. Catalog of sale no. 589. October 2000.

Chamberlain, Georgia Stamm. *American Medals and Medalists*. Annandale, VA: Turnpike Press, 1963.

The Coin Collector's Journal. New York: J.W. Scott & Co., 1870s and 1880s.

Coin World. Sidney, OH, 1960 to date.

Collet, Mark W., J. Ledyard Hodge, and Alfred B. Taylor. *Catalogue of American Store Cards &c., With Space for Marking the Condition, Price, Rarity, &c., of Each Piece, Designed for the Use and Convenience of Collectors*. Philadelphia, circa January 1860.

Collins, Jack. *Selections From the Collection of Washingtonia From the Estate of F.C.C. Boyd*. South Gate, CA, 1991.

The Colonial Newsletter. Huntsville, AL: Colonial Newsletter Foundation; now sponsored by the American Numismatic Society.

Crosby, Sylvester S. *The Early Coins of America*. Boston, 1875.

Culver, Virginia. "The Medal Collector's Corner: Stonewall Jackson Medal." *The Numismatist* (March 1968): 307.

DeLorey, Tom K. "Counterfeit Indian Peace Medals." *COINage*, March 1996.

Densmore, Christopher. *Red Jacket: Iroquois Diplomat and Orator*. Syracuse, NY: Syracuse University Press, 1999.

DeWitt, J. Doyle. *Alfred S. Robinson, Hartford Numismatist*. Hartford: Connecticut Historical Society, 1968.

———. *A Century of Campaign Buttons: 1789–1959*. Hartford, CT, 1959.

Dickeson, Montroville W. *American Numismatical Manual*. Philadelphia, PA, 1859.

Doty, Richard G., ed. *The Token: America's Other Money*. Coinage of the Americas Conference Proceedings, no. 10. New York: American Numismatic Society, 1994.

Forrer, Leonard. *Biographical Dictionary of Medallists*. London, 1923.

"Franklin's Celebrated Line, 'Eripuit Coelo Fulmen,' &c." *The United States Magazine and Democratic Review* 15, no. 78 (December 1844): 625–627.

SELECTED BIBLIOGRAPHY

"Francis Lovelace and the Recapture of New Netherlands, 1668–1674." *The National Magazine: A Monthly Journal of American History*, June 1892, 2–22.

Fuld, George, and Melvin Fuld. *Civil War Store Cards*. Iola, WI: Krause Publications, various years.

———. "Medallic Memorials to Franklin." *The Numismatist* 69, no. 12 (December 1956).

———. *Patriotic Civil War Tokens*. Iola, WI: Krause Publications, various years.

Greenslet, Phil W. *The Medals of Franklin: A Catalog of Medals, Tokens, Medallions, and Plaques Issued in Honor of Franklin*. Edited by David E. Schenkman. Lake Mary, FL: Token and Medal Society, 1993.

Hibler, Harold E., and Charles V. Kappen. *So-Called Dollars*. New York: Coin and Currency Institute, 1963.

Hickcox, John H. *An Historical Account of American Coinage*. Albany, NY, 1858.

The Historical Magazine. Morrisania, NY, 1850s and 1860s.

Hoch, Alfred, ed. *Selected Articles on the Subject of American Tokens Reprinted From "The Numismatist" (1904–1938)*. Lake Mary, FL: Token and Medal Society, 1969.

Holland, Frederic May. "King Voltaire." *The Open Court*, February 17, 1887.

Hough, Franklin B. "General Department: Notice of the 'Castorland Half Dollar' (So Called)." *The Historical Magazine, and Notes and Queries Concerning the Antiquities*, February 1860, 33.

Hudson, R.J. "The Kittanning Medal (or Armstrong Medal)." Western Pennsylvania Numismatic Society Presentation, September 1963. http://www.coin-library.com/wpns.

Journal of the Civil War Token Society (a.k.a. *The Copperhead Courier*). 1960s to present.

Julian, R.W. *Medals of the United States Mint: The First Century, 1792–1892*. El Cajon, CA: Token and Medal Society, 1977.

Kenney, Richard D. *Early American Medalists and Die-Sinkers Prior to the Civil War*. New York: Wayte Raymond, 1954.

Laws, Rita. *Indian Peace Medals and Related Items: Collecting the Symbols of Peace and Friendship*. 2nd ed. Harrah, OK, 2005.

Leon, Theophile E. "The Castorland Token." *The Numismatist* (April 1919).

Lossing, Benson J. *A Field-Book of the Revolution*. 2 vols. New York, 1852.

Loubat, Jacques Florimond. *The Medallic History of the United States of America, 1776–1876*. 1878.

Low, Lyman H. *Hard Times Tokens: An Arrangement of Jackson Cents Issued For and Against the United States Bank*. New York, 1899.

Luftschein, Susan. *One Hundred Years of American Medallic Art: 1845–1945*. Ithaca, NY: Cornell University Press, 1995.

MacNeil, Neil. *The President's Medal, 1789–1977*. New York: Clarkson Potter, 1977.

Mease, James. "Description of Some of the Medals Struck in Relation to the Important Events in North America, Before and Since the Declaration of Independence by the United States." *The Saturday Magazine*, January 25, 1822, 6.

Miller, Donald M. *A Catalogue of U.S. Store Cards or Merchants' Tokens*. Indiana, PA, 1962.

Minutes of the Friendly Association for Regaining and Preserving Peace with the Indians by Pacific Measures, 1755–1757. Friends Historical Library, Swarthmore, PA.

New York Times. "Hotels Which Flourished More Than Fifty Years Ago." June 7, 1903, 32.

———. "Inquest on Saltus to Be Held Tomorrow." June 26, 1922, 10.

———. "Old Tokens and Medals: Unique Collection of Metallic Store Cards Used in New York Early in This Century." December 19, 1897, 9.

Norton's Literary Letter. New York, 1857–1860.

Numisma (house organ published by Édouard Frossard). 1877–1891.

Numismatic News. Iola, WI: Krause Publications, 1952 to present.

The Numismatist. 1888 to present.

Orosz, Joel J. *The Eagle That Is Forgotten: Pierre Eugène du Simitière, Founding Father of American Numismatics*. Wolfeboro, NH, 1988.

Paltsits, Victor Hugo, ed. *Minutes of the Executive Council of the Province of New York: Administration of Francis Lovelace, 1668–1673*. Albany, NY, 1910.

Pilcher, Edith. *Castorland: French Refugees in the Western Adirondacks 1793–1814*. Harrison, NY: Harbor Hills Books, 1985.

Prime, William Cowper. *Coins, Medals and Seals, Ancient and Modern, Illustrated and Described, With a Sketch of the History of Coins and Coinage. . . .* New York: Harper Bros., 1861.

Prucha, Francis P. *Indian Peace Medals in American History*. Norman: University of Oklahoma Press, 1994.

Raymond, Wayte. *Standard Catalogue of U.S. Coins and Tokens*. New York, 1942.

Ronaldson, James, Thomas Fletcher, Adam Ramage, Wm. H. Keating, and Samuel V. Merrick. "Domestic Manufactures: Premiums Offered by the Franklin Institute at Philadelphia." *The American Farmer*, March 11, 1825, 51.

The Round Table: A Saturday Review of Politics, Finance, Literature, Society and Art. January 18, 1864, 13, and January 26, 1867, 58.

Rulau, Russell. *Discovering America: The Coin Collecting Connection*. Iola, WI: Krause Publications, 1989.

———. *Standard Catalog of United States Tokens 1700–1900*. 4th ed. Iola, WI: Krause Publications, 2004.

Rulau, Russell, and George J. Fuld. *Medallic Portraits of Washington*. Iola, WI: Krause Publications, 1999.

Satterlee, Alfred H. *An Arrangement of Medals and Tokens, Struck in Honor of the Presidents of the United States, and of the Presidential Candidates, From the Administration of John Adams to That of Abraham Lincoln, Inclusive. Described Chiefly From Originals in the Possession of the Compiler and of Robert Hewitt, Jr., Esq.* New York, 1862.

Savannah Morning News. "The *Wanderer* Episode." Savannahnow.com/features.

Schornstein, Fred. *Bryan Money*. Lake Mary, FL: Token and Medal Society, 2001.

Schultz, April. "'The Pride of the Race Had Been Touched': The 1925 Norse American Immigration Centennial and Ethnic Identity." *Journal of American History* (March 1991): 1265–1295.

Snowden, James Ross. *The Medallic Memorials of Washington in the Mint of the United States*. Philadelphia, PA, 1861.

Stahl, Alan M., ed. *The Medal in America*. Coinage of the Americas Conference Proceedings, no. 4. New York: American Numismatic Society, 1987.

———. *The Medal in America: Vol. 2*. Coinage of the Americas Conference Proceedings, no. 13. New York: American Numismatic Society, 1997.

Stone, William L. *The Centennial History of New York City, From the Discovery to the Present Day*. 1876.

Sullivan, Edmund B. *American Political Badges and Medalets 1789–1892*. Lawrence, MA: Quarterman Publications, 1981.

Taxay, Don. *Scott's Comprehensive Catalogue of United States Coinage*. New York: Scott, 1971.

———. *The U.S. Mint and Coinage*. New York: Arco, 1966.

Thayer, Theodore. "The Friendly Association." *Pennsylvania Magazine of History and Biography*, October 1943, 336–376.

Token and Medal Society Journal. 1960s to present.

U.S. Department of the Treasury, United States Mint. *Annual Report of the Director of the Mint*. Philadelphia and Washington, DC, 1795 to present.

Vaux, Roberts. "A Discourse Delivered Before the Historical Society of the State of Pennsylvania." January 1, 1827.

———. "Indian Medal: Provincial History." *Casket*, no. 10 (October 1827): 383.

Witham, Stewart P. *Johann Matthaus Reich, also known as John Reich*. 1994.

Workingman's Advocate. Items. February 5, 1831, 4.

Wright, Benjamin P. "The American Store Cards or Business Tokens." *The Numismatist* (1898–1901).

Wyatt, Thomas. *Memoirs of the Generals, Commodores, and Other Commanders, Who Distinguished Themselves in the American Army and Navy During the War of the Revolution*. Philadelphia, 1848.

Yeoman, R.S. *A Guide Book of United States Coins*. Edited by Kenneth E. Bressett. Whitman Publishing, 1946 to present.

WANTED

SERIOUS CUSTOMERS FOR SERIOUS EXONUMIA!

PRESIDENTIAL COIN AND ANTIQUE COMPANY, INC., was formed in 1970 by H. Joseph Levine. Mr. Levine is a past President of the Token and Medal Society and is a former Vice President and Legal Counsel to the Civil War Token Society. He is a member of many specialized clubs in the broad field of exonumia. He is the author of the *Collectors Guide to Presidential Inaugural Medals and Memorabilia* and of numerous articles on the subject of tokens and medals published in the *Numismatist*, the journal of the American Numismatic Association. In addition, he has served as a consultant on various subjects to the National Portrait Gallery; the American Numismatic Association; the American Numismatic Society; and the Smithsonian Institution, National Numismatic Collection.

PRESIDENTIAL has been known for selling the finest-quality tokens and medals in a wide variety of collecting fields.

Through the years, we have handled major rarities in virtually every token and medal area of significance. Below are just a few of the areas in which we deal extensively.

- **Hard Times & 19th-Century Merchant Tokens**
- **Civil War Tokens**
- **Transportation Tokens**
- **So-Called Dollars**
- **All Kinds of Political Americana**
- **Betts Medals**
- **Indian Peace Medals**
- **U.S. Mint Medals**
- **World's Fair & Exposition Items**
- **Art Medals**
- **Official Presidential Inaugural Medals**

AT AUCTION

We offer material from all of the above areas—plus some. We conduct a major sale each year at Whitman's Baltimore Coin and Currency Convention and have periodic offerings on eBay under the name of MEDALSMAN. If you prefer to sell at auction, there is no better vehicle than our professionally cataloged illustrated sales. Our commission rate is a most reasonable 10%. For many years our catalogs have been considered collector's items themselves. Part I of our Sale of the Charles McSorley Collection of 19th-century political tokens earned the Numismatic Literary Guild Award for the Best Exonumia Catalog of 1997, and Mr. Levine was awarded the Carl W.A. Carlson Award for Outstanding Research and Writing in the Medal Field by the Medal Collectors of America. **Please contact us to request a complimentary copy of our next sale.**

PRIVATE-TREATY TRANSACTIONS

We both buy and sell on a direct basis. The great majority of coin dealers could not care less about tokens and medals, and their prices reflect that disinterest. PRESIDENTIAL has specialized in the token and medal field for 35-plus years and is positioned to deal fairly and knowledgeably with such material.

PRESIDENTIAL COIN & ANTIQUE CO., INC.
P.O. BOX 277, CLIFTON, VA 20124
571-321-2121 • JLevine968@aol.com

The American Numismatic Society

For a century and a half, the American Numismatic Society has been expanding the depth and breadth of our understanding of how numismatic artifacts tell the story of human civilization through time and across the world . . .

Collections—Nearly 800,000 items from around the world, dating from ancient times to the present, make the Society a unique and valuable resource for scholars and collectors alike

Library—A complete reference collection relating to the history of numismatics, including books, periodicals, manuscripts, monographs, photographs, pamphlets, auction catalogs, and microforms

Publications—Award-winning publications program, including the *ANS Magazine*, *American Journal of Numismatics*, *Numismatic Notes and Monographs*, *Ancient Coins in North American Collections*, *Colonial Newsletter*, *Coinage of the Americas Conference Proceedings*, and *Numismatic Literature*, as well as individual titles of special interest

Exhibitions—Long-term exhibit *Drachmas, Doubloons and Dollars: The History of Money* is located at the Federal Reserve Bank of New York, 33 Liberty Street, New York, NY; temporary exhibitions of items from the ANS's renowned collection; invitational exhibitions; numerous artifacts from the Society's collections on loan to permanent, temporary, and traveling museum exhibitions

Educational Programs—Eric P. Newman Graduate Summer Seminar; various public lecture series, forums, and symposia throughout the year; awards presentations; internships and grants

Archives—Collecting, preserving, and making accessible the historical records of the Society, including search aids, electronic lists, and an oral-history project

Online Resources—Access to a database of over 500,000 coins, online library catalog, digital publications, and a list-serve group

Be a part of this exceptional heritage by becoming a member of the American Numismatic Society.

For more information or to become a member please visit our website at
http://www.numismatics.org or email membership@numismatics.org

The object and mission of the Society shall be the creation and maintenance of the preeminent national institution advancing the study and public appreciation of coins, currency, medals, orders and decorations, and related objects of all cultures as historical and artistic documents and artifacts; by maintaining the foremost numismatic collection, museum, and library; by supporting scholarly research and publications; and by sponsoring educational and interpretive programs for diverse audiences.

MCA: Medal Collectors of America

The MCA is a numismatic club dedicated to the collection of art, historical, and topical medals. These medals are generally issued to show the medallic sculptor's skill and artistry, or to commemorate an event or person.

MCA's journal is *The Medal Collectors Advisory*, which is issued on a monthly basis. It contains club news and articles of interest to all members, some of which are off-printed into a stand-alone format. Contributors include some of the best-known medal collectors in the country. Most of the information they provide has never been published before.

MCA meets at the ANA Anniversary Convention in the summer and at the International Show in New York in January. Panel discussions and learned presentations are features of these meetings. Regional meetings may be held at a coin show near you at various times throughout the year.

If your interest lies with art, historical, or topical medals in general, MCA is the club for you. Dues are a modest $20 per year. Send your remittance now to our club Treasurer, whose address is below.

Mail your $20 dues to:
Barry Tayman
3115 Nestling Pine Court, Ellicott City, MD 21042

NAME

ADDRESS

CITY　　　　　　　　　　　　　　　STATE　　ZIP

E-MAIL

I learned about the MCA from

The Token and Medal Society

The Token and Medal Society, Inc. (TAMS), founded in 1960, is an educational and nonprofit organization for collectors and students of all forms of tokens, medals, badges and related items.

The principal aims of TAMS are:

- To promote and stimulate the study of tokens and medals.
- To showcase original research on medals and tokens in a bimonthly journal.
- To publish well-researched, standard catalogs of tokens and medals.
- To encourage writing and cataloging through annual awards for outstanding achievement.
- To assist collectors in attributing their "maverick" (location omitted) tokens.
- To aid collecting through free classified ads and frequent membership directories listing collecting specialties.

Benefits of Membership in the Token and Medal Society

Members receive six issues of the *TAMS Journal* each year, plus occasional Supplements. Included are:

- Articles by expert authors.
- Maverick column.
- Marketplace (each member is entitled to one free 25-word classified ad per issue).
- Paid advertisements.
- Officers' messages and reports.

TAMS has an extensive library of books and periodicals, including most essential token and medal references. Members only are entitled to borrow material from the library by mail for just the cost of round-trip postage and insurance.

Discounts on token and medal catalogs published by TAMS.

Assistance for authors in publishing needed catalogs.

How to Join

For a membership application and dues information, contact:

Rachel Irish, Secretary
101 W. Prairie Ctr. #323
Hayden, ID 83815

MRirish5@aol.com

WE HAVE BEEN SELLING THE WORLD'S FINEST COLLECTIONS OF COINS, TOKENS, MEDALS, AND PAPER MONEY FOR OVER SEVEN DECADES

LET US BE OF SERVICE TO YOU!

Lawrence R. Stack • Christine Karstedt • Harvey G. Stack • Q. David Bowers

Call today to include your collection in one of our spectacular events.

123 West 57th Street • New York, NY 10019 • 800-566/2580 • Fax 212-245-5018
P.O. Box 1804 • Wolfeboro, NH 03894 • 866-811-1804 • Fax 603-569-3875

Auctions • Appraisals • Retail • Since 1935

www.stacks.com • email: auction@stacks.com

VISIT US AT STACKS.COM FOR ON-LINE CATALOGUES, COLOR IMAGES AND INTERACTIVE BIDDING